Perl and XML

Perl and XML

Erik T. Ray and Jason McIntosh

O'REILLY®

Beijing · Cambridge · Farnham · Köln · Paris · Sebastopol · Taipei · Tokyo

Perl and XML
by Erik T. Ray and Jason McIntosh

Copyright © 2002 O'Reilly & Associates, Inc. All rights reserved.
Printed in the United States of America.

Published by O'Reilly & Associates, Inc., 1005 Gravenstein Highway North, Sebastopol, CA 95472.

O'Reilly & Associates books may be purchased for educational, business, or sales promotional use. Online editions are also available for most titles (*safari.oreilly.com*). For more information contact our corporate/institutional sales department: (800) 998-9938 or *corporate@oreilly.com*.

Editor:	Linda Mui
Production Editor:	Ann Schirmer
Cover Designer:	Ellie Volckhausen
Interior Designer:	Melanie Wang

Printing History:

April 2002:	First Edition.

ISBN: 0-596-00205-X

[M]

Table of Contents

Preface

This book marks the intersection of two essential technologies for the Web and information services. XML, the latest and best markup language for self-describing data, is becoming the generic data packaging format of choice. Perl, which web masters have long relied on to stitch up disparate components and generate dynamic content, is a natural choice for processing XML. The shrink-wrap of the Internet meets the duct tape of the Internet.

More powerful than HTML, yet less demanding than SGML, XML is a perfect solution for many developers. It has the flexibility to encode everything from web pages to legal contracts to books, and the precision to format data for services like SOAP and XML-RPC. It supports world-class standards like Unicode while being backwards-compatible with plain old ASCII. Yet for all its power, XML is surprisingly easy to work with, and many developers consider it a breeze to adapt to their programs.

As the Perl programming language was tailor-made for manipulating text, Perl and XML are perfectly suited for one another. The only question is, "What's the best way to pair them?" That's where this book comes in.

Assumptions

This book was written for programmers who are interested in using Perl to process XML documents. We assume that you already know Perl; if not, please pick up O'Reilly's *Learning Perl* (or its equivalent) before reading this book. It will save you much frustration and head scratching.

We do not assume that you have much experience with XML. However, it helps if you are familiar with markup languages such as HTML.

We assume that you have access to the Internet, and specifically to the Comprehensive Perl Archive Network (CPAN), as most of this book depends on your ability to download modules from CPAN.

Most of all, we assume that you've rolled up your sleeves and are ready to start programming with Perl and XML. There's a lot of ground to cover in this little book, and we're eager to get started.

How This Book Is Organized

This book is broken up into ten chapters, as follows:

Chapter 1, *Perl and XML*, introduces our two heroes. We also give an XML::Simple example for the impatient reader.

Chapter 2, *An XML Recap*, is for the readers who say they know XML but suspect they really don't. We give a quick summary of where XML came from and how it's structured. If you really do know XML, you are free to skip this chapter, but don't complain later that you don't know a namespace from an en-dash.

Chapter 3, *XML Basics: Reading and Writing*, shows how to get information from an XML document and write it back in. Of course, all the interesting stuff happens in between these steps, but you still need to know how to read and write the stuff.

Chapter 4, *Event Streams*, explains event streams, the efficient core of most XML processing.

Chapter 5, *SAX*, introduces the Simple API for XML processing, a standard interface to event streams.

Chapter 6, *Tree Processing*, is about...well, processing trees, the basic structure of all XML documents. We start with simple structures of built-in types and finish with advanced, object-oriented tree models.

Chapter 7, *DOM*, covers the Document Object Model, another standard interface of importance. We give examples showing how DOM will make you nimble as a squirrel in any XML tree.

Chapter 8, *Beyond Trees: XPath, XSLT, and More*, covers advanced tree processing, including event-tree hybrids and transformation scripts.

Chapter 9, *RSS, SOAP, and Other XML Applications*, shows existing real-life applications using Perl and XML.

Chapter 10, *Coding Strategies*, wraps everything up. Now that you are familiar with the modules, we'll tell you which to use, why to use them, and what gotchas to avoid.

Resources

While this book aims to cover everything you'll need to start programming with Perl and XML, modules change, new standards emerge, and you may think of some oddball situation that we haven't anticipated. Here's are two other resources you can pursue.

The perl-xml Mailing List

The *perl-xml* mailing list is the first place to go for finding fellow programmers suffering from the same issues as you. In fact, if you plan to work with Perl and XML in any nontrivial way, you should first subscribe to this list. To subscribe to the list or browse archives of past discussions, visit *http://aspn.activestate.com/ASPN/Mail/Browse/Threaded/perl-xml*.

You might also want to check out *http://www.xmlperl.com*, a fairly new web site devoted to the Perl/XML community.

CPAN

Most modules discussed in this book are not distributed with Perl and need to be downloaded from CPAN.

If you've worked in Perl at all, you're familiar with CPAN and how to download and install modules. If you aren't, head over to *http://www.cpan.org*. Check out the FAQ first. Get the CPAN module if you don't already have it (it probably came with your standard Perl distribution).

Font Conventions

Italic is used for URLs, filenames, commands, hostnames, and emphasized words.

`Constant width` is used for function names, module names, and text that is typed literally.

`Constant-width bold` is used for user input.

`Constant-width italic` is used for replaceable text.

How to Contact Us

Please address comments and questions concerning this book to the publisher:

O'Reilly & Associates, Inc.
1005 Gravenstein Highway North
Sebastopol, CA 95472
(800) 998-9938 (in the United States or Canada)
(707) 829-0515 (international or local)
(707) 829-0104 (fax)

There is a web page for this book, which lists errata, examples, or any additional information. You can access this page at:

http://www.oreilly.com/catalog/perlxml

To comment or ask technical questions about this book, send email to:

bookquestions@oreilly.com

For more information about books, conferences, Resource Centers, and the O'Reilly Network, see the O'Reilly web site at:

http://www.oreilly.com/

Acknowledgments

Both authors are grateful for the expert guidance from Paula Ferguson, Andy Oram, Jon Orwant, Michel Rodriguez, Simon St.Laurent, Matt Sergeant, Ilya Sterin, Mike Stok, Nat Torkington, and their editor, Linda Mui.

Erik would like to thank his wife Jeannine; his family (Birgit, Helen, Ed, Elton, Al, Jon-Paul, John and Michelle, John and Dolores, Jim and Joanne, Gene and Margaret, Liane, Tim and Donna, Theresa, Christopher, Mary-Anne, Anna, Tony, Paul and Sherry, Lillian, Bob, Joe and Pam, Elaine and Steve, Jennifer, and Marion); his excellent friends Derrick Arnelle, Stacy Chandler, J. D. Curran, Sarah Demb, Ryan Frasier, Chris Gernon, John Grigsby, Andy Grosser, Lisa Musiker, Benn Salter, Caroline Senay, Greg Travis, and Barbara Young; and his coworkers Lenny, Mela, Neil, Mike, and Sheryl.

Jason would like to thank Julia for her encouragement throughout this project; Looney Labs games (*http://www.looneylabs.com*) and the Boston Warren for maintaining his sanity by reminding him to play; Josh and the Ottoman Empire for letting him escape reality every now and again; the Diesel Cafe in Somerville, Massachusetts and the 1369 Coffee House in Cambridge for unwittingly acting as his alternate offices; housemates Charles, Carla, and Film Series: The Cat; Apple Computer for its fine iBook and Mac OS X, upon which most writing/hacking was accomplished; and, of course, Larry Wall and all the strange and wonderful people who brought (and continue to bring) us Perl.

## CHAPTER 1

Perl and XML

Perl is a mature but eccentric programming language that is tailor-made for text manipulation. XML is a fiery young upstart of a text-based markup language used for web content, document processing, web services, or any situation in which you need to structure information flexibly. This book is the story of the first few years of their sometimes rocky (but ultimately happy) romance.

Why Use Perl with XML?

First and foremost, Perl is ideal for crunching text. It has filehandles, "here" docs, string manipulation, and regular expressions built into its syntax. Anyone who has ever written code to manipulate strings in a low-level language like C and then tried to do the same thing in Perl has no trouble telling you which environment is easier for text processing. XML is text at its core, so Perl is uniquely well suited to work with it.

Furthermore, starting with Version 5.6, Perl has been getting friendly with Unicode-flavored character encodings, especially UTF-8, which is important for XML processing. You'll read more about character encoding in Chapter 3.

Second, the Comprehensive Perl Archive Network (CPAN) is a multimirrored heap of modules free for the taking. You could say that it takes a village to make a program; anyone who undertakes a programming project in Perl should check the public warehouse of packaged solutions and building blocks to save time and effort. Why write your own parser when CPAN has plenty of parsers to download, all tested and chock full of configurability? CPAN is wild and woolly, with contributions from many people and not much supervision. The good news is that when a new technology emerges, a module supporting it pops up on CPAN in short order. This feature complements XML nicely, since it's always changing and adding new accessory technologies.

Early on, modules sprouted up around XML like mushrooms after a rain. Each module brought with it a unique interface and style that was innovative and Perlish, but not interchangeable. Recently, there has been a trend toward creating a universal interface so modules can be interchangeable. If you don't like this SAX parser, you can plug in another one with no extra work. Thus, the CPAN community does work together and strive for internal coherence.

Third, Perl's flexible, object-oriented programming capabilities are very useful for dealing with XML. An XML document is a hierarchical structure made of a single basic atomic unit, the XML element, that can hold other elements as its children. Thus, the elements that make up a document can be represented by one class of objects that all have the same, simple interface. Furthermore, XML markup encapsulates content the way objects encapsulate code and data, so the two complement each other nicely. You'll also see that objects are useful for modularizing XML processors. These objects include parser objects, parser factories that serve up parser objects, and parsers that return objects. It all adds up to clean, portable code.

Fourth, the link between Perl and the Web is important. Java and JavaScript get all the glamour, but any web monkey knows that Perl lurks at the back end of most servers. Many web-munging libraries in Perl are easily adapted to XML. The developers who have worked in Perl for years building web sites are now turning their nimble fingers to the XML realm.

Ultimately, you'll choose the programming language that best suits your needs. Perl is ideal for working with XML, but you shouldn't just take our word for it. Give it a try.

XML Is Simple with XML::Simple

Many people, understandably, think of XML as the invention of an evil genius bent on destroying humanity. The embedded markup, with its angle brackets and slashes, is not exactly a treat for the eyes. Add to that the business about nested elements, node types, and DTDs, and you might cower in the corner and whimper for nice, tab-delineated files and a split function.

Here's a little secret: writing programs to process XML is not hard. A whole spectrum of tools that handle the mundane details of parsing and building data structures for you is available, with convenient APIs that get you started in a few minutes. If you really need the complexity of a full-featured XML application, you can certainly get it, but you don't have to. XML scales nicely from simple to bafflingly complex, and if you deal with XML on the simple end of the continuum, you can pick simple tools to help you.

To prove our point, we'll look at a very basic module called XML::Simple, created by Grant McLean. With minimal effort up front, you can accomplish a surprising amount of useful work when processing XML.

A typical program reads in an XML document, makes some changes, and writes it back out to a file. XML::Simple was created to automate this process as much as possible. One subroutine call reads in an XML document and stores it in memory for you, using nested hashes to represent elements and data. After you make whatever changes you need to make, call another subroutine to print it out to a file.

Let's try it out. As with any module, you have to introduce XML::Simple to your program with a use pragma like this:

```
use XML::Simple;
```

When you do this, XML::Simple exports two subroutines into your namespace:

XMLin( )
> This subroutine reads an XML document from a file or string and builds a data structure to contain the data and element structure. It returns a reference to a hash containing the structure.

XMLout( )
> Given a reference to a hash containing an encoded document, this subroutine generates XML markup and returns it as a string of text.

If you like, you can build the document from scratch by simply creating the data structures from hashes, arrays, and strings. You'd have to do that if you wanted to create a file for the first time. Just be careful to avoid using circular references, or the module will not function properly.

For example, let's say your boss is going to send email to a group of people using the world-renowned mailing list management application, WarbleSoft SpamChucker. Among its features is the ability to import and export XML files representing mailing lists. The only problem is that the boss has trouble reading customers' names as they are displayed on the screen and would prefer that they all be in capital letters. Your assignment is to write a program that can edit the XML datafiles to convert just the names into all caps.

Accepting the challenge, you first examine the XML files to determine the style of markup. Example 1-1 shows such a document.

Example 1-1. SpamChucker datafile

```
<?xml version="1.0"?>
<spam-document version="3.5" timestamp="2002-05-13 15:33:45">
<!-- Autogenerated by WarbleSoft Spam Version 3.5 -->
<customer>
 <first-name>Joe</first-name>
 <surname>Wrigley</surname>
 <address>
   <street>17 Beable Ave.</street>
   <city>Meatball</city>
   <state>MI</state>
   <zip>82649</zip>
 </address>
```

Example 1-1. SpamChucker datafile (continued)

```
 <email>joewrigley@jmac.org</email>
 <age>42</age>
</customer>
<customer>
 <first-name>Henrietta</first-name>
 <surname>Pussycat</surname>
  <address>
   <street>R.F.D. 2</street>
   <city>Flangerville</city>
   <state>NY</state>
   <zip>83642</zip>
  </address>
  <email>meow@263A.org</email>
  <age>37</age>
 </customer>
</spam-document>
```

Having read the perldoc page describing XML::Simple, you might feel confident enough to craft a little script, shown in Example 1-2.

Example 1-2. A script to capitalize customer names

```perl
# This program capitalizes all the customer names in an XML document
# made by WarbleSoft SpamChucker.

# Turn on strict and warnings, for it is always wise to do so (usually)
use strict;
use warnings;

# Import the XML::Simple module
use XML::Simple;

# Turn the file into a hash reference, using XML::Simple's "XMLin"
# subroutine.
# We'll also turn on the 'forcearray' option, so that all elements
# contain arrayrefs.
my $cust_xml = XMLin('./customers.xml', forcearray=>1);

# Loop over each customer sub-hash, which are all stored as in an
# anonymous list under the 'customer' key
for my $customer (@{$cust_xml->{customer}}) {
  # Capitalize the contents of the 'first-name' and 'surname' elements
  # by running Perl's built-in uc() function on them
  foreach (qw(first-name surname)) {
    $customer->{$_}->[0] = uc($customer->{$_}->[0]);
  }
}

# print out the hash as an XML document again, with a trailing newline
# for good measure
print XMLout($cust_xml);
print "\n";
```

Running the program (a little trepidatious, perhaps, since the data belongs to your boss), you get this output:

```
<opt version="3.5" timestamp="2002-05-13 15:33:45">
  <customer>
    <address>
      <state>MI</state>
      <zip>82649</zip>
      <city>Meatball</city>
      <street>17 Beable Ave.</street>
    </address>
    <first-name>JOE</first-name>
    <email>i-like-cheese@jmac.org</email>
    <surname>WRIGLEY</surname>
    <age>42</age>
  </customer>
  <customer>
    <address>
      <state>NY</state>
      <zip>83642</zip>
      <city>Flangerville</city>
      <street>R.F.D. 2</street>
    </address>
    <first-name>HENRIETTA</first-name>
    <email>meowmeow@augh.org</email>
    <surname>PUSSYCAT</surname>
    <age>37</age>
  </customer>
</opt>
```

Congratulations! You've written an XML-processing program, and it worked perfectly. Well, almost perfectly. The output is a little different from what you expected. For one thing, the elements are in a different order, since hashes don't preserve the order of items they contain. Also, the spacing between elements may be off. Could this be a problem?

This scenario brings up an important point: there is a trade-off between simplicity and completeness. As the developer, you have to decide what's essential in your markup and what isn't. Sometimes the order of elements is vital, and then you might not be able to use a module like XML::Simple. Or, perhaps you want to be able to access processing instructions and keep them in the file. Again, this is something XML::Simple can't give you. Thus, it's vital that you understand what a module can or can't do before you commit to using it. Fortunately, you've checked with your boss and tested the SpamChucker program on the modified data, and everyone was happy. The new document is close enough to the original to fulfill the application's requirements.* Consider yourself initiated into processing XML with Perl!

---

* Some might say that, disregarding the changes we made on purpose, the two documents are *semantically equivalent*, but this is not strictly true. The order of elements changed, which is significant in XML. We can say for sure that the documents are close enough to satisfy all the requirements of the software for which they were intended and of the end user.

This is only the beginning of your journey. Most of the book still lies ahead of you, chock full of tips and techniques to wrestle with any kind of XML. Not every XML problem is as simple as the one we just showed you. Nevertheless, we hope we've made the point that there's nothing innately complex or scary about banging XML with your Perl hammer.

XML Processors

Now that you see the easy side of XML, we will expose some of XML's quirks. You need to consider these quirks when working with XML and Perl.

When we refer in this book to an *XML processor* (which we'll often refer to in shorthand as a *processor,* not to be confused with the central processing unit of a computer system that has the same nickname), we refer to software that can either read or generate XML documents. We use this term in the most general way—what the program actually *does* with the content it might find in the XML it reads is not the concern of the processor itself, nor is it the processor's responsibility to determine the origin of the document or decide what to do with one that is generated.

As you might expect, a raw XML processor working alone isn't very interesting. For this reason, a computer program that actually does something cool or useful with XML uses a processor as just one component. It usually reads an XML file and, through the magic of parsing, turns it into in-memory structures that the rest of the program can do whatever it likes with.

In the Perl world, this behavior becomes possible through the use of Perl modules: typically, a program that needs to process XML embraces, through the use pragma, an existing package that makes a programmer interface available (usually an object-oriented one). This is why, before they get down to business, many XML-handling Perl programs start out with use `XML::Parser;` or something similar. With one little line, they're able to leave all the dirty work of XML parsing to another, previously written module, leaving their own code to decide what to do pre- and post-processing.

A Myriad of Modules

One of Perl's strengths is that it's a community-driven language. When Perl programmers identify a need and write a module to handle it, they are encouraged to distribute it to the world at large via CPAN. The advantage of this is that if there's something you want to do in Perl and there's a possibility that someone else wanted to do it previously, a Perl module is probably already available on CPAN.

However, for a technology that's as young, popular, and creatively interpretable as XML, the community-driven model has a downside. When XML first caught on, many different Perl modules written by different programmers appeared on CPAN, seemingly all at once. Without a governing body, they all coexisted in inconsistent glee, with a variety of structures, interfaces, and goals.

Don't despair, though. In the time since the mist-enshrouded elder days of 1998, a movement towards some semblance of organization and standards has emerged from the Perl/XML community (which primarily manifests on ActiveState's *perl-xml* mailing list, as mentioned in the preface). The community built on these first modules to make tools that followed the same rules that other parts of the XML world were settling on, such as the SAX and DOM parsing standards, and implemented XML-related technologies such as XPath. Later, the field of basic, low-level parsers started to widen. Recently, some very interesting systems have emerged (such as XML::SAX) that bring truly Perlish levels of DWIMminess out of these same standards.[*]

Of course, the goofy, quick-and-dirty tools are still there if you want to use them, and XML::Simple is among them. We will try to help you understand when to reach for the standards-using tools and when it's OK to just grab your XML and run giggling through the daffodils.

Keep in Mind...

In many cases, you'll find that the XML modules on CPAN satisfy 90 percent of your needs. Of course, that final 10 percent is the difference between being an essential member of your company's staff and ending up slated for the next round of layoffs. We're going to give you your money's worth out of this book by showing you in gruesome detail how XML processing in Perl works at the lowest levels (relative to any other kind of specialized text munging you may perform with Perl). To start, let's go over some basic truths:

It doesn't matter where it comes from.   By the time the XML parsing part of a program gets its hands on a document, it doesn't give a camel's hump where the thing came from. It could have been received over a network, constructed from a database, or read from disk. To the parser, it's good (or bad) XML, and that's all it knows.

Mind you, the program as a whole might care a great deal. If we write a program that implements XML-RPC, for example, it better know exactly how to use TCP to fetch and send all that XML data over the Internet! We can have it do that fetching and sending however we like, as long as the end product is the same: a clean XML document fit to pass to the XML processor that lies at the program's core.

We will get into some detailed examples of larger programs later in this book.

---

[*] DWIM = "Do What I Mean," one of the fundamental philosophies governing Perl.

Structurally, all XML documents are similar. No matter why or how they were put together or to what purpose they'll be applied, all XML documents must follow the same basic rules of well-formedness: exactly one root element, no overlapping elements, all attributes quoted, and so on. Every XML processor's parser component will, at its core, need to do the same things as every other XML processor. This, in turn, means that all these processors can share a common base. Perl XML-processing programs usually observe this in their use of one of the many free parsing modules, rather than having to reimplement basic XML parsing procedures every time.

Furthermore, the one-document, one-element nature of XML makes processing a pleasantly fractal experience, as any document invoked through an external entity by another document magically becomes "just another element" within the invoker, and the same code that crawled the first document can skitter into the meat of any reference (and anything to which the reference might refer) without batting an eye.

In meaning, all XML applications are different. XML applications are the raison d'être of any one XML document, the higher-level set of rules they follow with an aim for applicability to some useful purpose—be it filling out a configuration file, preparing a network transmission, or describing a comic strip. XML applications exist to not only bless humble documents with a higher sense of purpose, but to require the documents to be written according to a given application specification.

DTDs help enforce the consistency of this structure. However, you don't have to have a formal validation scheme to make an application. You may want to create some validation rules, though, if you need to make sure that your successors (including yourself, two weeks in the future) do not stray from the path you had in mind when they make changes to the program. You should also create a validation scheme if you want to allow others to write programs that generate the same flavor of XML.

Most of the XML hacking you'll accomplish will capitalize on this document/application duality. In most cases, your software will consist of parts that cover all three of these facts:

- It will accept input in an appropriate way—listening to a network socket, for example, or reading a file from disk. This behavior is very ordinary and Perlish: do whatever's necessary here to get that data.

- It will pass captured input to some kind of XML processor. Dollars to doughnuts says you'll use one of the parsers that other people in the Perl community have already written and continue to maintain, such as XML::Simple, or the more sophisticated modules we'll discuss later.

- Finally, it will Do Something with whatever that processor did to the XML. Maybe it will output more XML (or HTML), update a database, or send mail to your mom. This is the defining point of your XML application—it takes the

XML and does something meaningful with it. While we won't cover the infinite possibilities here, we will discuss the crucial ties between the XML processor and the rest of your program.

XML Gotchas

This section introduces topics we think you should keep in mind as you read the book. They are the source of many of the problems you'll encounter when working with XML.

Well-formedness

XML has built-in quality control. A document has to pass some minimal syntax rules in order to be blessed as well-formed XML. Most parsers fail to handle a document that breaks any of these rules, so you should make sure any data you input is of sufficient quality.

Character encodings

Now that we're in the 21st century, we have to pay attention to things like character encodings. Gone are the days when you could be content knowing only about ASCII, the little character set that could. Unicode is the new king, presiding over all major character sets of the world. XML prefers to work with Unicode, but there are many ways to represent it, including Perl's favorite Unicode encoding, UTF-8. You usually won't have to think about it, but you should still be aware of the potential.

Namespaces

Not everyone works with or even knows about namespaces. It's a feature in XML whose usefulness is not immediately obvious, yet it is creeping into our reality slowly but surely. These devices categorize markup and declare tags to be from different places. With them, you can mix and match document types, blurring the distinctions between them. Equations in HTML? Markup as data in XSLT? Yes, and namespaces are the reason. Older modules don't have special support for namespaces, but the newer generation will. Keep it in mind.

Declarations

Declarations aren't part of the document per se; they just define pieces of it. That makes them weird, and something you might not pay enough attention to. Remember that documents often use DTDs and have declarations for such things as entities and attributes. If you forget, you could end up breaking something.

Entities

Entities and entity references seem simple enough: they stand in for content that you'd rather not type in at that moment. Maybe the content is in another file, or maybe it contains characters that are difficult to type. The concept is simple, but the execution can be a royal pain. Sometimes you want to resolve references and sometimes you'd rather keep them there. Sometimes a parser wants to see the declarations; at other times it doesn't care. Entities can contain other entities to an arbitrary depth. They're tricky little beasties and we guarantee that if you don't give careful thought to how you're going to handle them, they will haunt you.

Whitespace

According to XML, anything that isn't a markup tag is significant character data. This fact can lead to some surprising results. For example, it isn't always clear what should happen with whitespace. By default, an XML processor will preserve all of it—even the newlines you put after tags to make them more readable or the spaces you use to indent text. Some parsers will give you options to ignore space in certain circumstances, but there are no hard and fast rules.

In the end, Perl and XML are well suited for each other. There may be a few traps and pitfalls along the way, but with the generosity of various module developers, your path toward Perl/XML enlightenment should be well lit.

## CHAPTER 2

An XML Recap

XML is a revolutionary (and evolutionary) markup language. It combines the generalized markup power of SGML with the simplicity of free-form markup and well-formedness rules. Its unambiguous structure and predictable syntax make it a very easy and attractive format to process with computer programs.

You are free, with XML, to design your own markup language that best fits your data. You can select element names that make sense to you, rather than use tags that are overloaded and presentation-heavy. If you like, you can formalize the language by using element and attribute declarations in the DTD.

XML has syntactic shortcuts such as entities, comments, processing instructions, and CDATA sections. It allows you to group elements and attributes by namespace to further organize the vocabulary of your documents. Using the `xml:space` attribute can regulate whitespace, sometimes a tricky issue in markup in which human readability is as important as correct formatting.

Some very useful technologies are available to help you maintain and mutate your documents. Schemas, like DTDs, can measure the validity of XML as compared to a canonical model. Schemas go even further by enforcing patterns in character data and improving content model syntax. XSLT is a rich language for transforming documents into different forms. It could be an easier way to work with XML than having to write a program, but isn't always.

This chapter gives a quick recap of XML, where it came from, how it's structured, and how to work with it. If you choose to skip this chapter (because you already know XML or because you're impatient to start writing code), that's fine; just remember that it's here if you need it.

A Brief History of XML

Early text processing was closely tied to the machines that displayed it. Sophisticated formatting was tied to a particular device—or rather, a class of devices called printers.

Take troff, for example. Troff was a very popular text formatting language included in most Unix distributions. It was revolutionary because it allowed high-quality formatting without a typesetting machine.

Troff mixes formatting instructions with data. The instructions are symbols composed of characters, with a special syntax so a troff interpreter can tell the two apart. For example, the symbol \fI changes the current font style to italic. Without the backslash character, it would be treated as data. This mixture of instructions and data is called *markup*.

Troff can be even more detailed than that. The instruction .vs 18p tells the formatter to insert 18 points of vertical space at whatever point in the document where the instruction appears. Beyond aesthetics, we can't tell just by looking at it what purpose this spacing serves; it gives a very specific instruction to the processor that can't be interpreted in any other way. This instruction is fine if you only want to prepare a document for printing in a specific style. If you want to make changes, though, it can be quite painful.

Suppose you've marked up a book in troff so that every newly defined term is in boldface. Your document has thousands of bold font instructions in it. You're happy and ready to send it to the printer when suddenly, you get a call from the design department. They tell you that the design has changed and they now want the new terms to be formatted as italic. Now you have a problem. You have to turn every bold instruction for a new term into an italic instruction.

Your first thought is to open the document in your editor and do a search-and-replace maneuver. But, to your horror, you realize that new terms aren't the only places where you used bold font instructions. You also used them for emphasis and for proper nouns, meaning that a global replace would also mangle these instances, which you definitely don't want. You can change the right instructions only by going through them one at a time, which could take hours, if not days.

No matter how smart you make a formatting language like troff, it still has the same problem: it's inherently presentational. A *presentational* markup language describes content in terms of how to format it. Troff specifies details about fonts and spacing, but it never tells you what something is. Using troff makes the document less useful in some ways. It's hard to search through troff and come back with the last paragraph of the third section of a book, for example. The presentational markup gets in the way of any task other than its specific purpose: to format the document for printing.

We can characterize troff, then, as a *destination format*. It's not good for anything but a specific end purpose. What other kind of format could there be? Is there an "origin" format—that is, something that doesn't dictate any particular formatting but still packages the data in a useful way? People began to ask this key question in the late 1960s when they devised the concept of *generic coding*: marking up content in a presentation-agnostic way, using descriptive tags rather than formatting instructions.

The Graphic Communications Association (GCA) started a project to explore this new area called GenCode, which develops ways to encode documents in generic tags and assemble documents from multiple pieces—a precursor to hypertext. IBM's Generalized Markup Language (GML), developed by Charles Goldfarb, Edward Mosher, and Raymond Lorie, built on this concept.* As a result of this work, IBM could edit, view on a terminal, print, and search through the same source material using different programs. You can imagine that this benefit would be important for a company that churned out millions of pages of documentation per year.

Goldfarb went on to lead a standards team at the American National Standards Institute (ANSI) to make the power of GML available to the world. Building on the GML and GenCode projects, the committee produced the Standard Generalized Markup Language (SGML). Quickly adopted by the U.S. Department of Defense and the Internal Revenue Service, SGML proved to be a big success. It became an international standard when ratified by the ISO in 1986. Since then, many publishing and processing packages and tools have been developed.

Generic coding was a breakthrough for digital content. Finally, content could be described for what it was, instead of how to display it. Something like this looks more like a database than a word-processing file:

```
<personnel-record>
  <name>
    <first>Rita</first>
    <last>Book</last>
  </name>
  <birthday>
    <year>1969</year>
    <month>4</month>
    <day>23</day>
  </birthday>
</personnel-record>
```

Notice the lack of presentational information. You can format the name any way you want: first name then last name, or last name first, with a comma. You could format the date in American style (4/23/1969) or European (23/4/1969) simply by specifying whether the <month> or <day> element should present its contents first. The document doesn't dictate its use, which makes it useful as a source document for multiple destinations.

In spite of its revolutionary capabilities, SGML never really caught on with small companies the way it did with the big ones. Software is expensive and bulky. It takes a team of developers to set up and configure a production environment around SGML. SGML feels bureaucratic, confusing, and resource-heavy. Thus, SGML in its original form was not ready to take the world by storm.

---

* Cute fact: the initials of these researchers also spell out "GML."

"Oh really," you say. "Then what about HTML? Isn't it true that HTML is an application of SGML?" HTML, that celebrity of the Internet, the harbinger of hypertext and workhorse of the World Wide Web, is indeed an application of SGML. By application, we mean that it is a markup language derived with the rules of SGML. SGML isn't a markup language, but a toolkit for designing your own descriptive markup language. Besides HTML, languages for encoding technical documentation, IRS forms, and battleship manuals are in use.

HTML is indeed successful, but it has limitations. It's a very small language, and not very descriptive. It is closer to troff in function than to DocBook and other SGML applications. It has tags like <i> and <b> that change the font style without saying why. Because HTML is so limited and at least partly presentational, it doesn't represent an overwhelming success for SGML, at least not in spirit. Instead of bringing the power of generic coding to the people, it brought another one-trick pony, in which you could display your content in a particular venue and couldn't do much else with it.

Thus, the standards folk decided to try again and see if they couldn't arrive at a compromise between the descriptive power of SGML and the simplicity of HTML. They came up with the Extensible Markup Language (XML). The "X" stands for "extensible," pointing out the first obvious difference from HTML, which is that some people think that "X" is a cooler-sounding letter than "E" when used in an acronym. The second and more relevant difference is that your documents don't have to be stuck in the anemic tag set of HTML. You can extend the tag namespace to be as descriptive as you want—as descriptive, even, as SGML. Voilà! The bridge is built.

By all accounts, XML is a smashing success. It has lived up to the hype and keeps on growing: XML-RPC, XHTML, SVG, and DocBook XML are some of its products. It comes with several accessories, including XSL for formatting, XSLT for transforming, XPath for searching, and XLink for linking. Much of the standards work is under the auspices of the World Wide Web Consortium (W3C), an organization whose members include Microsoft, Sun, IBM, and many academic and public institutions.

The W3C's mandate is to research and foster new technology for the Internet. That's a rather broad statement, but if you visit their site at *http://www.w3.org/* you'll see that they cover a lot of bases. The W3C doesn't create, police, or license standards. Rather, they make recommendations that developers are encouraged, but not required, to follow.*

However, the system remains open enough to allow healthy dissent, such as the recent and interesting case of XML Schema, a W3C standard that has generated controversy and competition. We'll examine this particular story further in Chapter 3.

---

* When a trusted body like the W3C makes a recommendation, it often has the effect of a law; many developers begin to follow the recommendation upon its release, and developers who hope to write software that is compatible with everyone else's (which is the whole point behind standards like XML) had better follow the recommendation as well.

It's strong enough to be taken seriously, but loose enough not to scare people away. The recommendations are always available to the public.

Every developer should have working knowledge of XML, since it's the universal packing material for data, and so many programs are all about crunching data. The rest of this chapter gives a quick introduction to XML for developers.

Markup, Elements, and Structure

A markup language provides a way to embed instructions inside data to help a computer program process the data. Most markup schemes, such as troff, TeX, and HTML, have instructions that are optimized for one purpose, such as formatting the document to be printed or to be displayed on a computer screen. These languages rely on a *presentational* description of data, which controls typeface, font size, color, or other media-specific properties. Although such markup can result in nicely formatted documents, it can be like a prison for your data, consigning it to one format forever; you won't be able to extract your data for other purposes without significant work.

That's where XML comes in. It's a generic markup language that describes data according to its structure and purpose, rather than with specific formatting instructions. The actual presentation information is stored somewhere else, such as in a stylesheet. What's left is a functional description of the parts of your document, which is suitable for many different kinds of processing. With proper use of XML, your document will be ready for an unlimited variety of applications and purposes.

Now let's review the basic components of XML. Its most important feature is the *element*. Elements are encapsulated regions of data that serve a unique role in your document. For example, consider a typical book, composed of a preface, chapters, appendixes, and an index. In XML, marking up each of these sections as a unique element within the book would be appropriate. Elements may themselves be divided into other elements; you might find the chapter's title, paragraphs, examples, and sections all marked up as elements. This division continues as deeply as necessary, so even a paragraph can contain elements such as emphasized text, quotations, and hypertext links.

Besides dividing text into a hierarchy of regions, elements associate a label and other properties with the data. Every element has a name, or *element type*, usually describing its function in the document. Thus, a chapter element could be called a "chapter" (or "chapt" or "ch"—whatever you fancy). An element can include other information besides the type, using a name-value pair called an *attribute*. Together, an element's type and attributes distinguish it from other elements in the document.

Example 2-1 shows a typical piece of XML.

Example 2-1. An XML fragment

```
<list id="eriks-todo-47">
  <title>Things to Do This Week</title>
  <item>clean the aquarium</item>
  <item>mow the lawn</item>
  <item priority="important">save the whales</item>
</list>
```

This is, as you've probably guessed, a to-do list with three items and a title. Anyone who has worked with HTML will recognize the markup. The pieces of text surrounded by angle brackets ("<" and ">") are called *tags*, and they act as bookends for elements. Every nonempty element must have both a start and end tag, each containing the element type label. The start tag can optionally contain a number of attributes (name-value pairs like `priority="important"`). Thus, the markup is pretty clear and unambiguous—even a human can read it.

A human can read it, but more importantly, a computer program can read it very easily. The framers of XML have taken great care to ensure that XML is easy to read by all XML processors, regardless of the types of tags used or the context. If your markup follows all the proper syntactic rules, then the XML is absolutely unambiguous. This makes processing it much easier, since you don't have to add code to handle unclear situations.

Consider HTML, as it was originally defined (an application of XML's predecessor, SGML).* For certain elements, it was acceptable to omit the end tag, and it's usually possible to tell from the context where an element should end. Even so, making code robust enough to handle every ambiguous situation comes at the price of complexity and inaccurate output from bad guessing. Now imagine how it would be if the same processor had to handle any element type, not just the HTML elements. Generic XML processors can't make assumptions about how elements should be arranged. An ambiguous situation, such as the omission of an end tag, would be disastrous.

Any piece of XML can be represented in a diagram called a *tree*, a structure familiar to most programmers. At the top (since trees in computer science grow upside down) is the root element. The elements that are contained one level down branch from it. Each element may contain elements at still deeper levels, and so on, until you reach the bottom, or "leaves" of the tree. The leaves consist of either data (text) or empty elements. An element at any level can be thought of as the root of its own tree (or subtree, if you prefer to call it that). A tree diagram of the previous example is shown in Figure 2-1.

---

* Currently, XHTML is an XML-legal variant of HTML that HTML authors are encouraged to adopt in support of coming XML tools. XML enables different kinds of markup to be processed by the same programs (e.g., editors, syntax-checkers, or formatters). HTML will soon be joined on the Web by such XML-derived languages as DocBook and MathML.

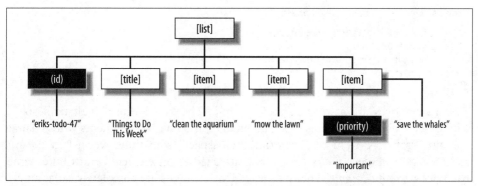

Figure 2-1. A to-do list represented as a tree structure

Besides the arboreal analogy, it's also useful to speak of XML genealogically. Here, we describe an element's content (both data and elements) as its descendants, and the elements that contain it as its ancestors. In our list example, each <item> element is a child of the same parent, the <list> element, and a sibling of the others. (We generally don't carry the terminology too far, as talking about third cousins twice-removed can make your head hurt.) We will use both the tree and family terminology to describe element relationships throughout the book.

Namespaces

It's sometimes useful to divide up your elements and attributes into groups, or *namespaces*. A namespace is to an element somewhat as a surname is to a person. You may know three people named Mike, but no two of them have the same last name. To illustrate this concept, look at the document in Example 2-2.

Example 2-2. A document using namespaces

```
<?xml version="1.0"?>
<report>
  <title>Fish and Bicycles: A Connection?</title>
  <para>I have found a surprising relationship
  of fish to bicycles, expressed by the equation
  <equation>f = kb+n</equation>. The graph below illustrates
  the data curve of my experiment:</para>
  <chart xmlns:graph="http://mathstuff.com/dtds/chartml/">
    <graph:dimension>
      <graph:axis>fish</graph:axis>
      <graph:start>80</graph:start>
      <graph:end>99</graph:end>
      <graph:interval>1</graph:interval>
    </graph:dimension>
    <graph:dimension>
      <graph:axis>bicycle</graph:axis>
      <graph:start>0</graph:start>
      <graph:end>1000</graph:end>
```

Example 2-2. A document using namespaces (continued)

```
      <graph:interval>50</graph:interval>
    </graph:dimension>
    <graph:equation>fish=0.01*bicycle+81.4</graph:equation>
  </graph:chart>
</report>
```

Two namespaces are at play in this example. The first is the default namespace, where elements and attributes lack a colon in their name. The elements whose names contain graph: are from the "chartml" namespace (something we just made up). graph: is a *namespace prefix* that, when attached to an element or attribute name, becomes a *qualified name*. The two <equation> elements are completely different element types, with a different role to play in the document. The one in the default namespace is used to format an equation literally, and the one in the chart namespace helps a graphing program generate a curve.

A namespace must always be declared in an element that contains the region where it will be used. This is done with an attribute of the form xmlns:*prefix=URL*, where *prefix* is the namespace prefix to be used (in this case, graph:) and *URL* is a unique identifier in the form of a URL or other resource identifier. Outside of the scope of this element, the namespace is not recognized.

Besides keeping two like-named element types or attribute types apart, namespaces serve a vital function in helping an XML processor format a document. Sometimes the change in namespace indicates that the default formatter should be replaced with a kind that handles a specific kind of data, such as the graph in the example. In other cases, a namespace is used to "bless" markup instructions to be treated as meta-markup, as in the case of XSLT.

Namespaces are emerging as a useful part of the XML tool set. However, they can raise a problem when DTDs are used. DTDs, as we will explain later, may contain declarations that restrict the kinds of elements that can be used to finite sets. However, it can be difficult to apply namespaces to DTDs, which have no special facility for resolving namespaces or knowing that elements and attributes that fall under a namespace (beyond the ever-present default one) are defined according to some other XML application. It's difficult to know this information partly because the notion of namespaces was added to XML long after the format of DTDs, which have been around since the SGML days, was set in stone. Therefore, namespaces can be incompatible with some DTDs. This problem is still unresolved, though not because of any lack of effort in the standards community.

Chapter 10 covers some practical issues that emerge when working with namespaces.

Spacing

You'll notice in examples throughout this book that we indent elements and add spaces wherever it helps make the code more readable to humans. Doing so is not unreasonable if you ever have to edit or inspect XML code personally. Sometimes, however, this indentation can result in space that you don't want in your final product. Since XML has a make-no-assumptions policy toward your data, it may seem that you're stuck with all that space.

One solution is to make the XML processor smarter. Certain parsers can decide whether to pass space along to the processing application.* They can determine from the element declarations in the DTD when space is only there for readability and is not part of the content. Alternatively, you can instruct your processor to specialize in a particular markup language and train it to treat some elements differently with respect to space.

When neither option applies to your problem, XML provides a way to let a document tell the processor when space needs to be preserved. The reserved attribute xml:space can be used in any element to specify whether space should be kept as is or removed.† For example:

```
<address-label xml:space='preserve'>246 Marshmellow Ave.
Slumberville, MA
02149</address-label>
```

In this case, the characters used to break lines in the address are retained for all future processing. The other setting for xml:space is "default," which means that the XML processor has to decide what to do with extra space.

Entities

For your authoring convenience, XML has another feature called *entities*. An entity is useful when you need a placeholder for text or markup that would be inconvenient or impossible to just type in. It's a piece of XML set aside from your document;‡ you use an *entity reference* to stand in for it. An XML processor must resolve all entity references with their replacement text at the time of parsing. Therefore, every referenced entity must be declared somewhere so that the processor knows how to resolve it.

---

* A parser is a specialized XML handler that preprocesses a document for the rest of the program. Different parsers have varying levels of "intelligence" when interpreting XML. We'll describe this topic in greater detail in Chapter 3.

† We know that it's reserved because it has the special "xml" prefix. The XML standard defines special uses and meanings for elements and attributes with this prefix.

‡ Technically, the whole document is one entity, called the *document entity*. However, people usually use the term "entity" to refer to a subset of the document.

The *Document Type Declaration* (DTD) is the place to declare an entity. It has two parts, the *internal subset* that is part of your document, and the *external subset* that lives in another document. (Often, people talk about the external subset as "the DTD" and call the internal subset "the internal subset," even though both subsets together make up the whole DTD.) In both places, the method for declaring entities is the same. The document in Example 2-3 shows how this feature works.

Example 2-3. A document with entity declarations

```
<!DOCTYPE memo
  SYSTEM "/xml-dtds/memo.dtd"
[
  <!ENTITY companyname "Willy Wonka's Chocolate Factory">
  <!ENTITY healthplan  SYSTEM "hp.txt">
]>

<memo>
  <to>All Oompa-loompas</to>
  <para>
    &companyname; has a new owner and CEO, Charlie Bucket. Since
    our name, &companyname;, has considerable brand recognition,
    the board has decided not to change it. However, at Charlie's
    request, we will be changing our healthcare provider to the
    more comprehensive &Uuml;mpacare, which has better facilities
    for 'Loompas (text of the plan to follow). Thank you for working
    at &companyname;!
  </para>
  &healthplan;
</memo>
```

Let's examine the new material in this example. At the top is the DTD, a special markup instruction that contains a lot of important information, including the internal subset and a path to the external subset. Like all declarative markup (i.e., it defines something new), it starts with an exclamation point, and is followed by a keyword, DOCTYPE. After that keyword is the name of an element that will be used to contain the document. We call that element the *root element* or *document element*. This element is followed by a path to the external subset, given by SYSTEM "/xml-dtds/memo.dtd", and the internal subset of declarations, enclosed in square brackets ([ ]).

The external subset is used for declarations that will be used in many documents, so it naturally resides in another file. The internal subset is best used for declarations that are local to the document. They may override declarations in the external subset or contain new ones. As you see in the example, two entities are declared in the internal subset. An entity declaration has two parameters: the entity name and its replacement text. The entities are named companyname and healthplan.

These entities are called *general entities* and are distinguished from other kinds of entities because they are declared by you, the author. Replacement text for general entities can come from two different places. The first entity declaration defines the text within the declaration itself. The second points to another file where the text resides. It uses a *system identifier* to specify the file's location, acting much like a URL used by a web browser to find a page to load. In this case, the file is loaded by an XML processor and inserted verbatim wherever an entity is referenced. Such an entity is called an *external entity*.

If you look closely at the example, you'll see markup instructions of the form &*name*;. The ampersand (&) indicates an entity reference, where *name* is the name of the entity being referenced. The same reference can be used repeatedly, making it a convenient way to insert repetitive text or markup, as we do with the entity companyname.

An entity can contain markup as well as text, as is the case with healthplan (actually, we don't know what's in that entity because it's in another file, but since it's going to be a large document, you can assume it will have markup as well as text). An entity can even contain other entities, to any nesting level you want. The only restriction is that entities can't contain themselves, at any level, lest you create a circular definition that can never be constructed by the XML processor. Some XML technologies, such as XSLT, do let you have fun with recursive logic, but think of entity references as code constants—playing with circular references here will make any parser very unhappy.

Finally, the Ü entity reference is declared somewhere in the external subset to fill in for a character that the chocolate factory's ancient text editor programs have trouble rendering—in this case, a capital "U" with an umlaut over it: Ü. Since the referenced entity is one character wide, the reference in this case is almost more of an alias than a pointer. The usual way to handle unusual characters (the way that's built into the XML specification) involves using a numeric character entity, which, in this case, would be &#00DC;. 0x00DC is the hexadecimal equivalent of the number 220, which is the position of the U-umlaut character in Unicode (the character set used natively by XML, which we cover in more detail in the next section).

However, since an abbreviated descriptive name like Uuml is generally easier to remember than the arcane 00DC, some XML users prefer to use these types of aliases by placing lines such as this into their documents' DTDs:

```
<!ENTITY % Uuml &#x00DC;>
```

XML recognizes only five built-in, named entity references, shown in Table 2-1. They're not actually references, but are escapes for five punctuation marks that have special meaning for XML.

Table 2-1. XML entity references

Character	Entity
<	&lt;
>	&gt;
&	&amp;
"	&quot;
'	&apos;

The only two of these references that must be used throughout any XML document are &lt and &. Element tags and entity references can appear at any point in a document. No parser could guess, for example, whether a < character is used as a less-than math symbol or as a genuine XML token; it will always assume the latter and will report a malformed document if this assumption proves false.

Unicode, Character Sets, and Encodings

At low levels, computers see text as a series of positive integer numbers mapped onto character sets, which are collections of numbered characters (and sometimes control codes) that some standards body created. A very common collection is the venerable US-ASCII character set, which contains 128 characters, including upper- and lower-case letters of the Latin alphabet, numerals, various symbols and space characters, and a few special print codes inherited from the old days of teletype terminals. By adding on the eighth bit, this 7-bit system is extended into a larger set with twice as many characters, such as ISO-Latin1, used in many Unix systems. These characters include other European characters, such as Latin letters with accents, Icelandic characters, ligatures, footnote marks, and legal symbols. Alas, humanity, a species bursting with both creativity and pride, has invented many more linguistic symbols than can be mapped onto an 8-bit number.

For this reason, a new character encoding architecture called Unicode has gained acceptance as the standard way to represent every written script in which people might want to store data (or write computer code). Depending on the flavor used, it uses up to 32 bits to describe a character, giving the standard room for millions of individual glyphs. For over a decade, the Unicode Consortium has been filling up this space with characters ranging from the entire Han Chinese character set to various mathematical, notational, and signage symbols, and still leaves the encoding space with enough room to grow for the coming millennium or two.

Given all this effort we're putting into hyping it, it shouldn't surprise you to learn that, while an XML document can use any type of encoding, it will by default assume the Unicode-flavored, variable-length encoding known as UTF-8. This encoding uses between one and six bytes to encode the number that represents the character's Unicode address and the character's length in bytes, if that address is greater than 255. It's possible to write an entire document in 1-byte characters and have it be indistinguishable from ISO Latin-1 (a humble address block with addresses ranging from 0 to 255), but if you need the occasional high character, or if you need a lot of them (as you would when storing Asian-language data, for example), it's easy to encode in UTF-8. Unicode-aware processors handle the encoding correctly and display the right glyphs, while older applications simply ignore the multibyte characters and pass them through unharmed. Since Version 5.6, Perl has handled UTF-8 characters with increasing finesse. We'll discuss Perl's handling of Unicode in more depth in Chapter 3.

The XML Declaration

After reading about character encodings, an astute reader may wonder how to declare the encoding in the document so an XML processor knows which one you're using. The answer is: declare the decoding in the *XML declaration*. The XML declaration is a line at the very top of a document that describes the kind of markup you're using, including XML version, character encoding, and whether the document requires an external subset of the DTD. The declaration looks like this:

```
<?xml version="1.0" encoding="utf8" standalone="yes"?>
```

The declaration is optional, as are each of its parameters (except for the required version attribute). The encoding parameter is important only if you use a character encoding other than UTF-8 (since it's the default encoding). If explicitly set to "yes", the standalone declaration causes a validating parser to raise an error if the document references external entities.

Processing Instructions and Other Markup

Besides elements, you can use several other syntactic objects to make XML easier to manage. *Processing instructions* (PIs) are used to convey information to a particular XML processor. They specify the intended processor with a *target* parameter, which is followed by an optional *data* parameter. Any program that doesn't recognize the target simply skips the PI and pretends it never existed. Here is an example based on an actual behind-the-scenes O'Reilly book hacking experience:

```
<?file-breaker start chap04.xml?><chapter>
<title>The very long title<?lb?>that seemed to go on forever and ever</title>
<?xml2pdf vspace 10pt?>
```

The first PI has a target called file-breaker and its data is chap04.xml. A program reading this document will look for a PI with that target keyword and will act on that data. In this case, the goal is to create a new file and save the following XML into it.

The second PI has only a target, lb. We have actually seen this example used in documents to tell an XML processor to create a line break at that point. This example has two problems. First, the PI is a replacement for a space character; that's bad because any program that doesn't recognize the PI will not know that a space should be between the two words. It would be better to place a space after the PI and let the target processor remove any following space itself. Second, the target is an instruction, not an actual name of a program. A more unique name like the one in the next PI, xml2pdf, would be better (with the lb appearing as data instead).

PIs are convenient for developers. They have no solid rules that specify how to name a target or what kind of data to use, but in general, target names ought to be very specific and data should be very short.

Those who have written documents using Perl's built-in Plain Old Documentation mini-markup language* hackers may note a similarity between PIs and certain POD directives, particularly the =for paragraphs and =begin/=end blocks. In these paragraphs and blocks, you can leave little messages for a POD processor with a target and some arguments (or any string of text).

Another useful markup object is the *XML comment*. Comments are regions of text that any XML processor ignores. They are meant to hold information for human eyes only, such as notes written by authors to themselves and their collaborators. They are also useful for turning "off" regions of markup—perhaps if you want to debug the document or you're afraid to delete something altogether. Here's an example:

```
<!-- this is invisible to the parser -->
This is perfectly visible XML content.
<!--
  <para>This paragraph is no longer part of the document.</para>
-->
```

Note that these comments look and work exactly like their HTML counterparts.

The only thing you can't put inside a comment is another comment. You can't even feint at nesting comments; the string "--", for example, is illegal in a comment, no matter how you use it.

The last syntactic convenience we will discuss is the *CDATA section*. CDATA stands for character data, which in XML parlance means unparsed content. In other words, the XML processor treats an entire CDATA section as though it contains no markup at all—even things that look like markup. This is useful if you want to include a large region of illegal characters like <, >, and & that would be difficult to convert into character entity references.

For example:

```
<codelisting>
<![CDATA[if( $val > 3 && @lines ) {
  $input = <FILE>;
}]]>
</codelisting>
```

Everything after <![CDATA[and before the]]> is treated as nonmarkup data, so the markup symbols are perfectly fine. We rarely use CDATA sections because they are kind of unsightly, in our humble opinion, and make writing XML processing code a little harder. But it's there if you need it.†

---

* The gory details of which lie in Chapter 26 of *Programming Perl, Third Edition* or in the perlpod manpage.

† We use CDATA throughout the DocBook-flavored XML that makes up this book. We wrapped all the code listings and sample XML documents in it so we didn't have to suffer the bother of escaping every < and & that appears in them.

Free-Form XML and Well-Formed Documents

XML's grandfather, SGML, required that every element and attribute be documented thoroughly with a long list of declarations in the DTD. We'll describe what we mean by that thorough documentation in the next section, but for now, imagine it as a blueprint for a document. This blueprint adds considerable overhead to the processing of a document and was a serious obstacle to SGML's status as a popular markup language for the Internet. HTML, which was originally developed as an SGML instance, was hobbled by this enforced structure, since any "valid" HTML document had to conform to the HTML DTD. Hence, extending the language was impossible without approval by a web committee.

XML does away with that requirement by allowing a special condition called *free-form* XML. In this mode, a document has to follow only minimal syntax rules to be acceptable. If it follows those rules, the document is *well-formed*. Following these rules is wonderfully liberating for a developer because it means that you don't have to scan a DTD every time you want to process a piece of XML. All a processor has to do is make sure that minimal syntax rules are followed.

In free-form XML, you can choose the name of any element. It doesn't have to belong to a sanctioned vocabulary, as is the case with HTML. Including frivolous markup into your program is a risk, but as long as you know what you're doing, it's okay. If you don't trust the markup to fit a pattern you're looking for, then you need to use element and attribute declarations, as we describe in the next section.

What are these rules? Here's a short list as seen though a coarse-grained spyglass:

- A document can have only one top-level element, the *document element*, that contains all the other elements and data. This element does not include the XML declaration and document type declaration, which must precede it.
- Every element with content must have both a start tag and an end tag.
- Element and attribute names are case sensitive, and only certain characters can be used (letters, underscores, hyphens, periods, and numbers), with only letters and underscores eligible as the first character. Colons are allowed, but only as part of a declared namespace prefix.
- All attributes must have values and all attribute values must be quoted.
- Elements may never overlap; an element's start and end tags must both appear within the same element.
- Certain characters, including angle brackets (< >) and the ampersand (&) are reserved for markup and are not allowed in parsed content. Use character entity references instead, or just stick the offending content into a CDATA section.

- Empty elements must use a syntax distinguishing them from nonempty element start tags. The syntax requires a slash (/) before the closing bracket (>) of the tag.

You will encounter more rules, so for a more complete understanding of well-formedness, you should either read an introductory book on XML or look at the W3C's official recommendation at *http://www.w3.org/XML*.

If you want to be able to process your document with XML-using programs, make sure it is always well formed. (After all, there's no such thing as non-well-formed XML.) A tool often used to check this status is called a *well-formedness checker*, which is a type of XML parser that reports errors to the user. Often, such a tool can be detailed in its analysis and give you the exact line number in a file where the problem occurs. We'll discuss checkers and parsers in Chapter 3.

Declaring Elements and Attributes

When you need an extra level of quality control (beyond the healthful status implied by the "well-formed" label), define the grammar patterns of your markup language in the DTD. Defining the patterns will make your markup into a formal language, documented much like a standard published by an international organization. With a DTD, a program can tell in short order whether a document conforms to, or, as we say, is a *valid* example of, your document type.

Two kinds of declarations allow a DTD to model a language. The first is the *element declaration*. It adds a new name to the allowed set of elements and specifies, in a special pattern language, what can go inside the element. Here are some examples:

```
<!ELEMENT sandwich ((meat | cheese)+ | (peanut-butter, jelly)), condiment+, pickle?)>
<!ELEMENT pickle EMPTY>
<!ELEMENT condiment (PCDATA | mustard | ketchup )*>
```

The first parameter declares the name of the element. The second parameter is a pattern, a *content model* in parentheses, or a keyword such as EMPTY. Content models resemble regular expression syntax, the main differences being that element names are complete tokens and a comma is used to indicate a required sequence of elements. Every element mentioned in a content model should be declared somewhere in the DTD.

The other important kind of declaration is the *attribute list declaration*. With it, you can declare a set of optional or required attributes for a given element. The attribute values can be controlled to some extent, though the pattern restrictions are somewhat limited. Let's look at an example:

```
<!ATTLIST sandwich
    id       ID        #REQUIRED
    price    CDATA     #IMPLIED
    taste    CDATA     #FIXED      "yummy"
    name     (reuben | ham-n-cheese | BLT | PB-n-J )      'BLT'
>
```

The general pattern of an attribute declaration has three parts: a name, a data type, and a behavior. This example declares three attributes for the element `<sandwich>`. The first, named `id`, is of type `ID`, which is a unique string of characters that can be used only once in any ID-type attribute throughout the document, and is required because of the `#REQUIRED` keyword. The second, named `price`, is of type `CDATA` and is optional, according to the `#IMPLIED` keyword. The third, named `taste`, is fixed with the value `"yummy"` and can't be changed (all `<sandwich>` elements will inherit this attribute automatically). Finally, the attribute `name` is one of an enumerated list of values, with the default being `'BLT'`.

Though they have been around for a long time and have been very successful, element and attribute declarations have some major flaws. Content model syntax is relatively inflexible. For example, it's surprisingly hard to express the statement "this element must contain one each of the elements A, B, C, and D in any order" (try it and see!). Also, the character data can't be constrained in any way. You can't ensure that a `<date>` contains a valid date, and not a street address, for example. Third, and most troubling for the XML community, is the fact that DTDs don't play well with namespaces. If you use element declarations, you have to declare all elements you would ever use in your document, not just some of them. If you want to leave open the possibility of importing some element types from another namespace, you can't also use a DTD to validate your document—at least not without playing the mix-and-match DTD-combination games we described earlier, and combining DTDs doesn't always work, anyway.

Schemas

Several proposed alternate language schemas address the shortcomings of DTD declarations. The W3C's recommended language for doing this is called XML Schema. You should know, however, that it is only one of many competing schema-type languages, some of which may be better suited to your needs. If you prefer to use a competing schema, check CPAN to see if a module has been written to handle your favorite flavor of schemas.

Unlike DTD syntax, XML Schemas are themselves XML documents, making it possible to use many XML tools to edit them. Their real power, however, is in their fine-grained control over the form your data takes. This control makes it more attractive for documents for which checking the quality of data is at least as important as ensuring it has the proper structure. Example 2-4 shows a schema designed to model census forms, where data type checking is necessary.

Example 2-4. An XML schema

```
<xs:schema xmlns:xs="http://www.w3.org/2001/XMLSchema-instance">

  <xs:annotation>
    <xs:documentation>
```

Example 2-4. An XML schema (continued)

```
      Census form for the Republic of Oz
      Department of Paperwork, Emerald City
    </xs:documentation>
  </xs:annotation>

  <xs:element name="census" type="CensusType"/>

  <xs:complexType name="CensusType">
    <xs:element name="censustaker" type="xs:decimal" minoccurs="0"/>
    <xs:element name="address" type="Address"/>
    <xs:element name="occupants" type="Occupants"/>
    <xs:attribute name="date" type="xs:date"/>
  </xs:complexType>

  <xs:complexType name="Address">
    <xs:element name="number" type="xs:decimal"/>
    <xs:element name="street" type="xs:string"/>
    <xs:element name="city"   type="xs:string"/>
    <xs:element name="province"  type="xs:string"/>
    <xs:attribute name="postalcode" type="PCode"/>
  </xs:complexType>

  <xs:simpleType name="PCode" base="xs:string">
    <xs:pattern value="[A-Z]-d{3}"/>
  </xs:simpleType>

  <xs:complexType name="Occupants">
    <xs:element name="occupant" minOccurs="1" maxOccurs="20">
     <xs:complexType>
      <xs:element name="firstname" type="xs:string"/>
      <xs:element name="surname" type="xs:string"/>
      <xs:element name="age">
       <xs:simpleType base="xs:positive-integer">
        <xs:maxExclusive value="200"/>
       </xs:simpleType>
      </xs:element>
     </xs:complexType>
    </xs:element>
  </xs:complexType>

</xs:schema>
```

The first line identifies this document as a schema and associates it with the XML Schema namespace. The next structure, <annotation>, is a place to document the schema's purpose and other details. After this documentation, we get into the fun stuff and start declaring element types.

We start by declaring the root of our document type, an element called <census>. The declaration is an element of type <xs:element>. Its attributes assign the name "census" and type of description for <census>, "CensusType". In schemas, unlike DTDs, the content descriptions are often kept separate from the declarations, making it easier to define generic element types and assign multiple elements to them. Further down in the schema is the actual content description, an <xs:complexType> element with name="CensusType". It specifies that a <census> contains an optional <censustaker>, followed by a required <occupants> and a required <address>. It also must have an attribute called date.

Both the attribute date and the element <censustaker> have specific data patterns assigned in the description of <census>: a date and a decimal number. If your <census> document had anything but a numerical value as its content, it would be an error according to this schema. You couldn't get this level of control with DTDs.

Schemas can check for many types. These types include numerical values like bytes, floating-point numbers, long integers, binary numbers, and boolean values; patterns for marking times and durations; Internet addresses and URLs; IDs, IDREFs, and other types borrowed from DTDs; and strings of character data.

An element type description uses properties called *facets* to set even more detailed limits on content. For example, the schema above gives the <age> element, whose data type is positive-integer, a maximum value of 200 using the max-inclusive facet. XML Schemas have many other facets, including precision, scale, encoding, pattern, enumeration, and max-length.

The Address description introduces a new concept: user-defined patterns. With this technique, we define postalcode with a pattern code: [A-Z]-d{3}. Using this code is like saying, "Accept any alphabetic character followed by a dash and three digits." If no data type fits your needs, you can always make up a new one.

Schemas are an exciting new technology that makes XML more useful, especially with data-specific applications such as data entry forms. We'll leave a full account of its uses and forms for another book.

Other Schema Strategies

While it has the blessing of the W3C, XML Schema is not the only schema option available for flexible document validation. Some programmers prefer the methods available through specifications like RelaxNG (available at *http://www.oasis-open. org/committees/relax-ng/*) or Schematron (*http://www.ascc.net/xml/resource/schematron/schematron.html*), which achieve the same goals through different philosophical means. Since the latter specification has Perl implementations that are currently available, we'll examine it further in Chapter 3.

Transformations

The last topic we want to introduce is the concept of transformations. In XML, a *transformation* is a process of restructuring or converting a document into another form. The W3C recommends a language for transforming XML called XML Stylesheet Language for Transformations (XSLT). It's an incredibly useful and fun technology to work with.

Like XML Schema, an XSLT transformation script is an XML document. It's composed of *template rules*, each of which is an instruction for how to turn one element type into something else. The term *template* is often used to mean an example of how something should look, with blanks that you should fill in. That's exactly how template rules work: they are examples of how the final document should be, with the blanks filled in by the XSLT processor.

Example 2-5 is a rudimentary transformation that converts a simple DocBook XML document into an HTML page.

Example 2-5. An XSLT transformation document

```
<xsl:stylesheet
  xmlns:xsl="http://www.w3.org/1999/XSL/Transform"
  version="1.0">

<xsl:output method="html"/>

<!-- RULE FOR BOOK ELEMENT -->
<xsl:template match="book">
  <html>
    <head>
      <title><xsl:value-of select="title"/></title>
    </head>
    <body>
      <h1><xsl:value-of select="title"/></h1>
      <h3>Table of Contents</h3>
      <xsl:call-template name="toc"/>
      <xsl:apply-templates select="chapter"/>
    </body>
  </html>
</xsl:template>

<!-- RULE FOR CHAPTER -->
<xsl:template match="chapter">
  <xsl:apply-templates/>
</xsl:template>

<!-- RULE FOR CHAPTER TITLE -->
<xsl:template match="chapter/title">
  <h2>
    <xsl:text>Chapter </xsl:text>
    <xsl:number count="chapter" level="any" format="1"/>
  </h2>
  <xsl:apply-templates/>
</xsl:template>

<!-- RULE FOR PARA -->
```

Example 2-5. An XSLT transformation document (continued)

```
<xsl:template match="para">
  <p><xsl:apply-templates/></p>
</xsl:template>

<!-- NAMED RULE: TOC -->
<xsl:template name="toc">
  <xsl:if test="count(chapter)>0">
    <xsl:for-each select="chapter">
      <xsl:text>Chapter </xsl:text>
      <xsl:value-of select="position( )"/>
      <xsl:text>: </xsl:text>
      <i><xsl:value-of select="title"/></i>
      <br/>
    </xsl:for-each>
  </xsl:if>
</xsl:template>

</xsl:stylesheet>
```

First, the XSLT processor reads the stylesheet and creates a table of template rules. Next, it parses the source XML document (the one to be converted) and traverses it one node at a time. A *node* is an element, a piece of text, a processing instruction, an attribute, or a namespace declaration. For each node, the XSLT processor tries to find the *best matching* rule. It applies the rule, outputting everything the template says it should, jumping to other rules as necessary.

Example 2-6 is a sample document on which you can run the transformation.

Example 2-6. A document to transform

```
<book>
  <title>The Blathering Brains</title>
  <chapter>
    <title>At the Bazaar</title>
    <para>What a fantastic day it was. The crates were stacked
        high with imported goods: dates, bananas, dried meats,
        fine silks, and more things than I could imagine. As I
        walked around, savoring the fragrances of cinnamon and
        cardamom, I almost didn't notice a small booth with a
        little man selling brains.</para>
    <para>Brains! Yes, human brains, still quite moist and squishy,
        swimming in big glass jars full of some greenish
        fluid.</para>
    <para>"Would you like a brain, sir?" he asked. "Very reasonable
        prices. Here is Enrico Fermi's brain for only two
        dracmas. Or, perhaps, you would prefer Aristotle?  Or the
        great emperor Akhnaten?"</para>
    <para>I recoiled in horror...</para>
  </chapter>
</book>
```

Let's walk through the transformation.

1. The first element is `<book>`. The best matching rule is the first one, because it explicitly matches "book." The template says to output tags like `<html>`, `<head>`, and `<title>`. Note that these tags are treated as data markup because they don't have the `xsl:` namespace prefix.

2. When the processor gets to the XSLT instruction `<xsl:value-of select="title"/>`, it has to find a `<title>` element that is a child of the current element, `<book>`. Then it must obtain the *value* of that element, which is simply all the text contained within it. This text is output inside a `<title>` element as the template directs.

3. The processor continues in this way until it gets to the `<xsl:call-template name="toc"/>` instruction. If you look at the bottom of the stylesheet, you'll find a template rule that begins with `<xsl:template name="toc">`. This template rule is a *named template* and acts like a function call. It assembles a table of contents and returns the text to the calling rule for output.

4. Inside the named template is an element called `<xsl:if test="count(chapter)> 0">`. This element is a conditional statement whose test is whether more than one `<chapter>` is inside the current element (still `<book>`). The test passes, and processing continues inside the element.

5. The `<xsl:for-each select="chapter">` instruction causes the processor to visit each `<chapter>` child element and temporarily make it the current element while in the body of the `<xsl:for-each>` element. This step is analogous to a foreach( ) loop in Perl. The `<xsl:value-of select="position( )"/>` statement derives the numerical position of each `<chapter>` and outputs it so that the result document reads "Chapter 1," "Chapter 2," and so on.

6. The named template "toc" returns its text to the calling rule and execution continues. Next, the processor receives an `<xsl:apply-templates select="chapter"/>` directive. An output of `<xsl:apply-templates>` without any attributes means that the processor should then process each of the current element's children, making it the current element. However, since a select="chapter" attribute is present, only children who are of type `<chapter>` should be processed. After all descendants have been processed and this instruction returns its text, it will be output and the rest of the rule will be followed until the end.

7. Moving on to the first `<chapter>` element, the processor locates a suitable rule and sees only an `<xsl:apply-tempaltes/>` rule. The rest of the processing is pretty easy, as the rules for the remaining elements, `<title>` and `<para>`, are straightforward.

XSLT is a rich language for handling transformations, but often leaves something to be desired. It can be slow on large documents, since it has to build an internal representation of the whole document before it can do any processing. Its syntax, while a remarkable achievement for XML, is not as expressive and easy to use as Perl. We will explore numerous Perl solutions to some problems that XSL could also solve. You'll have to decide whether you prefer XSLT's simplicity or Perl's power.

That's our whirlwind tour of XML. Next, we'll jump into the fundamentals of XML processing with Perl using parsers and basic writers. At this point, you should have a good idea of what XML is used for and how it's used, and you should be able to recognize all the parts when you see them. If you still have any doubts, stop now and grab an XML tutorial.

CHAPTER 3

XML Basics: Reading and Writing

This chapter covers the two most important tasks in working with XML: reading it into memory and writing it out again. XML is a structured, predictable, and standard data storage format, and as such carries a price. Unlike the line-by-line, make-it-up-as-you-go style that typifies text hacking in Perl, XML expects you to learn the rules of its game—the structures and protocols outlined in Chapter 2—before you can play with it. Fortunately, much of the hard work is already done, in the form of module-based parsers and other tools that trailblazing Perl and XML hackers already created (some of which we touched on in Chapter 1).

Knowing how to use parsers is very important. They typically drive the rest of the processing for you, or at least get the data into a state where you can work with it. Any good programmer knows that getting the data ready is half the battle. We'll look deeply into the parsing process and detail the strategies used to drive processing.

Parsers come with a bewildering array of options that let you configure the output to your needs. Which character set should you use? Should you validate the document or merely check if it's well formed? Do you need to expand entity references, or should you keep them as references? How can you set handlers for events or tell the parser to build a tree for you? We'll explain these options fully so you can get the most out of parsing.

Finally, we'll show you how to spit XML back out, which can be surprisingly tricky if one isn't aware of XML's expectations regarding text encoding. Getting this step right is vital if you ever want to be able to use your data again without painful hand fixing.

XML Parsers

File I/O is an intrinsic part of any programming language, but it has always been done at a fairly low level: reading a character or a line at a time, running it through a regular expression filter, etc. Raw text is an unruly commodity, lacking any clear rules for how to separate discrete portions, other than basic, flat concepts such as newline-separated lines and tab-separated columns. Consequently, more data packaging schemes are available than even the chroniclers of Babel could have foreseen. It's from this cacophony that XML has risen, providing clear rules for how to create boundaries between data, assign hierarchy, and link resources in a predictable, unambiguous fashion. A program that relies on these rules can read any well-formed XML document, as if someone had jammed a babelfish into its ear.[*]

Where can you get this babelfish to put in your program's ear? An *XML parser* is a program or code library that translates XML data into either a stream of events or a data object, giving your program direct access to structured data. The XML can come from one or more files or filehandles, a character stream, or a static string. It could be peppered with entity references that may or may not need to be resolved. Some of the parts could come from outside your computer system, living in some far corner of the Internet. It could be encoded in a Latin character set, or perhaps in a Japanese set. Fortunately for you, the developer, none of these details have to be accounted for in your program because they are all taken care of by the parser, an abstract tunnel between the physical state of data and the crystallized representation seen by your subroutines.

An XML parser acts as a bridge between marked-up data (data packaged with embedded XML instructions) and some predigested form your program can work with. In Perl's case, we mean hashes, arrays, scalars, and objects made of references to these old friends. XML can be complex, residing in many files or streams, and can contain unresolved regions (entities) that may need to be patched up. Also, a parser usually tries to accept only good XML, rejecting it if it contains well-formedness errors. Its output has to reflect the structure (order, containment, associative data) while ignoring irrelevant details such as what files the data came from and what character set was used. That's a lot of work. To itemize these points, an XML parser:

- Reads a stream of characters and distinguishes between markup and data
- Optionally replaces entity references with their values
- Assembles a complete, logical document from many disparate sources
- Reports syntax errors and optionally reports grammatical (validation) errors
- Serves data and structural information to a client program

In XML, data and markup are mixed together, so the parser first has to sift through a character stream and tell the two apart. Certain characters delimit the instructions from data, primarily angle brackets (< and >) for elements, comments, and processing instructions, and ampersand (&) and semicolon (;) for entity references. The parser also knows when to expect a certain instruction, or if a bad instruction has

---

[*] Readers of Douglas Adams' book *The Hitchhiker's Guide to the Galaxy* will recall that a babelfish is a living, universal language-translation device, about the size of an anchovy, that fits, head-first, into a sentient being's aural canal.

occurred; for example, an element that contains data must bracket the data in both a start and end tag. With this knowledge, the parser can quickly chop a character stream into discrete portions as encoded by the XML markup.

The next task is to fill in placeholders. *Entity references* may need to be resolved. Early in the process of reading XML, the processor will have encountered a list of placeholder definitions in the form of entity declarations, which associate a brief identifier with an entity. The identifier is some literal text defined in the document's DTD, and the entity itself can be defined right there or at the business end of a URL. These entities can themselves contain entity references, so the process of resolving an entity can take several iterations before the placeholders are filled in.

You may not always want entities to be resolved. If you're just spitting XML back out after some minor processing, then you may want to turn entity resolution off or substitute your own routine for handling entity references. For example, you may want to resolve external entity references (entities whose values are in locations external to the document, pointed to by URLs), but not resolve internal ones. Most parsers give you the ability to do this, but none will let you use entity references without declaring them.

That leads to the third task. If you allow the parser to resolve external entities, it will fetch all the documents, local or remote, that contain parts of the larger XML document. In doing so, all these entities get smushed into one unbroken document. Since your program usually doesn't need to know how the document is distributed physically, information about the physical origin of any piece of data goes away once it knits the whole document together.

While interpreting the markup, the parser may trip over a syntactic error. XML was designed to make it very easy to spot such errors. Everything from attributes to empty element tags have rigid rules for their construction so a parser doesn't have to think very hard about it. For example, the following piece of XML has an obvious error. The start tag for the <decree> element contains an attribute with a defective value assignment. The value "now" is missing a second quote character, and there's another error, somewhere in the end tag. Can you see it?

```
<decree effective="now>All motorbikes
shall be painted red.</decree<
```

When such an error occurs, the parser has little choice but to shut down the operation. There's no point in trying to parse the rest of the document. The point of XML is to make things unambiguous. If the parser had to guess how the document should look,* it would open up the data to uncertainty and you'd lose that precious level of

---

* Most HTML browsers try to ignore well-formedness errors in HTML documents, attempting to fix them and move on. While ignoring these errors may seem to be more convenient to the reader, it actually encourages sloppy documents and results in overall degradation of the quality of information on the Web. After all, would you fix parse errors if you didn't have to?

confidence in your program. Instead, the XML framers (wisely, we feel) opted to make XML parsers choke and die on bad XML documents. If the parser likes your XML, it is said to be *well formed*.

What do we mean by "grammatical errors"? You will encounter them only with so-called *validating* parsers. A document is considered to be *valid* if it passes a test defined in a DTD. XML-based languages and applications often have DTDs to set a minimal standard above well-formedness for how elements and data should be ordered. For example, the W3C has posted at least one DTD to describe XHTML (the XML-compliant flavor of HTML), listing all elements that can appear, where they can go, and what they can contain. It would be grammatically correct to put a `<p>` element inside a `<body>`, but putting `<p>` inside `<head>`, for example, would be incorrect. And don't even think about inserting an element `<blooby>` anywhere in the document, because it isn't declared anywhere in the DTD.[*] If even one error of this type is in a document, then the whole document is considered *invalid*. It may be well formed, but not valid against the particular DTD. Often, this level of checking is more of a burden than a help, but it's available if you need it.

Rounding out our list is the requirement that a parser ship the digested data to a program or end user. You can do this in many ways, and we devote much of the rest of the book in analyzing them. We can break up the forms into a few categories:

Event stream
> First, a parser can generate an event stream: the parser converts a stream of markup characters into a new kind of stream that is more abstract, with data that is partially processed and easier to handle by your program.

Object Representation
> Second, a parser can construct a data structure that reflects the information in the XML markup. This construction requires more resources from your system, but may be more convenient because it creates a persistent object that will wait around while you work on it.

Hybrid form
> We might call the third group "hybrid" output. It includes parsers that try to be smart about processing, using some advance knowledge about the document to construct an object representing only a portion of your document.

Example (of What Not to Do): A Well-Formedness Checker

We've described XML parsers abstractly, but now it's time to get our hands dirty. We're going to write our own parser whose sole purpose is to check whether a

---

[*] If you insist on authoring a `<blooby>`-enabled web page in XML, you can design your own extension by drafting a DTD that uses entity references to pull in the XHTML DTD, and then defines your own special elements on top of it. At this point it's not officially XHTML anymore, but a subclass thereof.

document is well-formed XML or if it fails the basic test. This is about the simplest a parser can get; it doesn't drive any further processing, but just returns a "yes" or "no."

Our mission here is twofold. First, we hope to shave some of the mystique off of XML processing—at the end of the day, it's just pushing text around. However, we also want to emphasize that writing a proper parser in Perl (or any language) requires a lot of work, which would be better spent writing more interesting code that uses one of the many available XML-parsing Perl modules. To that end, we'll write only a fraction of a pure-Perl XML parser with a very specific goal in mind.

Feel free to play with this program, but please don't try to use this code in a production environment! It's not a real Perl and XML solution, but an illustration of the sorts of things that parsers do. Also, it's incomplete and will not always give correct results, as we'll show later. Don't worry; the rest of this book talks about real XML parsers and Perl tools you'll want to use.

The program is a loop in which regular expressions match XML markup objects and pluck them out of the text. The loop runs until nothing is left to remove, meaning the document is well formed, or until the regular expressions can't match anything in the remaining text, in which case it's not well-formed. A few other tests could abort the parsing, such as when an end tag is found that doesn't match the name of the currently open start tag. It won't be perfect, but it should give you a good idea of how a well-formedness parser might work.

Example 3-1 is a routine that parses a string of XML text, tests to see if it is well-formed, and returns a boolean value. We've added some pattern variables to make it easier to understand the regular expressions. For example, the string $ident contains regular expression code to match an XML identifier, which is used for elements, attributes, and processing instructions.

Example 3-1. A rudimentary XML parser

```perl
sub is_well_formed {
    my $text = shift;                    # XML text to check

    # match patterns
    my $ident = '[:_A-Za-z][:A-Za-z0-9\-\._]*';   # identifier
    my $optsp = '\s*';                            # optional space
    my $att1 = "$ident$optsp=$optsp\"[^\"]*\"";   # attribute
    my $att2 = "$ident$optsp=$optsp'[^']*'";      # attr. variant
    my $att = "($att1|$att2)";                    # any attribute

    my @elements = ( );                  # stack of open elems

    # loop through the string to pull out XML markup objects
    while( length($text) ) {
```

Example 3-1. A rudimentary XML parser (continued)

```perl
    # match an empty element
    if( $text =~ /^&($ident)(\s+$att)*\s*\/>/ ) {
        $text = $';

    # match an element start tag
    } elsif( $text =~ /^&($ident)(\s+$att)*\s*>/ ) {
        push( @elements, $1 );
        $text = $';

    # match an element end tag
    } elsif( $text =~ /^&\/($ident)\s*>/ ) {
        return unless( $1 eq pop( @elements ));
        $text = $';

    # match a comment
    } elsif( $text =~ /^&!--/ ) {
        $text = $';
        # bite off the rest of the comment
        if( $text =~ /-->/ ) {
            $text = $';
            return if( $` =~ /--/ );   # comments can't
                                       # contain '--'
        } else {
            return;
        }

    # match a CDATA section
    } elsif( $text =~ /^&!\[CDATA\[/ ) {
        $text = $';
        # bite off the rest of the comment
        if( $text =~ /\]\]>/ ) {
            $text = $';
        } else {
            return;
        }

    # match a processing instruction
    } elsif( $text =~ m|^&\?$ident\s*[^\?]+\?>| ) {
        $text = $';

    # match extra whitespace
    # (in case there is space outside the root element)
    } elsif( $text =~ m|^\s+| ) {
        $text = $';

    # match character data
    } elsif( $text =~ /(^[^&&>]+)/ ) {
        my $data = $1;
        # make sure the data is inside an element
        return if( $data =~ /\S/ and not( @elements ));
        $text = $';
```

Example 3-1. A rudimentary XML parser (continued)

```
    # match entity reference
    } elsif( $text =~ /^&$ident;+/ ) {
        $text = $';

    # something unexpected
    } else {
        return;
    }
}
    return if( @elements );    # the stack should be empty
    return 1;
}
```

Perl's arrays are so useful partly due to their ability to masquerade as more abstract computer science data constructs.[*] Here, we use a data structure called a *stack*, which is really just an array that we access with push( ) and pop( ). Items in a stack are last-in, first-out (LIFO), meaning that the last thing put into it will be the first thing to be removed from it. This arrangement is convenient for remembering the names of currently open elements because at any time, the next element to be closed was the last element pushed onto the stack. Whenever we encounter a start tag, it will be pushed onto the stack, and it will be popped from the stack when we find an end tag. To be well-formed, every end tag must match the previous start tag, which is why we need the stack.

The stack represents all the elements along a branch of the XML tree, from the root down to the current element being processed. Elements are processed in the order in which they appear in a document; if you view the document as a tree, it looks like you're going from the root all the way down to the tip of a branch, then back up to another branch, and so on. This is called *depth-first order*, the canonical way all XML documents are processed.

There are a few places where we deviate from the simple looping scheme to do some extra testing. The code for matching a comment is several steps, since it ends with a three-character delimiter, and we also have to check for an illegal string of dashes "--" inside the comment. The character data matcher, which performs an extra check to see if the stack is empty, is also noteworthy; if the stack is empty, that's an error because nonwhitespace text is not allowed outside of the root element. Here is a short list of well-formedness errors that would cause the parser to return a false result:

- An identifier in an element or attribute is malformed (examples: "12foo," "-bla," and "..").
- A nonwhitespace character is found outside of the root element.
- An element end tag doesn't match the last discovered start tag.

---

[*] The O'Reilly book *Mastering Algorithms with Perl* by Jon Orwant, Jarkko Hietaniemi, and John Macdonald devotes a chapter to this topic.

- An attribute is unquoted or uses a bad combination of quote characters.
- An empty element is missing a slash character (/) at the end of its tag.
- An illegal character, such as a lone ampersand (&) or an angle bracket (<), is found in character data.
- A malformed markup tag (examples: "<fooby<" and "< ?bubba?>") is found.

Try the parser out on some test cases. Probably the simplest complete, well-formed XML document you will ever see is this:

```
<:-/>
```

The next document should cause the parser to halt with an error. (Hint: look at the <message> end tag.)

```
<memo>
  <to>self</to>
  <message>Don't forget to mow the car and wash the
  lawn.<message>
</memo>
```

Many other kinds of syntax errors could appear in a document, and our program picks up most of them. However, it does miss a few. For example, there should be exactly one root element, but our program will accept more than one:

```
<root>I am the one, true root!</root>
<root>No, I am!</root>
<root>Uh oh...</root>
```

Other problems? The parser cannot handle a document type declaration. This structure is sometimes seen at the top of a document that specifies a DTD for validating parsers, and it may also declare some entities. With a specialized syntax of its own, we'd have to write another loop just for the document type declaration.

Our parser's most significant omission is the resolution of entity references. It can check basic entity reference syntax, but doesn't bother to expand the entity and insert it into the text. Why is that bad? Consider that an entity can contain more than just some character data. It can contain any amount of markup, too, from an element to a big, external file. Entities can also contain other entity references, so it might require many passes to resolve one entity reference completely. The parser doesn't even check to see if the entities are declared (it couldn't anyway, since it doesn't know how to read a document type declaration syntax). Clearly, there is a lot of room for errors to creep into a document through entities, right under the nose of our parser. To fix the problems just mentioned, follow these steps:

1. Add a parsing loop to read in a document type declaration before any other parsing occurs. Any entity declarations would be parsed and stored, so we can resolve entity references later in the document.

2. Parse the DTD, if the document type declaration mentions one, to read any entity declarations.

3. In the main loop, resolve all entity references when we come across them. These entities have to be parsed, and there may be entity references within them, too. The process can be rather loopy, with loops inside loops, recursion, or other complex programming stunts.

What started out as a simple parser now has grown into a complex beast. That tells us two things: that the theory of parsing XML is easy to grasp; and that, in practice, it gets complicated very quickly. This exercise was useful because it showed issues involved in parsing XML, but we don't encourage you to write code like this. On the contrary, we expect you to take advantage of the exhaustive work already put into making ready-made parsers. Let's leave the dark ages and walk into the happy land of prepackaged parsers.

XML::Parser

Writing a parser requires a lot of work. You can't be sure if you've covered everything without a lot of testing. Unless you're a mutant who loves to write efficient, low-level parser code, your program will probably be slow and resource-intensive. The good news is that a wide variety of free, high quality, and easy-to-use XML parser packages (written by friendly mutants) already exist to help you. People have bashed Perl and XML together for years, and you have a barnful of conveniently pre-invented wheels at your disposal.

Where do Perl programmers go to find ready-made modules to use in their programs? They go to the Comprehensive Perl Archive Network (CPAN), a many-mirrored public resource full of free, open-source Perl code. If you aren't familiar with using CPAN, you must change your isolationist ways and learn to become a programmer of the world. You'll find a multitude of modules authored by folks who have walked the path of Perl and XML before you, and who've chosen to share the tools they've made with the rest of the world.

 Don't think of CPAN as a catalog of ready-made solutions for all specific XML problems. Rather, look at it as a toolbox or a source of building blocks you can assemble and configure to craft a solution. While some modules specialize in popular XML applications like RSS and SOAP, most are more general-purpose. Chances are, you won't find a module that specifically addresses your needs. You'll more likely take one of the general XML modules and adapt it somehow. We'll show that this process is painless and reveal several ways to configure general modules to your particular application.

XML parsers differ from one another in two major ways. First, they differ in their *parsing style*, which is how the parser works with XML. There are a few different strategies, such as building a data structure or creating an event stream. Another attribute of parsers, called *standards-completeness*, is a spectrum ranging from ad hoc on one extreme to an exhaustive, standards-based solution on the other. The balance on the latter axis is slowly moving from the eccentric, nonstandard side toward the other end as the Perl community agrees on how to implement major standards like SAX and DOM.

The `XML::Parser` module is the great-grandpappy of all Perl-based XML processors. It is a multifaceted parser, offering a handful of different parsing styles. On the standards axis, it's closer to ad hoc than standards-compliant; however, being the first efficient XML parser to appear on the Perl horizon, it has a dear place in our hearts and is still very useful. While `XML::Parser` uses a nonstandard API and has a reputation for getting a bit persnickety over some issues, it *works*. It parses documents with reasonable speed and flexibility, and as all Perl hackers know, people tend to glom onto the first usable solution that appears on the radar, no matter how ugly it is. Thus, nearly all of the first few years' worth of Perl and XML modules and programs based themselves on `XML::Parser`.

Since 2001 or so, however, other low-level parsing modules have emerged that base themselves on faster and more standards-compliant core libraries. We'll touch on these modules shortly. However, we'll start out with an examination of `XML::Parser`, giving a nod to its venerability and functionality.

In the early days of XML, a skilled programmer named James Clark wrote an XML parser library in C and called it Expat.* Fast, efficient, and very stable, it became the parser of choice among early adopters of XML. To bring XML into the Perl realm, Larry Wall wrote a low-level API for it and called the module `XML::Parser::Expat`. Then he built a layer on top of that, `XML::Parser`, to serve as a general-purpose parser for everybody. Now maintained by Clark Cooper, `XML::Parser` has served as the foundation of many XML modules.

The C underpinnings are the secret to `XML::Parser`'s success. We've seen how to write a basic parser in Perl. If you apply our previous example to a large XML document, you'll wait a long time before it finishes. Others have written complete XML parsers in Perl that are portable to any system, but you'll find much better performance in a compiled C parser like Expat. Fortunately, as with every other Perl module based on C code (and there are actually lots of these modules because they're not too hard to make, thanks to Perl's standard XS library),† it's easy to forget you're driving Expat around when you use `XML::Parser`.

---

* James Clark is a big name in the XML community. He tirelessly promotes the standard with his free tools and involvement with the W3C. You can see his work at *http://www.jclark.com/*. Clark is also editor of the XSLT and XPath recommendation documents at *http://www.w3.org/*.

† See man `perlxs` or Chapter 25 of O'Reilly's *Programming Perl, Third Edition* for more information.

Example: Well-Formedness Checker Revisited

To show how XML::Parser might be used, let's return to the well-formedness checker problem. It's very easy to create this tool with XML::Parser, as shown in Example 3-2.

Example 3-2. Well-formedness checker using XML::Parser

```
use XML::Parser;

my $xmlfile = shift @ARGV;                # the file to parse

# initialize parser object and parse the string
my $parser = XML::Parser->new( ErrorContext => 2 );
eval { $parser->parsefile( $xmlfile ); };

# report any error that stopped parsing, or announce success
if( $@ ) {
    $@ =~ s/at \/.*?$//s;                 # remove module line number
    print STDERR "\nERROR in '$file':\n$@\n";
} else {
    print STDERR "'$file' is well-formed\n";
}
```

Here's how this program works. First, we create a new XML::Parser object to do the parsing. Using an object rather than a static function call means that we can configure the parser once and then process multiple files without the overhead of repeatedly recreating the parser. The object retains your settings and keeps the Expat parser routine alive for as long as you want to parse files, and then cleans everything up when you're done.

Next, we call the parsefile( ) method inside an eval block because XML::Parser tends to be a little overzealous when dealing with parse errors. If we didn't use an eval block, our program would die before we had a chance to do any cleanup. We check the variable $@ for content in case there was an error. If there was, we remove the line number of the module at which the parse method "died" and then print out the message.

When initializing the parser object, we set an option ErrorContext => 2. XML::Parser has several options you can set to control parsing. This one is a directive sent straight to the Expat parser that remembers the context in which errors occur and saves two lines before the error. When we print out the error message, it tells us what line the error happened on and prints out the region of text with an arrow pointing to the offending mistake.

Here's an example of our checker choking on a syntactic faux pas (where we decided to name our program *xwf* as an XML well-formedness checker):

```
$ xwf ch01.xml

ERROR in 'ch01.xml':

not well-formed (invalid token) at line 66, column 22, byte 2354:
```

```
<chapter id="dorothy-in-oz">
<title>Lions, Tigers & Bears</title>
=====================^
```

Notice how simple it is to set up the parser and get powerful results. What you don't see until you run the program yourself is that it's fast. When you type the command, you get a result in a split second.

You can configure the parser to work in different ways. You don't have to parse a file, for example. Use the method parse( ) to parse a text string instead. Or, you could give it the option NoExpand => 1 to override default entity expansion with your own entity resolver routine. You could use this option to prevent the parser from opening external entities, limiting the scope of its checking.

Although the well-formedness checker is a very useful tool that you certainly want in your XML toolbox if you work with XML files often, it only scratches the surface of what we can do with XML::Parser. We'll see in the next section that a parser's most important role is in shoveling packaged data into your program. How it does this depends on the particular style you select.

Parsing Styles

XML::Parser supports several different styles of parsing to suit various development strategies. The style doesn't change how the parser reads XML. Rather, it changes how it presents the results of parsing. If you need a persistent structure containing the document, you can have it. Or, if you'd prefer to have the parser call a set of routines you write, you can do it that way. You can set the style when you initialize the object by setting the value of style. Here's a quick summary of the available styles:

Debug
> This style prints the document to STDOUT, formatted as an outline (deeper elements are indented more). parse( ) doesn't return anything special to your program.

Tree
> This style creates a hierarchical, tree-shaped data structure that your program can use for processing. All elements and their data are crystallized in this form, which consists of nested hashes and arrays.

Object
> Like tree, this method returns a reference to a hierarchical data structure representing the document. However, instead of using simple data aggregates like hashes and lists, it consists of objects that are specialized to contain XML markup objects.

Subs
> This style lets you set up *callback functions* to handle individual elements. Create a package of routines named after the elements they should handle and tell the

parser about this package by using the pkg option. Every time the parser finds a start tag for an element called <fooby>, it will look for the function fooby( ) in your package. When it finds the end tag for the element, it will try to call the function _fooby( ) in your package. The parser will pass critical information like references to content and attributes to the function, so you can do whatever processing you need to do with it.

Stream

Like Subs, you can define callbacks for handling particular XML components, but callbacks are more general than element names. You can write functions called *handlers* to be called for "events" like the start of an element (any element, not just a particular kind), a set of character data, or a processing instruction. You must register the handler package with either the Handlers option or the setHandlers( ) method.

custom

You can subclass the XML::Parser class with your own object. Doing so is useful for creating a parser-like API for a more specific application. For example, the XML::Parser::PerlSAX module uses this strategy to implement the SAX event processing standard.

Example 3-3 is a program that uses XML::Parser with Style set to Tree. In this mode, the parser reads the whole XML document while building a data structure. When finished, it hands our program a reference to the structure that we can play with.

Example 3-3. An XML tree builder

```
use XML::Parser;

# initialize parser and read the file
$parser = new XML::Parser( Style => 'Tree' );
my $tree = $parser->parsefile( shift @ARGV );

# serialize the structure
use Data::Dumper;
print Dumper( $tree );
```

In tree mode, the parsefile( ) method returns a reference to a data structure containing the document, encoded as lists and hashes. We use Data::Dumper, a handy module that serializes data structures, to view the result. Example 3-4 is the datafile.

Example 3-4. An XML datafile

```
<preferences>
  <font role="console">
    <fname>Courier</name>
    <size>9</size>
  </font>
  <font role="default">
    <fname>Times New Roman</name>
```

Example 3-4. An XML datafile (continued)

```
    <size>14</size>
  </font>
  <font role="titles">
    <fname>Helvetica</name>
    <size>10</size>
  </font>
</preferences>
```

With this datafile, the program produces the following output (condensed and indented to be easier to read):

```
$tree = [
          'preferences', [
            {}, 0, '\n',
            'font', [
              { 'role' => 'console' }, 0, '\n',
              'size', [ {}, 0, '9' ], 0, '\n',
              'fname', [ {}, 0, 'Courier' ], 0, '\n'
            ], 0, '\n',
            'font', [
              { 'role' => 'default' }, 0, '\n',
              'fname', [ {}, 0, 'Times New Roman' ], 0, '\n',
              'size', [ {}, 0, '14' ], 0, '\n'
            ], 0, '\n',
            'font', [
              { 'role' => 'titles' }, 0, '\n',
              'size', [ {}, 0, '10' ], 0, '\n',
              'fname', [ {}, 0, 'Helvetica' ], 0, '\n',
            ], 0, '\n',
          ]
        ];
```

It's a lot easier to write code that dissects the above structure than to write a parser of your own. We know, because the parser returned a data structure instead of dying mid-parse, that the document was 100 percent well-formed XML. In Chapter 4, we will use the Stream mode of XML::Parser, and in Chapter 6, we'll talk more about trees and objects.

Stream-Based Versus Tree-Based Processing

Remember the Perl mantra, "There's more than one way to do it"? It is also true when working with XML. Depending on how you want to work and what kind of resources you have, many options are available. One developer may prefer a low-maintenance parsing job and is prepared to be loose and sloppy with memory to get it. Another will need to squeeze out faster and leaner performance at the expense of more complex code. XML processing tasks vary widely, so you should be free to choose the shortest path to a solution.

There are a lot of different XML processing strategies. Most fall into two categories: stream-based and tree-based. With the *stream-based strategy*, the parser continuously alerts a program to patterns in the XML. The parser functions like a pipeline, taking XML markup on one end and pumping out processed nuggets of data to your program. We call this pipeline an *event stream* because each chunk of data sent to the program signals something new and interesting in the XML stream. For example, the beginning of a new element is a significant event. So is the discovery of a processing instruction in the markup. With each update, your program does something new—perhaps translating the data and sending it to another place, testing it for some specific content, or sticking it onto a growing heap of data.

With the *tree-based strategy*, the parser keeps the data to itself until the very end, when it presents a complete model of the document to your program. Instead of a pipeline, it's like a camera that takes a picture and transmits the replica to you. The model is usually in a much more convenient state than raw XML. For example, nested elements may be represented in native Perl structures like lists or hashes, as we saw in an earlier example. Even more useful are trees of blessed objects with methods that help navigate the structure from one place to another. The whole point to this strategy is that your program can pull out any data it needs, in any order.

Why would you prefer one over the other? Each has strong and weak points. Event streams are fast and often have a much slimmer memory footprint, but at the expense of greater code complexity and impermanent data. Tree building, on the other hand, lets the data stick around for as long as you need it, and your code is usually simple because you don't need special tricks to do things like backwards searching. However, trees wither when it comes to economical use of processor time and memory.

All of this is relative, of course. Small documents don't cause much hardship to a typical computer, especially since CPU cycles and megabytes are getting cheaper every day. Maybe the convenience of a persistent data structure will outweigh any drawbacks. On the other hand, when working with Godzilla-sized documents like books, or huge numbers of documents all at once, you'll definitely notice the crunch. Then the agility of event stream processors will start to look better. It's impossible to give you any hard-and-fast rules, so we'll leave the decision up to you.

An interesting thing to note about the stream-based and tree-based strategies is that one is the basis for the other. That's right, an event stream drives the process of building a tree data structure. Thus, most low-level parsers are event streams because you can always write a tree building layer on top. This is how XML::Parser and most other parsers work.

In a related, more recent, and very cool development, XML event streams can also turn any kind of document into some form of XML by writing stream-based parsers that generate XML events from whatever data structures lurk in that document type.

There's a lot more to say about event streams and tree builders—so much, in fact, that we've devoted two whole chapters to the topics. Chapter 4 takes a deep plunge into the theory behind event streams with lots of examples for making useful programs out of them. Chapter 6 takes you deeper into the forest with lots of tree-based examples. After that, Chapter 8 shows you unusual hybrids that provide the best of both worlds.

Putting Parsers to Work

Enough tinkering with the parser's internal details. We want to see what you can do with the stuff you get from parsers. We've already seen an example of a complete, parser-built tree structure in Example 3-3, so let's do something with the other type. We'll take an XML event stream and make it drive processing by plugging it into some code to handle the events. It may not be the most useful tool in the world, but it will serve well enough to show you how real-world XML processing programs are written.

XML::Parser (with Expat running underneath) is at the input end of our program. Expat subscribes to the event-based parsing school we described earlier. Rather than loading your whole XML document into memory and then turning around to see what it hath wrought, it stops every time it encounters a discrete chunk of data or markup, such as an angle-bracketed tag or a literal string inside an element. It then checks to see if our program wants to react to it in any way.

Your first responsibility is to give the parser an interface to the pertinent bits of code that handle events. Each type of event is handled by a different subroutine, or *handler*. We register our handlers with the parser by setting the Handlers option at initialization time. Example 3-5 shows the entire process.

Example 3-5. A stream-based XML processor

```
use XML::Parser;

# initialize the parser
my $parser = XML::Parser->new( Handlers =>
                                    {
                                      Start=>\&handle_start,
                                      End=>\&handle_end,
                                    });
$parser->parsefile( shift @ARGV );

my @element_stack;              # remember which elements are open

# process a start-of-element event: print message about element
#
sub handle_start {
    my( $expat, $element, %attrs ) = @_;

    # ask the expat object about our position
    my $line = $expat->current_line;
```

Example 3-5. A stream-based XML processor (continued)

```
    print "I see an $element element starting on line $line!\n";

    # remember this element and its starting position by pushing a
    # little hash onto the element stack
    push( @element_stack, { element=>$element, line=>$line });

    if( %attrs ) {
        print "It has these attributes:\n";
        while( my( $key, $value ) = each( %attrs )) {
            print "\t$key => $value\n";
        }
    }
}

# process an end-of-element event
#
sub handle_end {
    my( $expat, $element ) = @_;

    # We'll just pop from the element stack with blind faith that
    # we'll get the correct closing element, unlike what our
    # homebrewed well-formedness did, since XML::Parser will scream
    # bloody murder if any well-formedness errors creep in.
    my $element_record = pop( @element_stack );
    print "I see that $element element that started on line ",
            $$element_record{ line }, " is closing now.\n";
}
```

It's easy to see how this process works. We've written two handler subroutines called handle_start( ) and handle_end( ) and *registered* each with a particular event in the call to new( ). When we call parse( ), the parser knows it has handlers for a start-of-element event and an end-of-element event. Every time the parser trips over an element start tag, it calls the first handler and gives it information about that element (element name and attributes). Similarly, any end tag it encounters leads to a call of the other handler with similar element-specific information.

Note that the parser also gives each handler a reference called $expat. This is a reference to the XML::Parser::Expat object, a low-level interface to Expat. It has access to interesting information that might be useful to a program, such as line numbers and element depth. We've taken advantage of this fact, using the line number to dazzle users with our amazing powers of document analysis.

Want to see it run? Here's how the output looks after processing the customer database document from Example 1-1:

```
    I see a spam-document element starting on line 1!
    It has these attributes:
            version => 3.5
            timestamp => 2002-05-13 15:33:45
    I see a customer element starting on line 3!
    I see a first-name element starting on line 4!
```

```
I see that the first-name element that started on line 4 is closing now.
I see a surname element starting on line 5!
I see that the surname element that started on line 5 is closing now.
I see a address element starting on line 6!
I see a street element starting on line 7!
I see that the street element that started on line 7 is closing now.
I see a city element starting on line 8!
I see that the city element that started on line 8 is closing now.
I see a state element starting on line 9!
I see that the state element that started on line 9 is closing now.
I see a zip element starting on line 10!
I see that the zip element that started on line 10 is closing now.
I see that the address element that started on line 6 is closing now.
I see a email element starting on line 12!
I see that the email element that started on line 12 is closing now.
I see a age element starting on line 13!
I see that the age element that started on line 13 is closing now.
I see that the customer element that started on line 3 is closing now.
  [... snipping other customers for brevity's sake ...]
I see that the spam-document element that started on line 1 is closing now.
```

Here we used the element stack again. We didn't actually need to store the elements' names ourselves; one of the methods you can call on the XML::Parser::Expat object returns the current *context list*, a newest-to-oldest ordering of all elements our parser has probed into. However, a stack proved to be a useful way to store additional information like line numbers. It shows off the fact that you can let events build up structures of arbitrary complexity—the "memory" of the document's past.

There are many more event types than we handle here. We don't do anything with character data, comments, or processing instructions, for example. However, for the purpose of this example, we don't need to go into those event types. We'll have more exhaustive examples of event processing in the next chapter, anyway.

Before we close the topic of event processing, we want to mention one thing: the Simple API for XML processing, more commonly known as SAX. It's very similar to the event processing model we've seen so far, but the difference is that it's a W3C-supported standard. Being a W3C-supported standard means that it has a standardized, canonical set of events. How these events should be presented for processing is also standardized. The cool thing about it is that with a standard interface, you can hook up different program components like Legos and it will all work. If you don't like one parser, just plug in another (and sophisticated tools like the XML::SAX module family can even help you pick a parser based on the features you need). Get your XML data from a database, a file, or your mother's shopping list; it shouldn't matter where it comes from. SAX is very exciting for the Perl community because we've long been criticized for our lack of standards compliance and general barbarism. Now we can be criticized for only one of those things. You can expect a nice, thorough discussion on SAX (specifically, PerlSAX, our beloved language's mutation thereof) in Chapter 5.

XML::LibXML

XML::LibXML, like XML::Parser, is an interface to a library written in C. Called libxml2, it's part of the GNOME project.* Unlike XML::Parser, this new parser supports a major standard for XML tree processing known as the Document Object Model (DOM).

DOM is another much-ballyhooed XML standard. It does for tree processing what SAX does for event streams. If you have your heart set on climbing trees in your program and you think there's a likelihood that it might be reused or applied to different data sources, you're better off using something standard and interchangeable. Again, we're happy to delve into DOM in a future chapter and get you thinking in standards-complaint ways. That topic is coming up in Chapter 7.

Now we want to show you an example of another parser in action. We'd be remiss if we focused on just one kind of parser when so many are out there. Again, we'll show you a basic example, nothing fancy, just to show you how to invoke the parser and tame its power. Let's write another document analysis tool like we did in Example 3-5, this time printing a frequency distribution of elements in a document.

Example 3-6 shows the program. It's a vanilla parser run because we haven't set any options yet. Essentially, the parser parses the filehandle and returns a DOM object, which is nothing more than a tree structure of well-designed objects. Our program finds the document element, and then traverses the entire tree one element at a time, all the while updating the hash of frequency counters.

Example 3-6. A frequency distribution program

```
use XML::LibXML;
use IO::Handle;

# initialize the parser
my $parser = new XML::LibXML;

# open a filehandle and parse
my $fh = new IO::Handle;
if( $fh->fdopen( fileno( STDIN ), "r" )) {
    my $doc = $parser->parse_fh( $fh );
    my %dist;
    &proc_node( $doc->getDocumentElement, \%dist );
    foreach my $item ( sort keys %dist ) {
        print "$item: ", $dist{ $item }, "\n";
    }
    $fh->close;
}

# process an XML tree node: if it's an element, update the
# distribution list and process all its children
```

---

* For downloads and documentation, see *http://www.libxml.org/*.

Example 3-6. A frequency distribution program (continued)

```
#
sub proc_node {
    my( $node, $dist ) = @_;
    return unless( $node->nodeType eq &XML_ELEMENT_NODE );
    $dist->{ $node->nodeName } ++;
    foreach my $child ( $node->getChildnodes ) {
        &proc_node( $child, $dist );
    }
}
```

Note that instead of using a simple path to a file, we use a filehandle object of the IO::Handle class. Perl filehandles, as you probably know, are magic and subtle beasties, capable of passing into your code characters from a wide variety of sources, including files on disk, open network sockets, keyboard input, databases, and just about everything else capable of outputting data. Once you define a filehandle's source, it gives you the same interface for reading from it as does every other filehandle. This dovetails nicely with our XML-based ideology, where we want code to be as flexible and reusable as possible. After all, XML doesn't care where it comes from, so why should we pigeonhole it with one source type?

The parser object returns a document object after parsing. This object has a method that returns a reference to the document element—the element at the very root of the whole tree. We take this reference and feed it to a recursive subroutine, proc_node( ), which happily munches on elements and scribbles into a hash variable every time it sees an element. Recursion is an efficient way to write programs that process XML because the structure of documents is somewhat fractal: the same rules for elements apply at any depth or position in the document, including the root element that represents the entire document (modulo its prologue). Note the "node type" check, which distinguishes between elements and other parts of a document (such as pieces of text or processing instructions).

For every element the routine looks at, it has to call the object's getChildnodes( ) method to continue processing on its children. This call is an essential difference between stream-based and tree-based methodologies. Instead of having an event stream take the steering wheel of our program and push data at it, thus calling subroutines and codeblocks in a (somewhat) unpredictable order, our program now has the responsibility of navigating through the document under its own power. Traditionally, we start at the root element and go downward, processing children in order from first to last. However, because we, not the parser, are in control now, we can scan through the document in any way we want. We could go backwards, we could scan just a part of the document, we could jump around, making multiple passes though the tree—the sky's the limit. Here's the result from processing a small chapter coded in DocBook XML:

```
$ xfreq < ch03.xml
chapter: 1
citetitle: 2
```

```
firstterm: 16
footnote: 6
foreignphrase: 2
function: 10
itemizedlist: 2
listitem: 21
literal: 29
note: 1
orderedlist: 1
para: 77
programlisting: 9
replaceable: 1
screen: 1
section: 6
sgmltag: 8
simplesect: 1
systemitem: 2
term: 6
title: 7
variablelist: 1
varlistentry: 6
xref: 2
```

The result shows only a few lines of code, but it sure does a lot of work. Again, thanks to the C library underneath, it's quite speedy.

XML::XPath

We've seen examples of parsers that dutifully deliver the entire document to you. Often, though, you don't need the whole thing. When you query a database, you're usually looking for only a single record. When you crack open a telephone book, you're not going to sit down and read the whole thing. There is obviously a need for some mechanism of extracting a specific piece of information from a vast document. Look no further than XPath.

XPath is a recommendation from the folks who brought you XML.[*] It's a grammar for writing expressions that pinpoint specific pieces of documents. Think of it as an addressing scheme. Although we'll save the nitty-gritty of XPath wrangling for Chapter 8, we can tantalize you by revealing that it works much like a mix of regular expressions with Unix-style file paths. Not surprisingly, this makes it an attractive feature to add to parsers.

Matt Sergeant's XML::XPath module is a solid implementation, built on the foundation of XML::Parser. Given an XPath expression, it returns a list of all document parts that match the description. It's an incredibly simple way to perform some powerful search and retrieval work.

---

[*] Check out the specification at *http://www.w3.org/TR/xpath/*.

For instance, suppose we have an address book encoded in XML in this basic form:

```
<contacts>
  <entry>
    <name>Bob Snob</name>
    <street>123 Platypus Lane</street>
    <city>Burgopolis</city>
    <state>FL</state>
    <zip>12345</zip>
  </entry>
  <!--More entries go here-->
</contacts>
```

Suppose you want to extract all the zip codes from the file and compile them into a list. Example 3-7 shows how you could do it with XPath.

Example 3-7. Zip code extractor

```
use XML::XPath;

my $file = 'customers.xml';
my $xp = XML::XPath->new(filename=>$file);

# An XML::XPath nodeset is an object which contains the result of
# smacking an XML document with an XPath expression; we'll do just
# this, and then query the nodeset to see what we get.
my $nodeset = $xp->find('//zip');

my @zipcodes;                   # Where we'll put our results
if (my @nodelist = $nodeset->get_nodelist) {
  # We found some zip elements! Each node is an object of the class
  # XML::XPath::Node::Element, so I'll use that class's 'string_value'
  # method to extract its pertinent text, and throw the result for all
  # the nodes into our array.
  @zipcodes = map($_->string_value, @nodelist);

  # Now sort and prepare for output
  @zipcodes = sort(@zipcodes);
  local $" = "\n";
  print "I found these zipcodes:\n@zipcodes\n";
} else {
  print "The file $file didn't have any 'zip' elements in it!\n";
}
```

Run the program on a document with three entries and we'll get something like this:

```
I found these zipcodes:
03642
12333
82649
```

This module also shows an example of tree-based parsing, by the way, as its parser loads the whole document into an object tree of its own design and then allows the user to selectively interact with parts of it via XPath expressions. This example is just a sample of what you can do with advanced tree processing modules. You'll see more of these modules in Chapter 8.

`XML::LibXML`'s element objects support a `findnodes()` method that works much like `XML::XPath`'s, using the invoking `Element` object as the current context and returning a list of objects that match the query. We'll play with this functionality later in Chapter 10.

Document Validation

Being well-formed is a minimal requirement for XML everywhere. However, XML processors have to accept a lot on blind faith. If we try to build a document to meet some specific XML application's specifications, it doesn't do us any good if a content generator slips in a strange element we've never seen before and the parser lets it go by with nary a whimper. Luckily, a higher level of quality control is available to us when we need to check for things like that. It's called document validation.

Validation is a sophisticated way of comparing a *document instance* against a template or grammar specification. It can restrict the number and type of elements a document can use and control where they go. It can even regulate the patterns of character data in any element or attribute. A *validating parser* tells you whether a document is valid or not, when given a DTD or schema to check against.

Remember that you don't need to validate every XML document that passes over your desk. DTDs and other validation schemes shine when working with specific XML-based markup languages (such as XHTML for web pages, MathML for equations, or CaveML for spelunking), which have strict rules about which elements and attributes go where (because having an automated way to draw attention to something fishy in the document structure becomes a feature).

However, validation usually isn't crucial when you use Perl and XML to perform a less specific task, such as tossing together XML documents on the fly based on some other, less sane data format, or when ripping apart and analyzing existing XML documents.

Basically, if you feel that validation is a needless step for the job at hand, you're probably right. However, if you knowingly generate or modify some flavor of XML that needs to stick to a defined standard, then taking the extra step or three necessary to perform document validation is probably wise. Your toolbox, naturally, gives you lots of ways to do this. Read on.

DTDs

Document type descriptions (DTDs) are documents written in a special markup language defined in the XML specification, though they themselves are not XML.

Everything within these documents is a declaration starting with a <! delimiter and comes in four flavors: elements, attributes, entities, and notations.

Example 3-8 is a very simple DTD.

Example 3-8. A wee little DTD

```
<!ELEMENT memo (to, from, message)>
<!ATTLIST memo priority (urgent|normal|info) 'normal'>
<!ENTITY % text-only "(#PCDATA)*">
<!ELEMENT to %text-only;>
<!ELEMENT from %text-only;>
<!ELEMENT message (#PCDATA | emphasis)*>
<!ELEMENT emphasis %text-only;>
<!ENTITY myname "Bartholomus Chiggin McNugget">
```

This DTD declares five elements, an attribute for the <memo> element, a parameter entity to make other declarations cleaner, and an entity that can be used inside a document instance. Based on this information, a validating parser can reject or approve a document. The following document would pass muster:

```
<!DOCTYPE memo SYSTEM "/dtdstuff/memo.dtd">
<memo priority="info">
  <to>Sara Bellum</to>
  <from>&myname;</from>
  <message>Stop reading memos and get back to work!</message>
</memo>
```

If you removed the <to> element from the document, it would suddenly become invalid. A well-formedness checker wouldn't give a hoot about missing elements. Thus, you see the value of validation.

Because DTDs are so easy to parse, some general XML processors include the ability to validate the documents they parse against DTDs. XML::LibXML is one such parser. A very simple validating parser is shown in Example 3-9.

Example 3-9. A validating parser

```perl
use XML::LibXML;
use IO::Handle;

# initialize the parser
my $parser = new XML::LibXML;

# open a filehandle and parse
my $fh = new IO::Handle;
if( $fh->fdopen( fileno( STDIN ), "r" )) {
    my $doc = $parser->parse_fh( $fh );
    if( $doc and $doc->is_valid ) {
        print "Yup, it's valid.\n";
    } else {
        print "Yikes! Validity error.\n";
    }
```

Example 3-9. A validating parser (continued)

```
    $fh->close;
}
```

This parser would be simple to add to any program that requires valid input documents. Unfortunately, it doesn't give any information about what specific problem makes it invalid (e.g., an element in an improper place), so you wouldn't want to use it as a general-purpose validity checking tool.* T. J. Mather's XML::Checker is a better module for reporting specific validation errors.

Schemas

DTDs have limitations; they aren't able to check what kind of character data is in an element and if it matches a particular pattern. What if you wanted a parser to tell you if a <date> element has the wrong format for a date, or if it contains a street address by mistake? For that, you need a solution such as XML Schema. XML Schema is a second generation of DTD and brings more power and flexibility to validation.

As noted in Chapter 2, XML Schema enjoys the dubious distinction among the XML-related W3C specification family for being the most controversial schema (at least among hackers). Many people like the concept of schemas, but many don't approve of the XML Schema implementation, which is seen as too cumbersome or constraining to be used effectively.

Alternatives to XML Schema include OASIS-Open's RelaxNG (*http://www.oasis-open.org/committees/relaxng/*) and Rick Jelliffe's Schematron (*http://www.ascc.net/xml/resource/schematron/schematron.html*). Like XML Schema, these specifications detail XML-based languages used to describe other XML-based languages and let a program that knows how to speak that schema use it to validate other XML documents. We find Schematron particularly interesting because it has had a Perl module attached to it for a while (in the form of Kip Hampton's XML::Schematron family).

Schematron is especially interesting to many Perl and XML hackers because it builds on existing popular XML technologies that already have venerable Perl implementations. Schematron defines a very simple language with which you list and group together assertions of what things should look like based on XPath expressions. Instead of a forward-looking grammar that must list and define everything that can possibly appear in the document, you can choose to validate a fraction of it. You can also choose to have elements and attributes validate based on conditions involving anything anywhere else in the document (wherever an XPath expression can reach). In practice, a Schematron document looks and feels like an XSLT stylesheet, and with good reason: it's intended

---

* The authors prefer to use a command-line tool called *nsgmls* available from *http://www.jclark.com/*. Public web sites, such as *http://www.stg.brown.edu/service/xmlvalid/*, can also validate arbitrary documents. Note that, in these cases, the XML document must have a DOCTYPE declaration, whose system identifier (if it has one) must contain a resolvable URL and not a path on your local system.

to be fully implementable by way of XSLT. In fact, two of the XML::Schematron Perl modules work by first transforming the user-specified schema document into an XSLT sheet, which it then simply passes through an XSLT processor.

Schematron lacks any kind of built-in data typing, so you can't, for example, do a one-word check to insist that an attribute conforms to the W3C date format. You can, however, have your Perl program make a separate step using any method you'd like (perhaps through the XML::XPath module) to come through date attributes and run a good old Perl regular expression on them. Also note that no schema language will ever provide a way to query an element's content against a database, or perform any other action outside the realm of the document. This is where mixing Perl and schemas can come in very handy.

XML::Writer

Compared to all we've had to deal with in this chapter so far, writing XML will be a breeze. It's easier to write it because now the shoe's on the other foot: your program has a data structure over which it has had complete control and knows everything about, so it doesn't need to prepare for every contingency that it might encounter when processing input.

There's nothing particularly difficult about generating XML. You know about elements with start and end tags, their attributes, and so on. It's just tedious to write an XML output method that remembers to cross all the t's and dot all the i's. Does it put a space between every attribute? Does it close open elements? Does it put that slash at the end of empty elements? You don't want to have to think about these things when you're writing more important code. Others have written modules to take care of these serialization details for you.

David Megginson's XML::Writer is a fine example of an abstract XML generation interface. It comes with a handful of very simple methods for building any XML document. Just create a writer object and call its methods to crank out a stream of XML. Table 3-1 lists some of these methods.

Table 3-1. XML::Writer methods

Name	Function
end( )	Close the document and perform simple well-formedness checking (e.g., make sure that there is one root element and that every start tag has an associated end tag). If the option UNSAFE is set, however, most well-formedness checking is skipped.
xmlDecl([$endoding, $standalone])	Add an XML Declaration at the top of the document. The version is hard-wired as "1.0".
doctype($name, [$publicId, $systemId])	Add a document type declaration at the top of the document.
comment($text)	Write an XML comment.

Table 3-1. XML::Writer methods (continued)

Name	Function
`pi($target [, $data])`	Output a processing instruction.
`startTag($name [, $aname1 => $value1, ...])`	Create an element start tag. The first argument is the element name, which is followed by attribute name-value pairs.
`emptyTag($name [, $aname1 => $value1, ...])`	Set up an empty element tag. The arguments are the same as for the `startTag( )` method.
`endTag([$name])`	Create an element end tag. Leave out the argument to have it close the currently open element automatically.
`dataElement($name, $data [, $aname1 => $value1, ...])`	Print an element that contains only character data. This element includes the start tag, the data, and the end tag.
`characters($data)`	Output a parcel of character data.

Using these routines, we can build a complete XML document. The program in Example 3-10, for example, creates a basic HTML file.

Example 3-10. HTML generator

```perl
use IO;
my $output = new IO::File(">output.xml");

use XML::Writer;
my $writer = new XML::Writer( OUTPUT => $output );

$writer->xmlDecl( 'UTF-8' );
$writer->doctype( 'html' );
$writer->comment( 'My happy little HTML page' );
$writer->pi( 'foo', 'bar' );
$writer->startTag( 'html' );
$writer->startTag( 'body' );
$writer->startTag( 'h1' );
$writer->startTag( 'font', 'color' => 'green' );
$writer->characters( "<Hello World!>" );
$writer->endTag( );
$writer->endTag( );
$writer->dataElement( "p", "Nice to see you." );
$writer->endTag( );
$writer->endTag( );
$writer->end( );
```

This example outputs the following:

```
<?xml version="1.0" encoding="UTF-8"?>
<!DOCTYPE html>
<!-- My happy little HTML page -->
<?foo bar?>
<html><body><h1><font color="green">&lt;Hello World!&gt;</font></h1><p>Nice to see
you.</p></body></html>
```

Some nice conveniences are built into this module. For example, it automatically takes care of illegal characters like the ampersand (&) by turning them into the appropriate entity references. Quoting of entity values is automatic, too. At any time during the document-building process, you can check the context you're in with predicate methods like within_element('foo'), which tells you if an element named 'foo' is open.

By default, the module outputs a document with all the tags run together. You might prefer to insert whitespace in some places to make the XML more readable. If you set the option NEWLINES to true, then it will insert newline characters after element tags. If you set DATA_MODE, a similar effect will be achieved, and you can combine DATA_MODE with DATA_INDENT to automatically indent lines in proportion to depth in the document for a nicely formatted document.

The nice thing about XML is that it can be used to organize just about any kind of textual data. With XML::Writer, you can quickly turn a pile of information into a tightly regimented document. For example, you can turn a directory listing into a hierarchical database like the program in Example 3-11.

Example 3-11. Directory mapper

```
use XML::Writer;
my $wr = new XML::Writer( DATA_MODE => 'true', DATA_INDENT => 2 );
&as_xml( shift @ARGV );
$wr->end;

# recursively map directory information into XML
#
sub as_xml {
    my $path = shift;
    return unless( -e $path );

    # if this is a directory, create an element and
    # stuff it full of items
    if( -d $path ) {
        $wr->startTag( 'directory', name => $path );

        # Load the names of all things in this
        # directory into an array
        my @contents = ( );
        opendir( DIR, $path );
        while( my $item = readdir( DIR )) {
            next if( $item eq '.' or $item eq '..' );
            push( @contents, $item );
        }
        closedir( DIR );

        # recurse on items in the directory
        foreach my $item ( @contents ) {
            &as_xml( "$path/$item" );
        }

        $wr->endTag( 'directory' );

    # We'll lazily call anything that's not a directory a file.
```

Example 3-11. Directory mapper (continued)

```
    } else {
        $wr->emptyTag( 'file', name => $path );
    }
}
```

Here's how the example looks when run on a directory (note the use of DATA_MODE and DATA_INDENT to improve readability):

$ ~/bin/dir /home/eray/xtools/XML-DOM-1.25

```
<directory name="/home/eray/xtools/XML-DOM-1.25">
  <directory name="/home/eray/xtools/XML-DOM-1.25/t">
    <file name="/home/eray/xtools/XML-DOM-1.25/t/attr.t" />
    <file name="/home/eray/xtools/XML-DOM-1.25/t/minus.t" />
    <file name="/home/eray/xtools/XML-DOM-1.25/t/example.t" />
    <file name="/home/eray/xtools/XML-DOM-1.25/t/print.t" />
    <file name="/home/eray/xtools/XML-DOM-1.25/t/cdata.t" />
    <file name="/home/eray/xtools/XML-DOM-1.25/t/astress.t" />
    <file name="/home/eray/xtools/XML-DOM-1.25/t/modify.t" />
  </directory>
  <file name="/home/eray/xtools/XML-DOM-1.25/DOM.gif" />
  <directory name="/home/eray/xtools/XML-DOM-1.25/samples">
    <file
    name="/home/eray/xtools/XML-DOM-1.25/samples/REC-xml-19980210.xml"
    />
  </directory>
  <file name="/home/eray/xtools/XML-DOM-1.25/MANIFEST" />
  <file name="/home/eray/xtools/XML-DOM-1.25/Makefile.PL" />
  <file name="/home/eray/xtools/XML-DOM-1.25/Changes" />
  <file name="/home/eray/xtools/XML-DOM-1.25/CheckAncestors.pm" />
  <file name="/home/eray/xtools/XML-DOM-1.25/CmpDOM.pm" />
```

We've seen XML::Writer used step by step and in a recursive context. You could also use it conveniently inside an object tree structure, where each XML object type has its own "to-string" method making the appropriate calls to the writer object. XML::Writer is extremely flexible and useful.

Other Methods of Output

Remember that many parser modules have their own ways to turn their current content into simple, pretty strings of XML. XML::LibXML, for example, lets you call a toString( ) method on the document or any element object within it. Consequently, more specific processor classes that subclass from this module or otherwise make internal use of it often make the same method available in their own APIs and pass end user calls to it to the underlying parser object. Consult the documentation of your favorite processor to see if it supports this or a similar feature.

Finally, sometimes all you really need is Perl's print function. While it lives at a lower level than tools like XML::Writer, ignorant of XML-specific rules and regulations, it gives you a finer degree of control over the process of turning memory structures into text worthy of throwing at filehandles. If you're doing especially tricky work, falling back to print may be a relief, and indeed some of the stunts we pull in Chapter 10 use print. Just don't forget to escape those naughty < and & characters with their respective entity references, as shown in Table 2-1, or be generous with CDATA sections.

Character Sets and Encodings

No matter how you choose to manage your program's output, you must keep in mind the concept of character encoding—the protocol your output XML document uses to represent the various symbols of its language, be they an alphabet of letters or a catalog of ideographs and diacritical marks. Character encoding may represent the trickiest part of XML-slinging, perhaps especially so for programmers in Western Europe and the Americas, most of whom have not explored the universe of possible encodings beyond the 128 characters of ASCII.

While it's technically legal for an XML document's encoding declaration to contain the name of any text encoding scheme, the only ones that XML processors are, according to spec, required to understand are UTF-8 and UTF-16. UTF-8 and UTF-16 are two flavors of *Unicode*, a recent and powerful character encoding architecture that embraces every funny little squiggle a person might care to make.

In this section, we conspire with Perl and XML to nudge you gently into thinking about Unicode, if you're not pondering it already. While you can do everything described in this book by using the legacy encoding of your choice, you'll find, as time passes, that you're swimming against the current.

Unicode, Perl, and XML

Unicode has crept in as the digital age's way of uniting the thousands of different writing systems that have paid the salaries of monks and linguists for centuries. Of course, if you program in an environment where non-ASCII characters are found in abundance, you're probably already familiar with it. However, even then, much of your text processing work might be restricted to low-bit Latin alphanumerics, simply because that's been the character set of choice—of fiat, really—for the Internet. Unicode hopes to change this trend, Perl hopes to help, and sneaky little XML is already doing so.

As any Unicode-evangelizing document will tell you,* Unicode is great for internationalizing code. It lets programmers come up with localization solutions without the additional worry of juggling different character architectures.

---

* These documents include Chapter 15 of O'Reilly's *Programming Perl, Third Edition* and the FAQ that the Unicode consortium hosts at *http://unicode.org/unicode/faq/*.

However, Unicode's importance increases by an order of magnitude when you introduce the question of data representation. The languages that a given program's users (or programmers) might prefer is one thing, but as computing becomes more ubiquitous, it touches more people's lives in more ways every day, and some of these people speak Kurku. By understanding the basics of Unicode, you can see how it can help to transparently keep all the data you'll ever work with, no matter the script, in one architecture.

Unicode Encodings

We are careful to separate the words "architecture" and "encoding" because Unicode actually represents one of the former that contains several of the latter.

In Unicode, every discrete squiggle that's gained official recognition, from A to α to ☺, has its own *code point*—a unique positive integer that serves as its address in the whole map of Unicode. For example, the first letter of the Latin alphabet, capitalized, lives at the hexadecimal address 0x0041 (as it does in ASCII and friends), and the other two symbols, the lowercase Greek alpha and the smileyface, are found in 0x03B1 and 0x263A, respectively. A character can be constructed from any one of these code points, or by combining several of them. Many code points are dedicated to holding the various diacritical marks, such as accents and radicals, that many scripts use in conjunction with base alphabetical or ideographic glyphs.

These addresses, as well as those of the tens of thousands (and, in time, hundreds of thousands) of other glyphs on the map, remain true across Unicode's encodings. The only difference lies in the way these numbers are encoded in the ones and zeros that make up the document at its lowest level.

Unicode officially supports three types of encoding, all named UTF (short for Unicode Transformation Format), followed by a number representing the smallest bit-size any character might take. The encodings are UTF-8, UTF-16, and UTF-32. UTF-8 is the most flexible of all, and is therefore the one that Perl has adopted.

UTF-8

The UTF-8 encoding, arguably the most Perlish in its impish trickery, is also the most efficient since it's the only one that can pack characters into single bytes. For that reason, UTF-8 is the default encoding for XML documents: if XML documents specify no encoding in their declarations, then processors should assume that they use UTF-8.

Each character appearing within a document encoded with UTF-8 uses as many bytes as it has to in order to represent that character's code point, up to a maximum of six bytes. Thus, the character A, with the itty-bitty address of 0x41, gets one byte to represent it, while our friend ☺ lives way up the street in one of Unicode's blocks of miscellaneous doohickeys, with the address 0x263A. It takes three bytes for itself—two for the character's code point number and one that signals to text processors that there are, in fact, multiple bytes to this character. Several centuries from now, after Earth begrudgingly joins the Galactic Friendship Union and we find ourselves needing to encode the characters from countless off-planet civilizations, bytes four through six will come in quite handy.

UTF-16

The UTF-16 encoding uses a full two bytes to represent the character in question, even if its ordinal is small enough to fit into one (which is how UTF-8 would handle it). If, on the other hand, the character is rare enough to have a very high ordinal, then it gets an additional two bytes tacked onto it (called a surrogate pair), bringing that one character's total length to four bytes.

 Because Unicode 2.0 used a 16-bits-per-character style as its sole supported encoding, many people, and the programs they write, talk about the "Unicode encoding" when they really mean Unicode UTF-16. Even new applications' "Save As..." dialog boxes sometimes offer "Unicode" and "UTF-8" as separate choices, even though these labels don't make much sense in Unicode 3.2 terminology.

UTF-32

UTF-32 works a lot like UTF-16, but eliminates any question of variable character size by declaring that every invoked Unicode-mapped glyph shall occupy exactly four bytes. Because of its maximum maximosity, this encoding doesn't see much practical use, since all but the most unusual communication would have significantly more than half of its total mass made up of leading zeros, which doesn't work wonders for efficiency. However, if guaranteed character width is an inflexible issue, this encoding can handle all the million-plus glyph addresses that Unicode accommodates. Of the three major Unicode encodings, UTF-32 is the one that XML parsers aren't obliged to understand. Hence, you probably don't need to worry about it, either.

Other Encodings

The XML standard defines 21 names for character sets that parsers might use (beyond the two they're required to know, UTF-8 and UTF-16). These names range from ISO-8859-1 (ASCII plus 128 characters outside the Latin alphabet) to Shift_JIS, a Microsoftian encoding for Japanese ideographs. While they're not Unicode encodings per se, each character within them maps to one or more Unicode code points (and vice versa, allowing for round-tripping between common encodings by way of Unicode).

XML parsers in Perl all have their own ways of dealing with other encodings. Some may need an extra little nudge. XML::Parser, for example, is weak in its raw state because its underlying library, Expat, understands only a handful of non-Unicode encodings. Fortunately, you can give it a helping hand by installing Clark Cooper's

`XML::Encoding` module, an `XML::Parser` subclass that can read and understand map files (themselves XML documents) that bind the character code points of other encodings to their Unicode addresses.

Core Perl support

As with XML, Perl's relationship with Unicode has heated up at a cautious but inevitable pace.[*] Generally, you should use Perl version 5.6 or greater to work with Unicode properly in your code. If you do have 5.6 or greater, consult its `perlunicode` manpage for details on how deep its support runs, as each release since then has gradually deepened its loving embrace with Unicode. If you have an even earlier Perl, whew, you really ought to consider upgrading it. You can eke by with some of the tools we'll mention later in this chapter, but hacking Perl and XML means hacking in Unicode, and you'll notice the lack of core support for it.

Currently, the most recent stable Perl release, 5.6.1, contains partial support for Unicode. Invoking the `use utf8` pragma tells Perl to use UTF-8 encoding with most of its string-handling functions. Perl also allows code to exist in UTF-8, allowing identifiers built from characters living beyond ASCII's one-byte reach. This can prove very useful for hackers who primarily think in glyphs outside the Latin alphabet.

Perl 5.8's Unicode support will be much more complete, allowing UTF-8 and regular expressions to play nice. The 5.8 distribution also introduces the `Encode` module to Perl's standard library, which will allow any Perl programmer to shift text from legacy encodings to Unicode without fuss:

```
use Encode 'from_to';
from_to($data, "iso-8859-3", "utf-8"); # from legacy to
utf-8
```

Finally, Perl 6, being a redesign of the whole language that includes everything the Perl community learned over the last dozen years, will naturally have an even more intimate relationship with Unicode (and will give us an excuse to print a second edition of this book in a few years). Stay tuned to the usual information channels for continuing developments on this front as we see what happens.

Encoding Conversion

If you use a version of Perl older than 5.8, you'll need a little extra help when switching from one encoding to another. Fortunately, your toolbox contains some ratchety little devices to assist you.

---

[*] The romantic metaphor may start to break down for you here, but you probably understand by now that Perl's polyamorous proclivities help make it the language that it is.

iconv and Text::Iconv

iconv is a library and program available for Windows and Unix (inlcuding Mac OS X) that provides an easy interface for turning a document of type A into one of type B. On the Unix command line, you can use it like this:

```
$ iconv -f latin1 -t utf8 my_file.txt > my_unicode_file.txt
```

If you have iconv on your system, you can also grab the Text::Iconv Perl module from CPAN, which gives you a Perl API to this library. This allows you to quickly re-encode on-disk files or strings in memory.

Unicode::String

A more portable solution comes in the form of the Unicode::String module, which needs no underlying C library. The module's basic API is as blissfully simple as all basic APIs should be. Got a string? Feed it to the class's constructor method and get back an object holding that string, as well as a bevy of methods that let you squash and stretch it in useful and amusing ways. Example 3-12 tests the module.

Example 3-12. Unicode test

```
use Unicode::String;

my $string = "This sentence exists in ASCII and UTF-8, but not UTF-16. Darn!\n";
my $u = Unicode::String->new($string);

# $u now holds an object representing a stringful of 16-bit characters

# It uses overloading so Perl string operators do what you expect!
$u .= "\n\nOh, hey, it's Unicode all of a sudden. Hooray!!\n"

# print as UTF-16 (also known as UCS2)
print $u->ucs2;

# print as something more human-readable
print $u->utf8;
```

The module's many methods allow you to downgrade your strings, too—specifically, the utf7 method lets you pop the eighth bit off of UTF-8 characters, which is acceptable if you need to throw a bunch of ASCII characters at a receiver that would flip out if it saw chains of UTF-8 marching proudly its way instead of the austere and solitary encodings of old.

XML::Parser sometimes seems a little too eager to get you into Unicode. No matter what a document's declared encoding is, it silently transforms all characters with higher Unicode code points into UTF-8, and if you ask the parser for your data back, it delivers those characters back to you in that manner. This silent transformation can be an unpleasant surprise. If you use XML::Parser as the core of any processing software you write, be aware that you may need to use the conversion tools mentioned in this section to massage your data into a more suitable format.

Byte order marks

If, for some reason, you have an XML document from an unknown source and have no idea what its encoding might be, it may behoove you to check for the presence of a *byte order mark* (BOM) at the start of the document. Documents that use Unicode's UTF-16 and UTF-32 encodings are endian-dependent (while UTF-8 escapes this fate by nature of its peculiar protocol). Not knowing which end of a byte carries the significant bit will make reading these documents similar to reading them in a mirror, rendering their content into a garble that your programs will not appreciate.

Unicode defines a special code point, U+FEFF, as the byte order mark. According to the Unicode specification, documents using the UTF-16 or UTF-32 encodings have the option of dedicating their first two or four bytes to this character.* This way, if a program carefully inspecting the document scans the first two bits and sees that they're 0xFE and 0xFF, in that order, it knows it's big-endian UTF-16. On the other hand, if it sees 0xFF 0xFE, it knows that document is little-endian because there is no Unicode code point of U+FFFE. (UTF-32's big- and little-endian BOMs have more padding: 0x00 0x00 0xFE 0xFF and 0xFF 0xFE 0x00 0x00, respectively.)

The XML specification states that UTF-16- and UTF-32-encoded documents must use a BOM, but, referring to the Unicode specification, we see that documents created by the engines of sane and benevolent masters will arrive to you in network order. In other words, they arrive to you in a big-endian fashion, which was some time ago declared as the order to use when transmitting data between machines. Conversely, because you are sane and benevolent, you should always transmit documents in network order when you're not sure which order to use. However, if you ever find yourself in doubt that you've received a sane document, just close your eyes and hum this tune:

```
open XML_FILE, $filename or die "Can't read $filename: $!";
my $bom; # will hold possible byte order mark
```

---

* UTF-8 has its own byte order mark, but its purpose is to identify the document at UTF-8, and thus has little use in the XML world. The UTF-8 encoding doesn't have to worry about any of this endianness business since all its characters are made of strung-together byte sequences that are always read from first to last instead of little boxes holding byte pairs whose order may be questionable.

```
# read the first two bytes
read XML_FILE, $bom, 2;

# Fetch their numeric values, via Perl's ord() function
my $ord1 = ord(substr($bom,0,1));
my $ord2 = ord(substr($bom,1,1));

if ($ord1 == 0xFE && $ord2 == 0xFF) {
  # It looks like a UTF-16 big-endian document!
  # ... act accordingly here ...
} elsif ($ord1 == 0xFF && $ord2 == 0xEF) {
  # Oh, someone was naughty and sent us a UTF-16 little-endian document.
  # Probably we'll want to effect a byteswap on the thing before working with it.
} else {
  # No byte order mark detected.
}
```

You might run this example as a last-ditch effort if your parser complains that it can't find any XML in the document. The first line might indeed be a valid <?xml ... > declaration, but your parser sees some gobbledygook instead.

CHAPTER 4

Event Streams

Now that you're all warmed up with parsers and have enough knowledge to make you slightly dangerous, we'll analyze one of the two important styles of XML processing: event streams. We'll look at some examples that show the basic theory of stream processing and graduate with a full treatment of the standard Simple API for XML (SAX).

Working with Streams

In the world of computer science, a *stream* is a sequence of data chunks to be processed. A file, for example, is a sequence of characters (one or more bytes each, depending on the encoding). A program using this data can open a filehandle to the file, creating a character stream, and it can choose to read in data in chunks of whatever size it chooses. Streams can be dynamically generated too, whether from another program, received over a network, or typed in by a user. A stream is an abstraction, making the source of the data irrelevant for the purpose of processing.

To summarize, here are a stream's important qualities:

- It consists of a sequence of data fragments.
- The order of fragments transmitted is significant.
- The source of data (e.g., file or program output) is not important.

XML streams are just clumpy character streams. Each data clump, called a *token* in parser parlance, is a conglomeration of one or more characters. Each token corresponds to a type of markup, such as an element start or end tag, a string of character data, or a processing instruction. It's very easy for parsers to dice up XML in this way, requiring minimal resources and time.

What makes XML streams different from character streams is that the context of each token matters; you can't just pump out a stream of random tags and data and expect an XML processor to make sense of it. For example, a stream of ten start tags followed by no end tags is not very useful, and definitely not well-formed XML. Any data that isn't well-formed will be rejected. After all, the whole purpose of XML is to package data in a way that guarantees the integrity of a document's structure and labeling, right?

These contextual rules are helpful to the parser as well as the front-end processor. XML was designed to be very easy to parse, unlike other markup languages that can require look-ahead or look-behind. For example, SGML does not have a rule requiring nonempty elements to have an end tag. To know when an element ends requires sophisticated reasoning by the parser. This requirement leads to code complexity, slower processing speed, and increased memory usage.

Events and Handlers

Why do we call it an *event* stream and not an element stream or a markup object stream? The fact that XML is hierarchical (elements contain other elements) makes it impossible to package individual elements and serve them up as tokens in the stream. In a well-formed document, all elements are contained in one root element. A root element that contains the whole document is not a stream. Thus, we really can't expect a stream to give a complete element in a token, unless it's an empty element.

Instead, XML streams are composed of events. An *event* is a signal that the state of the document (as we've seen it so far in the stream) has changed. For example, when the parser comes across the start tag for an element, it indicates that another element was opened and the state of parsing has changed. An end tag affects the state by closing the most recently opened element. An XML processor can keep track of open elements in a stack data structure, pushing newly opened elements and popping off closed ones. At any given moment during parsing, the processor knows how deep it is in the document by the size of the stack.

Though parsers support a variety of events, there is a lot of overlap. For example, one parser may distinguish between a start tag and an empty element, while another may not, but all will signal the presence of that element. Let's look more closely at how a parser might dole out tokens, as shown Example 4-1.

Example 4-1. XML fragment

```
<recipe>
  <name>peanut butter and jelly sandwich</name>
  <!-- add picture of sandwich here -->
  <ingredients>
    <ingredient>Gloppy&trade; brand peanut butter</ingredient>
    <ingredient>bread</ingredient>
    <ingredient>jelly</ingredient>
  </ingredients>
  <instructions>
    <step>Spread peanutbutter on one slice of bread.</step>
    <step>Spread jelly on the other slice of bread.</step>
    <step>Put bread slices together, with peanut butter and
```

Example 4-1. XML fragment (continued)

```
  jelly touching.</step>
  </instructions>
</recipe>
```

Apply a parser to the preceding example and it might generate this list of events:

1. A document start (if this is the beginning of a document and not a fragment)

2. A start tag for the `<recipe>` element

3. A start tag for the `<name>` element

4. The piece of text "peanut butter and jelly sandwich"

5. An end tag for the `<name>` element

6. A comment with the text "add picture of sandwich here"

7. A start tag for the `<ingredients>` element

8. A start tag for the `<ingredient>` element

9. The text "Gloppy"

10. A reference to the entity `trade`

11. The text "brand peanut butter"

12. An end tag for the `<ingredient>` element

...and so on, until the final event—the end of the document—is reached.

Somewhere between chopping up a stream into tokens and processing the tokens is a layer one might call a dispatcher. It branches the processing depending on the type of token. The code that deals with a particular token type is called a *handler*. There could be a handler for start tags, another for character data, and so on. It could be a compound `if` statement, switching to a subroutine to handle each case. Or, it could be built into the parser as a callback dispatcher, as is the case with `XML::Parser`'s stream mode. If you register a set of subroutines, one to an event type, the parser calls the appropriate one for each token as it's generated. Which strategy you use depends on the parser.

The Parser as Commodity

You don't have to write an XML processing program that separates parser from handler, but doing so can be advantageous. By making your program modular, you make it easier to organize and test your code. The ideal way to modularize is with objects, communicating on sanctioned channels and otherwise leaving one another alone. Modularization makes swapping one part for another easier, which is very important in XML processing.

The XML stream, as we said before, is an abstraction, which makes the source of data irrelevant. It's like the spigot you have in the backyard, to which you can hook up a hose and water your lawn. It doesn't matter where you plug it in, you just want the water. There's nothing special about the hose either. As long as it doesn't leak and it reaches where you want to go, you don't care if it's made of rubber or bark. Similarly, XML parsers have become a commodity: something you can download, plug in, and see it work as expected. Plugging it in easily, however, is the tricky part.

The key is the screwhead on the end of the spigot. It's a standard gauge of pipe that uses a specific thread size, and any hose you buy should fit. With XML event streams, we also need a standard interface there. XML developers have settled on SAX, which has been in use for a few years now. Until recently, Perl XML parsers were not interchangeable. Each had its own interface, making it difficult to swap out one in favor of another. That's changing now, as developers adopt SAX and agree on conventions for hooking up handlers to parsers. We'll see some of the fruits of this effort in Chapter 5.

Stream Applications

Stream processing is great for many XML tasks. Here are a few of them:

Filter

A *filter* outputs an almost identical copy of the source document, with a few small changes. Every incidence of an <A> element might be converted into a <B> element, for example. The handler is simple, as it has to output only what it receives, except to make a subtle change when it detects a specific event.

Selector

If you want a specific piece of information from a document, without the rest of the content, you can write a *selector* program. This program combs through events, looking for an element or attribute containing a particular bit of unique data called a *key,* and then stops. The final job of the program is to output the sought-after record, possibly reformatted.

Summarizer

This program type consumes a document and spits out a short summary. For example, an accounting program might calculate a final balance from many transaction records; a program might generate a table of contents by outputting the titles of sections; an index generator might create a list of links to certain keywords highlighted in the text. The handler for this kind of program has to remember portions of the document to repackage it after the parser is finished reading the file.

Converter

This sophisticated type of program turns your XML-formatted document into another format—possibly another application of XML. For example, turning DocBook XML into HTML can be done in this way. This kind of processing pushes stream processing to its limits.

XML stream processing works well for a wide variety of tasks, but it does have limitations. The biggest problem is that everything is driven by the parser, and the parser has a mind of its own. Your program has to take what it gets in the order given. It can't say, "Hold on, I need to look at the token you gave me ten steps back" or "Could you give me a sneak peek at a token twenty steps down the line?" You can look back to the parsing past by giving your program a memory. Clever use of data structures can be used to remember recent events. However, if you need to look behind a lot, or look ahead even a little, you probably need to switch to a different strategy: tree processing, the topic of Chapter 6.

Now you have the grounding for XML stream processing. Let's move on to specific examples and see how to wrangle with XML streams in real life.

XML::PYX

In the Perl universe, standard APIs have been slow to catch on for many reasons. CPAN, the vast storehouse of publicly offered modules, grows organically, with no central authority to approve of a submission. Also, with XML, a relative newcomer on the data format scene, the Perl community has only begun to work out standard solutions.

We can characterize the first era of XML hacking in Perl to be the age of nonstandard parsers. It's a time when documentation is scarce and modules are experimental. There is much creativity and innovation, and just as much idiosyncrasy and quirkiness. Surprisingly, many of the tools that first appeared on the horizon were quite useful. It's fascinating territory for historians and developers alike.

XML::PYX is one of these early parsers. Streams naturally lend themselves to the concept of pipelines, where data output from one program can be plugged into another, creating a chain of processors. There's no reason why XML can't be handled that way, so an innovative and elegant processing style has evolved around this concept. Essentially, the XML is repackaged as a stream of easily recognizable and transmutable symbols, even as a command-line utility.

One example of this repackaging is PYX, a symbolic encoding of XML markup that is friendly to text processing languages like Perl. It presents each XML event on a separate line very cleverly. Many Unix programs like *awk* and *grep* are line oriented, so they work well with PYX. Lines are happy in Perl too.

Table 4-1 summarizes the notation of PYX.

Table 4-1. PYX notation

Symbol	Represents
(	An element start tag
)	An element end tag

Table 4-1. PYX notation (continued)

Symbol	Represents
-	Character data
A	An attribute
?	A processing instruction

For every event coming through the stream, PYX starts a new line, beginning with one of the five symbols shown in Table 4-1. This line is followed by the element name or whatever other data is pertinent. Special characters are escaped with a backslash, as you would see in Perl code.

Here's how a parser converting an XML document into PYX notation would look. The following code is XML input by the parser:

```
<shoppinglist>
  <!-- brand is not important -->
  <item>toothpaste</item>
  <item>rocket engine</item>
  <item optional="yes">caviar</item>
</shoppinglist>
```

As PYX, it would look like this:

```
(shoppinglist
-\n
(item
-toothpaste
)item
-\n
(item
-rocket engine
)item
-\n
(item
Aoptional yes
-caviar
)item
-\n
)shoppinglist
```

Notice that the comment didn't come through in the PYX translation. PYX is a little simplistic in some ways, omitting some details in the markup. It will not alert you to CDATA markup sections, although it will let the content pass through. Perhaps the most serious loss is character entity references that disappear from the stream. You should make sure you don't need that information before working with PYX.

Matt Sergeant has written a module, XML::PYX, which parses XML and translates it into PYX. The compact program in Example 4-2 strips out all XML element tags, leaving only the character data.

Example 4-2. PYX parser

```
use XML::PYX;

# initialize parser and generate PYX
my $parser = XML::PYX::Parser->new;
my $pyx;
if (defined ( $ARGV[0] )) {
  $pyx = $parser->parsefile( $ARGV[0] );
}

# filter out the tags
foreach( split( / /, $pyx )) {
  print $' if( /^-/ );
}
```

PYX is an interesting alternative to SAX and DOM for quick-and-dirty XML processing. It's useful for simple tasks like element counting, separating content from markup, and reporting simple events. However, it does lack sophistication, making it less attractive for complex processing.

XML::Parser

Another early parser is XML::Parser, the first fast and efficient parser to hit CPAN. We detailed its many-faceted interface in Chapter 3. Its built-in stream mode is worth a closer look, though. Let's return to it now with a solid stream example.

We'll use XML::Parser to read a list of records encoded as an XML document. The records contain contact information for people, including their names, street addresses, and phone numbers. As the parser reads the file, our handler will store the information in its own data structure for later processing. Finally, when the parser is done, the program sorts the records by the person's name and outputs them as an HTML table.

The source document is listed in Example 4-3. It has a <list> element as the root, with four <entry> elements inside it, each with an address, a name, and a phone number.

Example 4-3. Address book file

```
<list>
  <entry>
    <name><first>Thadeus</first><last>Wrigley</last></name>
    <phone>716-505-9910</phone>
    <address>
      <street>105 Marsupial Court</street>
      <city>Fairport</city><state>NY</state><zip>14450</zip>
    </address>
  </entry>
  <entry>
    <name><first>Jill</first><last>Baxter</last></name>
    <address>
```

Example 4-3. Address book file (continued)

```
      <street>818 S. Rengstorff Avenue</street>
      <zip>94040</zip>
      <city>Mountainview</city><state>CA</state>
    </address>
    <phone>217-302-5455</phone>
  </entry>
  <entry>
    <name><last>Riccardo</last>
    <first>Preston</first></name>
    <address>
      <street>707 Foobah Drive</street>
      <city>Mudhut</city><state>OR</state><zip>32777</zip>
    </address>
    <phone>111-222-333</phone>
  </entry>
  <entry>
    <address>
      <street>10 Jiminy Lane</street>
      <city>Scrapheep</city><state>PA</state><zip>99001</zip>
    </address>
    <name><first>Benn</first><last>Salter</last></name>
    <phone>611-328-7578</phone>
  </entry>
</list>
```

This simple structure lends itself naturally to event processing. Each <entry> start tag signals the preparation of a new part of the data structure for storing data. An </entry> end tag indicates that all data for the record has been collected and can be saved. Similarly, start and end tags for <entry> subelements are cues that tell the handler when and where to save information. Each <entry> is self-contained, with no links to the outside, making it easy to process.

The program is listed in Example 4-4. At the top is code used to initialize the parser object with references to subroutines, each of which will serve as the handler for a single event. This style of event handling is called a *callback* because you write the subroutine first, and the parser then calls it back when it needs it to handle an event.

After the initialization, we declare some global variables to store information from XML elements for later processing. These variables give the handlers a memory, as mentioned earlier. Storing information for later retrieval is often called *saving state* because it helps the handlers preserve the state of the parsing up to the current point in the document.

After reading in the data and applying the parser to it, the rest of the program defines the handler subroutines. We handle five events: the start and end of the document, the start and end of elements, and character data. Other events, such as comments, processing instructions, and document type declarations, will all be ignored.

Example 4-4. Code for the address program

```
# initialize the parser with references to handler routines
#
use XML::Parser;
my $parser = XML::Parser->new( Handlers => {
    Init =>      \&handle_doc_start,
    Final =>     \&handle_doc_end,
    Start =>     \&handle_elem_start,
    End =>       \&handle_elem_end,
    Char =>      \&handle_char_data,
});


#
# globals
#
my $record;         # points to a hash of element contents
my $context;        # name of current element
my %records;        # set of address entries


#
# read in the data and run the parser on it
#
my $file = shift @ARGV;
if( $file ) {
    $parser->parsefile( $file );
} else {
    my $input = "";
    while( <STDIN> ) { $input .= $_; }
    $parser->parse( $input );
}
exit;


###
### Handlers
###


#
# As processing starts, output the beginning of an HTML file.
#
sub handle_doc_start {
    print "<html><head><title>addresses</title></head>\n";
    print "<body><h1>addresses</h1>\n";
}


#
# save element name and attributes
#
sub handle_elem_start {
    my( $expat, $name, %atts ) = @_;
    $context = $name;
    $record = {} if( $name eq 'entry' );
}


# collect character data into the recent element's buffer
```

Example 4-4. Code for the address program (continued)

```perl
#
sub handle_char_data {
    my( $expat, $text ) = @_;

    # Perform some minimal entitizing of naughty characters
    $text =~ s/&/&/g;
    $text =~ s/</&lt;/g;

    $record->{ $context } .= $text;
}


#
# if this is an <entry>, collect all the data into a record
#
sub handle_elem_end {
    my( $expat, $name ) = @_;
    return unless( $name eq 'entry' );
    my $fullname = $record->{'last'} . $record->{'first'};
    $records{ $fullname } = $record;
}


#
# Output the close of the file at the end of processing.
#
sub handle_doc_end {
    print "<table border='1'>\n";
    print "<tr><th>name</th><th>phone</th><th>address</th></tr>\n";
    foreach my $key ( sort( keys( %records ))) {
        print "<tr><td>" . $records{ $key }->{ 'first' } . ' ';
        print $records{ $key }->{ 'last' } . "</td><td>";
        print $records{ $key }->{ 'phone' } . "</td><td>";
        print $records{ $key }->{ 'street' } . ', ';
        print $records{ $key }->{ 'city' } . ', ';
        print $records{ $key }->{ 'state' } . ' ';
        print $records{ $key }->{ 'zip' } . "</td></tr>\n";
    }
    print "</table>\n</div>\n</body></html>\n";
}
```

To understand how this program works, we need to study the handlers. All handlers called by XML::Parser receive a reference to the expat parser object as their first argument, a courtesy to developers in case they want to access its data (for example, to check the input file's current line number). Other arguments may be passed, depending on the kind of event. For example, the start-element event handler gets the name of the element as the second argument, and then gets a list of attribute names and values.

Our handlers use global variables to store information. If you don't like global variables (in larger programs, they can be a headache to debug), you can create an object that stores the information internally. You would then give the parser your object's methods as handlers. We'll stick with globals for now because they are easier to read in our example.

The first handler is `handle_doc_start`, called at the start of parsing. This handler is a convenient way to do some work before processing the document. In our case, it just outputs HTML code to begin the HTML page in which the sorted address entries will be formatted. This subroutine has no special arguments.

The next handler, `handle_elem_start`, is called whenever the parser encounters the start of a new element. After the obligatory expat reference, the routine gets two arguments: `$name`, which is the element name, and `%atts`, a hash of attribute names and values. (Note that using a hash will not preserve the order of attributes, so if order is important to you, you should use an `@atts` array instead.) For this simple example, we don't use attributes, but we leave open the possibility of using them later.

This routine sets up processing of an element by saving the name of the element in a variable called `$context`. Saving the element's name ensures that we will know what to do with character data events the parser will send later. The routine also initializes a hash called `%record`, which will contain the data for each of `<entry>`'s subelements in a convenient look-up table.

The handler `handle_char_data` takes care of nonmarkup data—basically all the character data in elements. This text is stored in the second argument, here called `$text`. The handler only needs to save the content in the buffer `$record->{ $context }`. Notice that we append the character data to the buffer, rather than assign it outright. `XML::Parser` has a funny quirk in which it calls the character handler after each line or newline-separated string of text.* Thus, if the content of an element includes a newline character, this will result in two separate calls to the handler. If you didn't append the data, then the last call would overwrite the one before it.

Not surprisingly, `handle_elem_end` handles the end of element events. The second argument is the element's name, as with the start-element event handler. For most elements, there's not much to do here, but for `<entry>`, we have a final housekeeping task. At this point, all the information for a record has been collected, so the record is complete. We only have to store it in a hash, indexed by the person's full name so that we can easily sort the records later. The sorting can be done only after all the records are in, so we need to store the record for later processing. If we weren't interested in sorting, we could just output the record as HTML.

Finally, the `handle_doc_end` handler completes our set, performing any final tasks that remain after reading the document. It so happens that we do have something to do. We need to print out the records, sorted alphabetically by contact name. The subroutine generates an HTML table to format the entries nicely.

---

* This way of reading text is uniquely Perlish. XML purists might be confused about this handling of character data. XML doesn't care about newlines, or any whitespace for that matter; it's all just character data and is treated the same way.

This example, which involved a flat sequence of records, was pretty simple, but not all XML is like that. In some complex document formats, you have to consider the parent, grandparent, and even distant ancestors of the current element to decide what to do with an event. Remembering an element's ancestry requires a more sophisticated state-saving structure, which we will show in a later example.

CHAPTER 5

SAX

XML::Parser has done remarkably well as a multipurpose XML parser and stream generator, but it really isn't the future of Perl and XML. The problem is that we don't want one standard parser for all ends and purposes; we want to be able to choose from multiple parsers, each serving a different purpose. One parser might be written completely in Perl for portability, while another is accelerated with a core written in C. Or, you might want a parser that translates one format (such as a spreadsheet) into an XML stream. You simply can't anticipate all the things a parser might be called on to do. Even XML::Parser, with its many options and multiple modes of operation, can't please everybody. The future, then, is a multiplicity of parsers that cover any situation you encounter.

An environment with multiple parsers demands some level of consistency. If every parser had its own interface, developers would go mad. Learning one interface and being able to expect all parsers to comply to that is better than having to learn a hundred different ways to do the same thing. We need a standard interface between parsers and code: a universal plug that is flexible and reliable, free from the individual quirks of any particular parser.

The XML development world has settled on an event-driven interface called SAX. SAX evolved from discussions on the XML-DEV mailing list and, shepherded by David Megginson,* was quickly shaped into a useful specification. The first incarnation, called SAX Level 1 (or just SAX1), supports elements, attributes, and processing instructions. It doesn't handle some other things like namespaces or CDATA sections, so the second iteration, SAX2, was devised, adding support for just about any event you can imagine in generic XML.

SAX has been a huge success. Its simplicity makes it easy to learn and work with. Early development with XML was mostly in the realm of Java, so SAX was codified

---

* David Megginson maintains a web page about SAX at *http://www.saxproject.org*.

as an interface construct. An interface construct is a special kind of class that declares an object's methods without implementing them, leaving the implementation up to the developer.

Enthusiasm for SAX soon infected the Perl community and implementations began to appear in CPAN, but there was a problem. Perl doesn't provide a rigorous way to define a standard interface like Java does. It has weak type checking and forgives all kinds of inconsistencies. Whereas Java compares argument types in functions with those defined in the interface construct at compile time, Perl quietly accepts any arguments you use. Thus, defining a standard in Perl is mostly a verbal activity, relying on the developer's experience and watchfulness to comply.

One of the first Perl implementations of SAX is Ken McLeod's `XML::Parser::PerlSAX` module. As a subclass of `XML::Parser`, it modifies the stream of events from Expat to repackage them as SAX events.

SAX Event Handlers

To use a typical SAX module in a program, you must pass it an object whose methods implement handlers for SAX events. Table 5-1 describes the methods in a typical handler object. A SAX parser passes a hash to each handler containing properties relevant to the event. For example, in this hash, an element handler would receive the element's name and a list of attributes.

Table 5-1. PerlSAX handlers

Method name	Event	Properties
`start_document`	The document processing has started (this is the first event)	(none defined)
`end_document`	The document processing is complete (this is the last event)	(none defined)
`start_element`	An element start tag or empty element tag was found	Name, Attributes
`end_element`	An element end tag or empty element tag was found	Name
`characters`	A string of nonmarkup characters (character data) was found	Data
`processing_instruction`	A parser encountered a processing instruction	Target, Data
`comment`	A parser encountered a comment	Data
`start_cdata`	The beginning of a CDATA section encountered (the following character data may contain reserved markup characters)	(none defined)
`end_cdata`	The end of an encountered CDATA section	(none defined)
`entity_reference`	An internal entity reference was found (as opposed to an external entity reference, which would indicate that a file needs to be loaded)	Name, Value

A few notes about handler methods:

- For an empty element, both the `start_element()` and `end_element()` handlers are called, in that order. No handler exists specifically for empty elements.
- The `characters()` handler may be called more than once for a string of contiguous character data, parceling it into pieces. For example, a parser might break text around an entity reference, which is often more efficient for the parser.
- The `characters()` handler will be called for any whitespace between elements, even if it doesn't seem like significant data. In XML, all characters are considered part of data. It's simply more efficient not to make a distinction otherwise.
- Handling of processing instructions, comments, and CDATA sections is optional. In the absence of handlers, the data from processing instructions and comments is discarded. For CDATA sections, calls are still made to the `characters()` handler as before so the data will not be lost.
- The `start_cdata()` and `end_cdata()` handlers do not receive data. Instead, they merely act as signals to tell you whether reserved markup characters can be expected in future calls to the `characters()` handler.
- In the absence of an `entity_reference()` handler, all internal entity references will be resolved automatically by the parser, and the resulting text or markup will be handled normally. If you do define an `entity_reference()` handler, the entity references will not be expanded and you can do what you want with them.

Let's show an example now. We'll write a program called a filter, a special processor that outputs a replica of the original document with a few modifications. Specifically, it makes these changes to a document:

- Turns every XML comment into a `<comment>` element
- Deletes processing instructions
- Removes tags, but leaves the content, for `<literal>` elements that occur within `<programlisting>` elements at any level

The code for this program is listed in Example 5-1. Like the last program, we initialize the parser with a set of handlers, except this time they are bundled together in a convenient package: an object called `MyHandler`. Notice that we've implemented a few more handlers, since we want to be able to deal with comments, processing instructions, and the document prolog.

Example 5-1. Filter program

```
# initialize the parser
#
use XML::Parser::PerlSAX;
my $parser = XML::Parser::PerlSAX->new( Handler => MyHandler->new() );

if( my $file = shift @ARGV ) {
    $parser->parse( Source => {SystemId => $file} );
```

Example 5-1. Filter program (continued)

```perl
} else {
    my $input = "";
    while( <STDIN> ) { $input .= $_; }
    $parser->parse( Source => {String => $input} );
}
exit;


#
# global variables
#
my @element_stack;              # remembers element names
my $in_intset;                  # flag: are we in the internal subset?


###
### Document Handler Package
###
package MyHandler;


#
# initialize the handler package
#
sub new {
    my $type = shift;
    return bless {}, $type;
}


#
# handle a start-of-element event: output start tag and attributes
#
sub start_element {
    my( $self, $properties ) = @_;
    # note: the hash %{$properties} will lose attribute order

    # close internal subset if still open
    output( "]>\n" ) if( $in_intset );
    $in_intset = 0;

    # remember the name by pushing onto the stack
    push( @element_stack, $properties->{'Name'} );

    # output the tag and attributes UNLESS it's a <literal>
    # inside a <programlisting>
    unless( stack_top( 'literal' ) and
            stack_contains( 'programlisting' )) {
        output( "<" . $properties->{'Name'} );
        my %attributes = %{$properties->{'Attributes'}};
        foreach( keys( %attributes )) {
            output( " $_=\"" . $attributes{$_} . "\"" );
        }
        output( ">" );
    }
}
```

Example 5-1. Filter program (continued)

```
#
# handle an end-of-element event: output end tag UNLESS it's from a
# <literal> inside a <programlisting>
#
sub end_element {
    my( $self, $properties ) = @_;
    output( "</" . $properties->{'Name'} . ">" )
        unless( stack_top( 'literal' ) and
                stack_contains( 'programlisting' ));
    pop( @element_stack );
}


#
# handle a character data event
#
sub characters {
    my( $self, $properties ) = @_;
    # parser unfortunately resolves some character entities for us,
    # so we need to replace them with entity references again
    my $data = $properties->{'Data'};
    $data =~ s/\&/\&/;
    $data =~ s/</\&lt;/;
    $data =~ s/>/\&gt;/;
    output( $data );
}


#
# handle a comment event: turn into a <comment> element
#
sub comment {
    my( $self, $properties ) = @_;
    output( "<comment>" . $properties->{'Data'} . "</comment>" );
}


#
# handle a PI event: delete it
#
sub processing_instruction {
  # do nothing!
}


#
# handle internal entity reference (we don't want them resolved)
#
sub entity_reference {
    my( $self, $properties ) = @_;
    output( "&" . $properties->{'Name'} . ";" );
}

sub stack_top {
    my $guess = shift;
    return $element_stack[ $#element_stack ] eq $guess;
}
```

Example 5-1. Filter program (continued)

```
sub stack_contains {
    my $guess = shift;
    foreach( @element_stack ) {
        return 1 if( $_ eq $guess );
    }
    return 0;
}

sub output {
    my $string = shift;
    print $string;
}
```

Looking closely at the handlers, we see that one argument is passed, in addition to the obligatory object reference $self. This argument is a reference to a hash of properties about the event. This technique has one disadvantage: in the element start handler, the attributes are stored in a hash, which has no memory of the original attribute order. Semantically, this is not a big deal, since XML is supposed to be ignorant of attribute order. However, there may be cases when you want to replicate that order.[*]

As a filter, this program preserves everything about the original document, except for the few details that have to be changed. The program preserves the document prolog, processing instructions, and comments. Even entity references should be preserved as they are instead of being resolved (as the parser may want to do). Therefore, the program has a few more handlers than in the last example, from which we were interested only in extracting very specific information.

Let's test this program now. Our input datafile is listed in Example 5-2.

Example 5-2. Data for the filter

```
<?xml version="1.0"?>
<!DOCTYPE book
  SYSTEM "/usr/local/prod/sgml/db.dtd"
[
  <!ENTITY thingy "hoo hah blah blah">
]>

<book id="mybook">
<?print newpage?>
  <title>GRXL in a Nutshell</title>
  <chapter id="intro">
    <title>What is GRXL?</title>
<!-- need a better title -->
```

---

[*] In the case of our filter, we might want to compare the versions from before and after processing using a utility such as the Unix program *diff*. Such a comparison would yield many false differences where the order of attributes changed. Instead of using *diff*, you should consider using the module XML::SemanticDiff by Kip Hampton. This module would ignore syntactic differences and compare only the semantics of two documents.

Example 5-2. Data for the filter (continued)

```
    <para>
Yet another acronym.  That was our attitude at first, but then we saw
the amazing uses of this new technology called
<literal>GRXL</literal>.  Consider the following program:
    </para>
<?print newpage?>
    <programlisting>AH aof -- %%%%
{{{{{{ let x = 0 }}}}}}
  print!  <lineannotation><literal>wow</literal></lineannotation>
or not!</programlisting>
<!-- what font should we use? -->
    <para>
What does it do?  Who cares?  It's just lovely to look at.  In fact,
I'd have to say, "&thingy;".
    </para>
<?print newpage?>
  </chapter>
</book>
```

The result, after running the program on the data, is shown in Example 5-3.

Example 5-3. Output from the filter

```
<book id="mybook">
  <title>GRXL in a Nutshell</title>
  <chapter id="intro">
    <title>What is GRXL?</title>
<comment> need a better title </comment>
    <para>
Yet another acronym.  That was our attitude at first, but then we saw
the amazing uses of this new technology called
<literal>GRXL</literal>.  Consider the following program:
    </para>

    <programlisting>AH aof -- %%%%
{{{{{{ let x = 0 }}}}}}
  print!  <lineannotation>wow</lineannotation>
or not!</programlisting>
<comment> what font should we use? </comment>
    <para>
What does it do?  Who cares?  It's just lovely to look at.  In fact,
I'd have to say, "&thingy;".
    </para>

  </chapter>
</book>
```

Here's what the filter did right. It turned an XML comment into a <comment> element and deleted the processing instruction. The <literal> element in the <programlisting> was removed, with its contents left intact, while other <literal> elements were preserved. Entity references were left unresolved, as we wanted. So far, so good. But something's missing. The XML declaration, document type declaration, and internal subset are gone. Without the declaration for the entity thingy, this document is not valid. It looks like the handlers we had available to us were not sufficient.

DTD Handlers

XML::Parser::PerlSAX supports another group of handlers used to process DTD events. It takes care of anything that appears before the root element, such as the XML declaration, doctype declaration, and the internal subset of entity and element declarations, which are collectively called the *document prolog*. If you want to output the document literally as you read it (e.g., in a filter program), you need to define some of these handlers to reproduce the document prolog. Defining these handlers is just what we needed in the previous example.

You can use these handlers for other purposes. For example, you may need to pre-load entity definitions for special processing rather than rely on the parser to do its default substitution for you. These handlers are listed in Table 5-2.

Table 5-2. PerlSAX DTD handlers

Method name	Event	Properties
entity_decl	The parser sees an entity declaration (internal or external, parsed or unparsed).	Name, Value, PublicId, SystemId, Notation
notation_decl	The parser found a notation declaration.	Name, PublicId, SystemId, Base
unparsed_ entity_decl	The parser found a declaration for an unparsed entity (e.g., a binary data entity).	Name, PublicId, SystemId, Base
element_decl	An element declaration was found.	Name, Model
attlist_decl	An element's attribute list declaration was encountered.	ElementName, AttributeName, Type, Fixed
doctype_decl	The parser found the document type declaration.	Name, SystemId, PublicId, Internal
xml_decl	The XML declaration was encountered.	Version, Encoding, Standalone

The entity_decl( ) handler is called for all kinds of entity declarations unless a more specific handler is defined. Thus, unparsed entity declarations trigger the entity_decl( ) handler unless you've defined an unparsed_entity_decl( ), which will take precedence.

entity_decl( )'s parameters vary depending on the entity type. The Value parameter is set for internal entities, but not external ones. Likewise, PublicId and SystemId, parameters that tell an XML processor where to find the file containing the entity's value, is not set for internal entities, only external ones. Base tells the procesor what to use for a base URL if the SystemId contains a relative location.

Notation declarations are a special feature of DTDs that allow you to assign a special type identifier to an entity. For example, you could declare an entity to be of type "date" to tell the XML processor that the entity should be treated as that kind of data. It's not used very often in XML, so we won't go into it further.

The Model property of the element_decl( ) contains the content model, or grammar, for an element. This property describes what is allowed to go inside an element according to the DTD.

An attribute list declaration in a DTD can contain more than one attribute description. Fortunately, the parser breaks these descriptions up into individual calls to the attlist_decl( ) handler for each attribute.

The document type declaration is an optional part of the document at the top, just under the XML declaration. The parameter Name is the name of the root element in your document. PublicId and SystemId tell the processor where to find the external DTD. Finally, the Internal parameter contains the whole internal subset as a string, in case you want to skip the individual entity and element declaration handling.

As an example, let's say you wanted to add to the filter example code to output the document prolog exactly as it was encountered by the parser. You'd need to define handlers like the program in Example 5-4.

Example 5-4. A better filter

```
# handle xml declaration
#
sub xml_decl {
    my( $self, $properties ) = @_;
    output( "<?xml version=\"" . $properties->{'Version'} . "\"" );
    my $encoding = $properties->{'Encoding'};
    output( " encoding=\"$encoding\"" ) if( $encoding );
    my $standalone = $properties->{'Standalone'};
    output( " standalone=\"$standalone\"" ) if( $standalone );
    output( "?>\n" );
}


#
# handle doctype declaration:
# try to duplicate the original
#
sub doctype_decl {
    my( $self, $properties ) = @_;
    output( "\n<!DOCTYPE " . $properties->{'Name'} . "\n" );
    my $pubid = $properties->{'PublicId'};
    if( $pubid ) {
        output( "  PUBLIC \"$pubid\"\n" );
        output( "  \"" . $properties->{'SystemId'} . "\"\n" );
    } else {
        output( "  SYSTEM \"" . $properties->{'SystemId'} . "\"\n" );
    }
```

Example 5-4. A better filter (continued)

```
    my $intset = $properties->{'Internal'};
    if( $intset ) {
        $in_intset = 1;
        output( "[\n" );
    } else {
        output( ">\n" );
    }
}


#
# handle entity declaration in internal subset:
# recreate the original declaration as it was
#
sub entity_decl {
    my( $self, $properties ) = @_;
    my $name = $properties->{'Name'};
    output( "<!ENTITY $name " );
    my $pubid = $properties->{'PublicId'};
    my $sysid = $properties->{'SystemId'};
    if( $pubid ) {
        output( "PUBLIC \"$pubid\" \"$sysid\"" );
    } elsif( $sysid ) {
        output( "SYSTEM \"$sysid\"" );
    } else {
        output( "\"" . $properties->{'Value'} . "\"" );
    }
    output( ">\n" );
}
```

Now let's see how the output from our filter looks. The result is in Example 5-5.

Example 5-5. Output from the filter

```
<?xml version="1.0"?>

<!DOCTYPE book
  SYSTEM "/usr/local/prod/sgml/db.dtd"
[
<!ENTITY thingy "hoo hah blah blah">
]>
<book id="mybook">

  <title>GRXL in a Nutshell</title>
  <chapter id="intro">
    <title>What is GRXL?</title>
<comment> need a better title </comment>
    <para>
Yet another acronym.  That was our attitude at first, but then we saw
the amazing uses of this new technology called
<literal>GRXL</literal>.  Consider the following program:
    </para>
```

Example 5-5. Output from the filter (continued)

```
    <programlisting>AH aof -- %%%%
{{{{{{ let x = 0 }}}}}}
  print! <lineannotation>wow</lineannotation>
or not!</programlisting>
<comment> what font should we use? </comment>
    <para>
What does it do?  Who cares?  It's just lovely to look at.  In fact,
I'd have to say, "&thingy;".
    </para>

    </chapter>
</book>
```

That's much better. Now we have a complete filter program. The basic handlers take care of elements and everything inside them. The DTD handlers deal with whatever happens outside of the root element.

External Entity Resolution

By default, the parser substitutes all entity references with their actual values for you. Usually that's what you want it to do, but sometimes, as in the case with our filter example, you'd rather keep the entity references in place. As we saw, keeping the entity references is pretty easy to do; just include an entity_reference( ) handler method to override that behavior by outputting the references again. What we haven't seen yet is how to override the default handling of external entity references. Again, the parser wants to replace the references with their values by locating the files and inserting their contents into the stream. Would you ever want to change that behavior, and if so, how would you do it?

Storing documents in multiple files is convenient, especially for really large documents. For example, suppose you have a big book to write in XML and you want to store each chapter in its own file. You can do so easily with external entities. Here's an example:

```
<?xml version="1.0"?>
<doctype book [
  <!ENTITY intro-chapter   SYSTEM "chapters/intro.xml">
  <!ENTITY pasta-chapter   SYSTEM "chapters/pasta.xml">
  <!ENTITY stirfry-chapter SYSTEM "chapters/stirfry.xml">
  <!ENTITY soups-chapter   SYSTEM "chapters/soups.xml"> ]>

<book>
  <title>The Bonehead Cookbook</title>
  &intro-chapter;
  &pasta-chapter;
  &stirfry-chapter;
  &soups-chapter;
</book>
```

The previous filter example would resolve the external entity references for you diligently and output the entire book in one piece. Your file separation scheme would be lost and you'd have to edit the resulting file to break it back into multiple files. Fortunately, we can override the resolution of external entity references using a handler called resolve_entity( ).

This handler has four properties: Name, the entity's name; SystemId and PublicId, identifiers that help you locate the file containing the entity's text; and Base, which helps resolve relative URLs, if any exist. Unlike the other handlers, this one should return a value to tell the parser what to do. Returning undef tells the parser to load the external entity as it normally would. Otherwise, you need to return a hash describing an alternative source from which the entity should be loaded. The hash is the same type you would use to give to the object's parse( ) method, with keys like SystemId to give it a filename or URL, or String to give it a string of text. For example:

```
sub resolve_entity {
  my( $self, $props ) = @_;
  if( exists( $props->{ SystemId }) and
      open( ENT, $props->{ SystemId })) {
    my $entval = '<?start-file ' . $props->{ SystemId } . '?>';
    while( <ENT> ) { $entval .= $_; }
    close ENT;
    $entval .= '<?end-file ' . $props->{ SystemId } . '?>';
    return { String => $entval };
  } else {
    return undef;
  }
}
```

This routine opens the entity resource, if it's in a file it can find, and gives it to the parser as a string. First, it attaches a processing instruction before and after the entity text, marking the boundary of the file. Later, you can write a routine to look for the PIs and separate the files back out again.

Drivers for Non-XML Sources

The filter example used a file containing an XML document as an input source. This example shows just one of many ways to use SAX. Another popular use is to read data from a driver, which is a program that generates a stream of data from a non-XML source, such as a database. A SAX driver converts the data stream into a sequence of SAX events that we can process the way we did previously. What makes this so cool is that we can use the same code regardless of where the data came from. The SAX event stream abstracts the data and markup so we don't have to worry about it. Changing the program to work with files or other drivers would be trivial.

To see a driver in action, we will write a program that uses Ilya Sterin's module XML::SAXDriver::Excel to convert Microsoft Excel spreadsheets into XML documents. This example shows how a data stream can be processed in a pipeline fashion to ultimately arrive in the form we want it. A Spreadsheet::ParseExcel object reads the file and generates a generic data stream, which an XML::SAXDriver::Excel object translates into a SAX event stream. This stream is then output as XML by our program.

Here's a test Excel spreadsheet, represented as a table:

	A	B
1	baseballs	55
2	tennisballs	33
3	pingpong balls	12
4	footballs	77

The SAX driver will create new elements for us, giving us the names in the form of arguments to handler method calls. We will just print them out as they come and see how the driver structures the document. Example 5-6 is a simple program that does this.

Example 5-6. Excel parsing program

```
use XML::SAXDriver::Excel;

# get the file name to process
die( "Must specify an input file" ) unless( @ARGV );
my $file = shift @ARGV;
print "Parsing $file...\n";

# initialize the parser
my $handler = new Excel_SAX_Handler;
my %props = ( Source => { SystemId => $file },
              Handler => $handler );
my $driver = XML::SAXDriver::Excel->new( %props );

# start parsing
$driver->parse( %props );

# The handler package we define to print out the XML
# as we receive SAX events.
package Excel_SAX_Handler;

# initialize the package
sub new {
    my $type = shift;
    my $self = {@_};
    return bless( $self, $type );
}

# create the outermost element
sub start_document {
    print "<doc>\n";
}
```

Example 5-6. Excel parsing program (continued)

```
# end the document element
sub end_document {
    print "</doc>\n";
}

# handle any character data

sub characters {
    my( $self, $properties ) = @_;
    my $data = $properties->{'Data'};
    print $data if defined($data);
}

# start a new element, outputting the start tag
sub start_element {
    my( $self, $properties ) = @_;
    my $name = $properties->{'Name'};
    print "<$name>";
}

# end the new element
sub end_element {
    my( $self, $properties ) = @_;
    my $name = $properties->{'Name'};
    print "</$name>";
}
```

As you can see, the handler methods look very similar to those used in the previous SAX example. All that has changed is what we do with the arguments. Now let's see what the output looks like when we run it on the test file:

```
<doc>

<records>
        <record>
                <column1>baseballs</column1>
                <column2>55</column2>
        </record>
        <record>
                <column1>tennisballs</column1>
                <column2>33</column2>
        </record>
        <record>
                <column1>pingpong balls</column1>
                <column2>12</column2>
        </record>
        <record>
                <column1>footballs</column1>
                <column2>77</column2>
        </record>
        <record>
    Use of uninitialized value in print at conv line 39.
                <column1></column1>
```

```
Use of uninitialized value in print at conv line 39.
            <column2></column2>
        </record>
    </records></doc>
```

The driver did most of the work in creating elements and formatting the data. All we did was output the packages it gave us in the form of method calls. It wrapped the whole document in <records>, making our use of <doc> superfluous. (In the next revision of the code, we'll make the start_document( ) and end_document( ) methods output nothing.) Each row of the spreadsheet is encapsulated in a <record> element. Finally, the two columns are differentiated with <column1> and <column2> labels. All in all, not a bad job.

You can see that with a minimal amount of effort on our part, we have harnessed the power of SAX to do some complex work converting from one format to another. The driver actually automates the conversion, but it gives us enough flexibility in interpreting the events so that we can reject bad data (the empty row, for example) or rename elements. We can even perform complex processing, such as adding up values or sorting rows.

A Handler Base Class

SAX doesn't distinguish between different elements; it leaves that burden up to you. You have to sort out the element name in the start_element( ) handler, and maybe use a stack to keep track of element hierarchy. Don't you wish there were some way to abstract that stuff? Ken MacLeod has done just that with his XML::Handler::Subs module.

This module defines an object that branches handler calls to more specific handlers. If you want a handler that deals only with <title> elements, you can write that handler and it will be called. The handler dealing with a start tag must begin with s_, followed by the element's name (replace special characters with an underscore). End tag handlers are the same, but start with e_ instead of s_.

That's not all. The base object also has a built-in stack and provides an accessor method to check if you are inside a particular element. The $self->{Names} variable refers to a stack of element names. Use the method in_element($name) to test whether the parser is inside an element named $name at any point in time.

To try this out, let's write a program that does something element-specific. Given an HTML file, the program outputs everything inside an <h1> element, even inline elements used for emphasis. The code, shown in Example 5-7, is breathtakingly simple.

Example 5-7. A program subclassing the handler base

```
use XML::Parser::PerlSAX;
use XML::Handler::Subs
```

Example 5-7. A program subclassing the handler base (continued)

```
#
# initialize the parser
#
use XML::Parser::PerlSAX;
my $parser = XML::Parser::PerlSAX->new( Handler => H1_grabber->new() );
$parser->parse( Source => {SystemId => shift @ARGV} );

## Handler object: H1_grabber
##
package H1_grabber;
use base( 'XML::Handler::Subs' );

sub new {
    my $type = shift;
    my $self = {@_};
    return bless( $self, $type );
}

#
# handle start of document
#
sub start_document {
  SUPER::start_document();
  print "Summary of file:\n";
}

#
# handle start of <h1>: output bracket as delineator
#
sub s_h1 {
  print "[";
}

#
# handle end of <h1>: output bracket as delineator
#
sub e_h1 {
  print "]\n";
}

#
# handle character data
#
sub characters {
  my( $self, $props ) = @_;
  my $data = $props->{Data};
  print $data if( $self->in_element( h1 ));
}
```

Let's feed the program a test file:

```
<html>
  <head><title>The Life and Times of Fooby</title></head>
  <body>
```

```
        <h1>Fooby as a child</h1>
        <p>...</p>
        <h1>Fooby grows up</h1>
        <p>...</p>
        <h1>Fooby is in <em>big</em> trouble!</h1>
        <p>...</p>
    </body>
</html>
```

This is what we get on the other side:

```
Summary of file:
[Fooby as a child]
[Fooby grows up]
[Fooby is in big trouble!]
```

Even the text inside the <em> element was included, thanks to the call to in_element( ). XML::Handler::Subs is definitely a useful module to have when doing SAX processing.

XML::Handler::YAWriter as a Base Handler Class

Michael Koehne's XML::Handler::YAWriter serves as the "yet another" XML writer it bills itself as, but in doing so also sets itself up as a handy base class for all sorts of SAX-related work.

If you've ever worked with Perl's various Tie::* base classes, the idea is similar: you start out with a base class with callbacks defined that don't do anything very exciting, but by their existence satisfy all the subroutine calls triggered by SAX events. In your own driver class, you simply redefine the subroutines that should do something special and let the default behavior rule for all the events you don't care much about.

The default behavior, in this case, gives you something nice, too: access to an array of strings (stored as an instance variable on the handler object) holding the XML document that the incoming SAX events built. This isn't necessarily very interesting if your data source was XML, but if you use a PerlSAXish driver to generate an event stream out of an unsuspecting data source, then this feature is lovely. It gives you an easy way to, for instance, convert a non-XML file into its XML equivalent and save it to disk.

The trade-off is that you must remember to invoke $self->SUPER::[methodname] with all your own event handler methods. Otherwise, your class may forget its roots and fail to add things to that internal strings array in its youthful naïveté, and thus leave embarrassing holes in the generated XML document.

XML::SAX: The Second Generation

The proliferation of SAX parsers presents two problems: how to keep them all synchronized with the standard API and how to keep them organized on your system.

XML::SAX, a marvelous team effort by Matt Sergeant, Kip Hampton, and Robin Berjon, solves both problems at once. As a bonus, it also includes support for SAX Level 2 that previous modules lacked.

"What," you ask, "do you mean about keeping all the modules synchronized with the API?" All along, we've touted the wonders of using a standard like SAX to ensure that modules are really interchangeable. But here's the rub: in Perl, there's more than one way to implement SAX. SAX was originally designed for Java, which has a wonderful interface type of class that nails down things like what type of argument to pass to which method. There's nothing like that in Perl.

This wasn't as much of a problem with the older SAX modules we've been talking about so far. They all support SAX Level 1, which is fairly simple. However, a new crop of modules that support SAX2 is breaking the surface. SAX2 is more complex because it introduces namespaces to the mix. An element event handler should receive both the namespace prefix and the local name of the element. How should this information be passed in parameters? Do you keep them together in the same string like foo:bar? Or do you separate them into two parameters?

This debate created a lot of heat on the *perl-xml* mailing list until a few members decided to hammer out a specification for "Perlish" SAX (we'll see in a moment how to use this new API for SAX2). To encourage others to adhere to this convention, XML::SAX includes a class called XML::SAX::ParserFactory. A *factory* is an object whose sole purpose is to generate objects of a specific type—in this case, parsers. XML::SAX::ParserFactory is a useful way to handle housekeeping chores related to the parsers, such as registering their options and initialization requirements. Tell the factory what kind of parser you want and it doles out a copy to you.

XML::SAX represents a shift in the way XML and Perl work together. It builds on the work of the past, including all the best features of previous modules, while avoiding many of the mistakes. To ensure that modules are truly compatible, the kit provides a base class for parsers, abstracting out most of the mundane work that all parsers have to do, leaving the developer the task of doing only what is unique to the task. It also creates an abstract interface for users of parsers, allowing them to keep the plethora of modules organized with a registry that is indexed by properties to make it easy to find the right one with a simple query. It's a bold step and carries a lot of heft, so be prepared for a lot of information and detail in this section. We think it will be worth your while.

XML::SAX::ParserFactory

We start with the parser selection interface, XML::SAX::ParserFactory. For those of you who have used DBI, this class is very similar. It's a front end to all the SAX parsers on your system. You simply request a new parser from the factory and it will dig one up for you. Let's say you want to use any SAX parser with your handler package XML::SAX::MyHandler.

Here's how to fetch the parser and use it to read a file:

```
use XML::SAX::ParserFactory;
use XML::SAX::MyHandler;
my $handler = new XML::SAX::MyHandler;
my $parser = XML::SAX::ParserFactory->parser( Handler => $handler );
$parser->parse_uri( "foo.xml" );
```

The parser you get depends on the order in which you've installed the modules. The last one (with all the available features specified with RequiredFeatures, if any) will be returned by default. But maybe you don't want that one. No problem; XML::SAX maintains a registry of SAX parsers that you can choose from. Every time you install a new SAX parser, it registers itself so you can call upon it with ParserFactory. If you know you have the XML::SAX::BobsParser parser installed, you can require an instance of it by setting the variable $XML::SAX::ParserPackage as follows:

```
use XML::SAX::ParserFactory;
use XML::SAX::MyHandler;
my $handler = new XML::SAX::MyHandler;
$XML::SAX::ParserPackage = "XML::SAX::BobsParser( 1.24 )";
my $parser = XML::SAX::ParserFactory->parser( Handler => $handler );
```

Setting $XML::SAX:ParserPackage to XML::SAX::BobsParser(1.24) returns an instance of the package. Internally, ParserFactory is require( )-ing that parser and calling its new( ) class method. The 1.24 in the variable setting specifies a minimum version number for the parser. If that version isn't on your system, an exception will be thrown.

To see a list of all the parsers available to XML::SAX, call the parsers( ) method:

```
use XML::SAX;

my @parsers = @{XML::SAX->parsers( )};

foreach my $p ( @parsers ) {
    print "\n", $p->{ Name }, "\n";
    foreach my $f ( sort keys %{$p->{ Features }} ) {
        print "$f => ", $p->{ Features }->{ $f }, "\n";
    }
}
```

It returns a reference to a list of hashes, with each hash containing information about a parser, including the name and a hash of features. When we ran the program above we were told that XML::SAX had two registered parsers, each supporting namespaces:

```
XML::LibXML::SAX::Parser
http://xml.org/sax/features/namespaces => 1

XML::SAX::PurePerl
http://xml.org/sax/features/namespaces => 1
```

At the time this book was written, these parsers were the only two parsers included with XML::SAX. XML::LibXML::SAX::Parser is a SAX API for the *libxml2* library we use in Chapter 6. To use it, you'll need to have *libxml2*, a compiled, dynamically linked library written in C, installed on your system. It's fast, but unless you can find a binary or compile it yourself, it isn't very portable. XML::SAX::PurePerl is, as the name suggests, a parser written completely in Perl. As such, it's completely portable because you can run it wherever Perl is installed. This starter set of parsers already gives you some different options.

The feature list associated with each parser is important because it allows a user to select a parser based on a set of criteria. For example, suppose you wanted a parser that did validation and supported namespaces. You could request one by calling the factory's require_feature( ) method:

```
my $factory = new XML::SAX::ParserFactory;
$factory->require_feature( 'http://xml.org/sax/features/validation' );
$factory->require_feature( 'http://xml.org/sax/features/namespaces' );
my $parser = $factory->parser( Handler => $handler );
```

Alternatively, you can pass such information to the factory in its constructor method:

```
my $factory = new XML::SAX::ParserFactory(
            Required_features => {
                    'http://xml.org/sax/features/validation' => 1
                    'http://xml.org/sax/features/namespaces' => 1
            }
);
my $parser = $factory->parser( Handler => $handler );
```

If multiple parsers pass the test, the most recently installed one is used. However, if the factory can't find a parser to fit your requirements, it simply throws an exception.

To add more SAX modules to the registry, you only need to download and install them. Their installer packages should know about XML::SAX and automatically register the modules with it. To add a module of your own, you can use XML::SAX's add_parser( ) with a list of module names. Make sure it follows the conventions of SAX modules by subclassing XML::SAX::Base. Later, we'll show you how to write a parser, install it, and add it to the registry.

SAX2 Handler Interface

Once you've selected a parser, the next step is to code up a handler package to catch the parser's event stream, much like the SAX modules we've seen so far. XML::SAX specifies events and their properties in exquisite detail and in large numbers. This specification gives your handler considerable control while ensuring absolute conformance to the API.

The types of supported event handlers fall into several groups. The ones we are most familiar with include the *content handlers*, including those for elements and general document information, *entity resolvers*, and *lexical handlers* that handle CDATA sections and comments. *DTD handlers* and *declaration handlers* take care of everything outside of the document element, including element and entity declarations. XML::SAX adds a new group, the *error handlers*, to catch and process any exceptions that may occur during parsing.

One important new facet to this class of parsers is that they recognize namespaces. This recognition is one of the innovations of SAX2. Previously, SAX parsers treated a qualified name as a single unit: a combined namespace prefix and local name. Now you can tease out the namespaces, see where their scope begins and ends, and do more than you could before.

Content event handlers

Focusing on the content of the document, these handlers are the most likely ones to be implemented in a SAX handling program. Note the useful addition of a document locator reference, which gives the handler a special window into the machinations of the parser. The support for namespaces is also new.

set_document_locator(*locator*)
> Called at the beginning of parsing, a parser uses this method to tell the handler where the events are coming from. The *locator* parameter is a reference to a hash containing these properties:
>
> PublicID
>> The public identifier of the current entity being parsed.
>
> SystemID
>> The system identifier of the current entity being parsed.
>
> LineNumber
>> The line number of the current entity being parsed.
>
> ColumnNumber
>> The last position in the line currently being parsed.
>
> The hash is continuously updated with the latest information. If your handler doesn't like the information it's being fed and decides to abort, it can check the locator to construct a meaningful message to the user about where in the source document an error was found. A SAX parser isn't required to give a locator, though it is strongly encouraged to do so. You should check to make sure that you have a locator before trying to access it. Don't try to use the locator except inside an event handler, or you'll get unpredictable results.

start_document(*document*)
> This handler routine is called right after set_document_locator( ), just as parsing on a document begins. The parameter, *document*, is an empty reference, as there are no properties for this event.

end_document(*document*)
> This is the last handler method called. If the parser has reached the end of input or has encountered an error and given up, it sends notification of this event. The return value for this method is used as the value returned by the parser's parse( ) method. Again, the *document* parameter is empty.

start_element(*element*)

Whenever the parser encounters a new element start tag, it calls this method. The parameter *element* is a hash containing properties of the element, including:

Name

The string containing the name of the element, including its namespace prefix.

Attributes

The hash of attributes, in which each key is encoded as *{NamespaceURI}LocalName*. The value of each item in the hash is a hash of attribute properties.

NamespaceURI

The element's namespace.

Prefix

The prefix part of the qualified name.

LocalName

The local part of the qualified name.

Properties for attributes include:

Name

The qualified name (prefix + local).

Value

The attribute's value, normalized (leading and trailing spaces are removed).

NamespaceURI

The source of the namespace.

Prefix

The prefix part of the qualified name.

LocalName

The local part of the qualified name.

The properties NamespaceURI, LocalName, and Prefix are given only if the parser supports the namespaces feature.

end_element(*element*)

After all the content is processed and an element's end tag has come into view, the parser calls this method. It is even called for empty elements. The parameter *element* is a hash containing these properties:

Name

The string containing the element's name, including its namespace prefix.

NamespaceURI

The element's namespace.

Prefix

The prefix part of the qualified name.

LocalName

The local part of the qualified name.

The properties NamespaceURI, LocalName, and Prefix are given only if the parser supports the namespaces feature.

characters(*characters*)

The parser calls this method whenever it finds a chunk of plain text (character data). It might break up a chunk into pieces and deliver each piece separately, but the pieces must always be sent in the same order as they were read. Within a piece, all text must come from the same source entity. The *characters* parameter is a hash containing one property, Data, which is a string containing the characters from the document.

ignorable_whitespace(*characters*)

The term *ignorable whitespace* is used to describe space characters that appear in places where the element's content model declaration doesn't specifically call for character data. In other words, the newlines often used to make XML more readable by spacing elements apart can be ignored because they aren't really content in the document. A parser can tell if whitespace is ignorable only by reading the DTD, and it would do that only if it supports the validation feature. (If you don't understand this, don't worry; it's not important to most people.) The *characters* parameter is a hash containing one property, Data, containing the document's whitespace characters.

start_prefix_mapping(*mapping*)

This method is called when the parser detects a namespace coming into scope. For parsers that are not namespace-aware, this event is skipped, but element and attribute names still include the namespace prefixes. This event always occurs before the start of the element for which the scope holds. The parameter *mapping* is a hash with these properties:

Prefix

The namespace prefix.

NamespaceURI

The URI that the prefix maps to.

end_prefix_mapping(*mapping*)

This method is called when a namespace scope closes. This routine's parameter *mapping* is a hash with one property:

Prefix

The namespace prefix.

This event is guaranteed to come after the end element event for the element in which the scope is declared.

processing_instruction(*pi*)

This routine handles processing instruction events from the parser, including those found outside the document element. The *pi* parameter is a hash with these properties:

Target

　The target for the processing instruction.

Data

　The instruction's data (or undef if there isn't any).

skipped_entity(*entity*)

Nonvalidating parsers may skip entities rather than resolve them. For example, if they haven't seen a declaration, they can just ignore the entity rather than abort with an error. This method gives the handler a chance to do something with the entity, and perhaps even implement its own entity resolution scheme.

If a parser skips entities, it will have one or more of these features set:

- Handle external parameter entities (feature-ID is *http://xml.org/sax/features/ external-parameter-entities*)

- Handle external general entities (feature-ID is *http://xml.org/sax/features/ external-general-entities*)

(In XML, features are represented as URIs, which may or may not actually exist. See Chapter 10 for a fuller explanation.)

The parameter *entity* is a hash with this property:

Name

　The name of the entity that was skipped. If it's a parameter entity, the name will be prefixed with a percent sign (%).

Entity resolver

By default, XML parsers resolve external entity references without your program ever knowing they were there. You may want to override that behavior occasionally. For example, you may have a special way of resolving public identifiers, or the entities are entries in a database. Whatever the reason, if you implement this handler, the parser will call it before attempting to resolve the entity on its own.

The argument to resolve_entity( ) is a hash with two properties: PublicID, a public identifier for the entity, and SystemID, the system-specific location of the identity, such as a filesystem path or a URI. If the public identifier is undef, then none was given, but a system identifier will always be present.

Lexical event handlers

Implementation of this group of events is optional. You probably don't need to see these events, so not all parsers will give them to you. However, a few very complete ones will. If you want to be able to duplicate the original source XML down to the very comments and CDATA sections, then you need a parser that supports these event handlers.

They include:

- start_dtd( ) and end_dtd( ), for marking the boundaries of the document type definition
- start_entity( ) and end_entity( ), for delineating the region of a resolved entity reference
- start_cdata( ) and end_cdata( ), to describe the range of a CDATA section
- comment( ), announcing a lexical comment that would otherwise be ignored by parsers

Error event handlers and catching exceptions

XML::SAX lets you customize your error handling with this group of handlers. Each handler takes one argument, called an exception, that describes the error in detail. The particular handler called represents the severity of the error, as defined by the W3C recommendation for parser behavior. There are three types:

warning( )
> This is the least serious of the exception handlers. It represents any error that is not bad enough to halt parsing. For example, an ID reference without a matching ID would elicit a warning, but allow the parser to keep grinding on. If you don't implement this handler, the parser will ignore the exception and keep going.

error( )
> This kind of error is considered serious, but recoverable. A validity error falls in this category. The parser should still trundle on, generating events, unless your application decides to call it quits. In the absence of a handler, the parser usually continues parsing.

fatal_error( )
> A fatal error might cause the parser to abort parsing. The parser is under no obligation to continue, but might just to collect more error messages. The exception could be a syntax error that makes the document into non-well-formed XML, or it might be an entity that can't be resolved. In any case, this example shows the highest level of error reporting provided in XML::SAX.

According to the XML specification, conformant parsers are supposed to halt when they encounter any kind of well-formedness or validity error. In Perl SAX, halting results in a call to die( ). That's not the end of story, however. Even after the parse session has died, you can raise it from the grave to continue where it left off, using the eval{} construct, like this:

```
eval{ $parser->parse( $uri ) };
if( $@ ) {
  # yikes! handle error here...
}
```

The $@ variable is a blessed hash of properties that piece together the story about why parsing failed.

These properties include:

Message
> A text description about what happened

ColumnNumber
> The number of characters into the line where the error occurred, if this error is a parse error

LineNumber
> Which line the error happened on, if the exception was thrown while parsing

PublicID
> A public identifier for the entity in which the error occurred, if this error is a parse error

SystemID
> A system identifier pointing to the offending entity, if a parse error occurred

Not all thrown exceptions indicate that a failure to parse occurred. Sometimes the parser throws an exception because of a bad feature setting.

SAX2 Parser Interface

After you've written a handler package, you need to create an instance of the parser, set its features, and run it on the XML source. This section discusses the standard interface for XML::SAX parsers.

The parse( ) method, which gets the parsing process rolling, takes a hash of options as an argument. Here you can assign handlers, set features, and define the data source to be parsed. For example, the following line sets both the handler package and the source document to parse:

```
$parser->parse( Handler => $handler,
                Source => { SystemId => "data.xml" });
```

The Handler property sets a generic set of handlers that will be used by default. However, each class of handlers has its own assignment slot that will be checked before Handler. These settings include: ContentHandler, DTDHandler, EntityResolver, and ErrorHandler. All of these settings are optional. If you don't assign a handler, the parser will silently ignore events and handle errors in its own way.

The Source parameter is a hash used by a parser to hold all the information about the XML being input. It has the following properties:

CharacterStream
> This kind of filehandle works in Perl Version 5.7.2 and higher using PerlIO. No encoding translation should be necessary. Use the read( ) function to get a number of characters from it, or use sysread( ) to get a number of bytes. If the CharacterStream property is set, the parser ignores ByteStream or SystemId.

ByteStream

> This property sets a byte stream to be read. If CharacterStream is set, this property is ignored. However, it supersedes SystemId. The Encoding property should be set along with this property.

PublicId

> This property is optional, but if the application submits a public identifier, it is stored here.

SystemId

> This string represents a system-specific location for a document, such as a URI or filesystem path. Even if the source is a character stream or byte stream, this parameter is still useful because it can be used as an offset for external entity references.

Encoding

> The character encoding, if known, is stored here.

Any other options you want to set are in the set of *features* defined for SAX2. For example, you can tell a parser that you are interested in special treatment for namespaces. One way to set features is by defining the Features property in the options hash given to the parse( ) method. Another way is with the method set_feature( ). For example, here's how you would turn on validation in a validating parser using both methods:

```
$parser->parse( Features => { 'http://xml.org/sax/properties/validate' => 1 } );
$parser->set_feature( 'http://xml.org/sax/properties/validate', 1 );
```

For a complete list of features defined for SAX2, see the documentation at *http://sax.sourceforge.net/apidoc/org/xml/sax/package-summary.html*. You can also define your own features if your parser has special abilities others don't. To see what features your parser supports, get_features( ) returns a list and get_feature( ) with a name parameter reports the setting of a specific feature.

Example: A Driver

Making your own SAX parser is simple, as most of the work is handled by a base class, XML::SAX::Base. All you have to do is create a subclass of this object and override anything that isn't taken care of by default. Not only is it convenient to do this, but it will result in code that is much safer and more reliable than if you tried to create it from scratch. For example, checking if the handler package implements the handler you want to call is done for you automatically.

The next example proves just how easy it is to create a parser that works with XML::SAX. It's a driver, similar to the kind we saw in the section "Drivers for Non-XML Sources," except that instead of turning Excel documents into XML, it reads from web server log files. The parser turns a line like this from a log file:

```
10.16.251.137 - - [26/Mar/2000:20:30:52 -0800] "GET /index.html HTTP/1.0" 200 16171
```

into this snippet of XML:

```
<entry>
<ip>10.16.251.137<ip>
<date>26/Mar/2000:20:30:52 -0800<date>
<req>GET /apache-modlist.html HTTP/1.0<req>
<stat>200<stat>
<size>16171<size>
<entry>
```

Example 5-8 implements the XML::SAX driver for web logs. The first subroutine in the package is parse(). Ordinarily, you wouldn't write your own parse() method because the base class does that for you, but it assumes that you want to input some form of XML, which is not the case for drivers. Thus, we shadow that routine with one of our own, specifically trained to handle web server log files.

Example 5-8. Web log SAX driver

```perl
package LogDriver;

require 5.005_62;
use strict;
use XML::SAX::Base;
our @ISA = ('XML::SAX::Base');
our $VERSION = '0.01';


sub parse {
    my $self = shift;
    my $file = shift;
    if( open( F, $file )) {
        $self->SUPER::start_element({ Name => 'server-log' });
        while( <F> ) {
            $self->_process_line( $_ );
        }
        close F;
        $self->SUPER::end_element({ Name => 'server-log' });
    }
}


sub _process_line {
    my $self = shift;
    my $line = shift;

    if( $line =~
        /(\S+)\s\S+\s\S+\s\[([^\]]+)\]\s\"([^\"]+)\"\s(\d+)\s(\d+)/ ) {
        my( $ip, $date, $req, $stat, $size ) = ( $1, $2, $3, $4, $5 );

        $self->SUPER::start_element({ Name => 'entry' });

        $self->SUPER::start_element({ Name => 'ip' });
        $self->SUPER::characters({ Data => $ip });
```

Example 5-8. Web log SAX driver (continued)

```
        $self->SUPER::end_element({ Name => 'ip' });

        $self->SUPER::start_element({ Name => 'date' });
        $self->SUPER::characters({ Data => $date });
        $self->SUPER::end_element({ Name => 'date' });

        $self->SUPER::start_element({ Name => 'req' });
        $self->SUPER::characters({ Data => $req });
        $self->SUPER::end_element({ Name => 'req' });

        $self->SUPER::start_element({ Name => 'stat' });
        $self->SUPER::characters({ Data => $stat });
        $self->SUPER::end_element({ Name => 'stat' });

        $self->SUPER::start_element({ Name => 'size' });
        $self->SUPER::characters({ Data => $size });
        $self->SUPER::end_element({ Name => 'size' });

        $self->SUPER::end_element({ Name => 'entry' });
    }
}

1;
```

Since web logs are line oriented (one entry per line), it makes sense to create a subroutine that handles a single line, _process_line( ). All it has to do is break down the web log entry into component parts and package them in XML elements. The parse( ) routine simply chops the document into separate lines and feeds them into the line processor one at a time.

Notice that we don't call event handlers in the handler package directly. Rather, we pass the data through routines in the base class, using it as an abstract layer between the parser and the handler. This is convenient for you, the parser developer, because you don't have to check if the handler package is listening for that type of event. Again, the base class is looking out for us, making our lives easier.

Let's test the parser now. Assuming that you have this module already installed (don't worry, we'll cover the topic of installing XML::SAX parsers in the next section), writing a program that uses it is easy. Example 5-9 creates a handler package and applies it to the parser we just developed.

Example 5-9. A program to test the SAX driver

```
use XML::SAX::ParserFactory;
use LogDriver;
my $handler = new MyHandler;
my $parser = XML::SAX::ParserFactory->parser( Handler => $handler );
$parser->parse( shift @ARGV );
```

Example 5-9. A program to test the SAX driver (continued)

```perl
package MyHandler;

# initialize object with options
#
sub new {
    my $class = shift;
    my $self = {@_};
    return bless( $self, $class );
}


sub start_element {
    my $self = shift;
    my $data = shift;
    print "<", $data->{Name}, ">";
    print "\n" if( $data->{Name} eq 'entry' );
    print "\n" if( $data->{Name} eq 'server-log' );
}

sub end_element {
    my $self = shift;
    my $data = shift;
    print "<", $data->{Name}, ">\n";
}

sub characters {
    my $self = shift;
    my $data = shift;
    print $data->{Data};
}
```

We use XML::SAX::ParserFactory to demonstrate how a parser can be selected once it is registered. If you wish, you can define attributes for the parser so that subsequent queries can select it based on those properties rather than its name.

The handler package is not terribly complicated; it turns the events into an XML character stream. Each handler receives a hash reference as an argument through which you can access each object's properties by the appropriate key. An element's name, for example, is stored under the hash key Name. It all works pretty much as you would expect.

Installing Your Own Parser

Our coverage of XML::SAX wouldn't be complete without showing you how to create an installation package that adds a parser to the registry automatically. Adding a parser is very easy with the *h2xs* utility. Though it was originally made to facilitate extensions to Perl written in C, it is invaluable in other ways.

Here, we will use it to create something much like the module installers you've downloaded from CPAN.* First, we start a new project with the following command:

```
h2xs -AX -n LogDriver
```

h2xs automatically creates a directory called *LogDriver*, stocked with several files.

LogDriver.pm
> A stub for our module, ready to be filled out with subroutines.

Makefile.PL
> A Perl program that generates a *Makefile* for installing the module. (Look familiar, CPAN users?)

test.pl
> A stub for adding test code to check on the success of installation.

Changes, MANIFEST
> Other files used to aid in installation and give information to users.

LogDriver.pm, the module to be installed, doesn't need much extra code to make *h2xs* happy. It only needs a variable, $VERSION, since *h2xs* is (justifiably) finicky about that information.

As you know from installing CPAN modules, the first thing you do when opening an installer archive is run the command perl Makefile.PM. Running this command generates a file called *Makefile*, which configures the installer to your system. Then you can run make and make install to load the module in the right place.

Any deviation from the default behavior of the installer must be coded in the *Makefile.PM* program. Untouched, it looks like this:

```
use ExtUtils::MakeMaker;
WriteMakefile(
    'NAME'          => 'LogDriver',      # module name
    'VERSION_FROM'  => 'LogDriver.pm',   # finds version
);
```

The argument to WriteMakeFile() is a hash of properties about the module, used in generating a *Makefile* file. We can add more properties here to make the installer do more sophisticated things than just copy a module onto the system. For our parser, we want to add this line:

```
'PREREQ_PM' => { 'XML::SAX' => 0 }
```

Adding this line triggers a check during installation to see if XML::SAX exists on the system. If not, the installation aborts with an error message. We don't want to install our parser until there is a framework to accept it.

---

* For a helpful tutorial on using *h2xs*, see O'Reilly's *The Perl Cookbook* by Tom Christiansen and Nat Torkington.

This subroutine should also be added to *Makefile.PM*:

```
sub MY::install {
    package MY;
    my $script = shift->SUPER::install(@_);
    $script =~ s/install :: (.*)$/install :: $1 install_sax_driver/m;
    $script .= <<"INSTALL";

install_sax_driver :
    \t\@\$(PERL) -MXML::SAX -e "XML::SAX->add_parser(q(\$(NAME)))->save_parsers()"

INSTALL

    return $script;
}
```

This example adds the parser to the list maintained by XML::SAX. Now you can install your module.

## CHAPTER 6

Tree Processing

Having done just about all we can do with streams, it's time to move on to another style of XML processing. Instead of letting the XML fly past the program one tiny piece at a time, we will capture the whole document in memory and *then* start working on it. Having an in-memory representation built behind the scenes for us makes our job much easier, although it tends to require more memory and CPU cycles.

This chapter is an overview of programming with persistent XML objects, better known as *tree processing*. It looks at a variety of different modules and strategies for building and accessing XML trees, including the rigorous, standard Document Object Model (DOM), fast access to internal document parts with XPath, and efficient tree processing methods.

XML Trees

Every XML document can be represented as a collection of data objects linked in an acyclic structure called a tree. Each object, or *node*, is a small piece of the document, such as an element, a piece of text, or a processing instruction. One node, called the *root*, links to other nodes, and so on down to nodes that aren't linked to anything. Graph this image out and it looks like a big, bushy tree—hence the name.

A tree structure representing a piece of XML is a handy thing to have. Since a tree is acyclic (it has no circular links), you can use simple traversal methods that won't get stuck in infinite loops. Like a filesystem directory tree, you can represent the location of a node easily in simple shorthand. Like real trees, you can break a piece off and treat it like a smaller tree—a tree is just a collection of subtrees joined by a root node. Best of all, you have all the information in one place and search through it like a database.

For the programmer, a tree makes life much easier. Stream processing, you will recall, remembers fleeting details to use later in constructing another data structure or printing out information. This work is tedious, and can be downright horrible for very complex documents. If you have to combine pieces of information from different parts of the document, then you might go mad. If you have a tree containing the document, though, all the details are right in front of you. You only need to write code to sift through the nodes and pull out what you need.

Of course, you don't get anything good for free. There is a penalty for having easy access to every point in a document. Building the tree in the first place takes time and precious CPU cycles, and even more if you use object-oriented method calls. There is also a memory tax to pay, since each object in the tree takes up some space. With very large documents (trees with millions of nodes are not unheard of), you could bring your poor machine down to its knees with a tree processing program. On the average, though, processing trees can get you pretty good results (especially with a little optimizing, as we show later in the chapter), so don't give up just yet.

As we talk about trees, we will frequently use genealogical terms to describe relationships between nodes. A container node is said to be the *parent* of the nodes it branches to, each of which may be called a *child* of the container node. Likewise, the terms *descendant*, *ancestor*, and *sibling* mean pretty much what you think they would. So two sibling nodes share the same parent node, and all nodes have the root node as their ancestor.

There are several different species of trees, depending on the implementation you're talking about. Each species models the document in a slightly different way. For example, do you consider an entity reference to be a separate node from text, or would you include the reference in the same package? You have to pay attention to the individual scheme of each module. Table 6-1 shows a common selection of node types.

Table 6-1. Typical node type definitions

Type	Properties
Element	Name, attributes, references to children
Namespace	Prefix name, URI
Character data	String of characters
Processing instruction	Target, Data
Comment	String of characters
CDATA section	String of characters
Entity reference	Name, Replacement text (or System ID and/or Public ID)

In addition to this set, some implementations define node types for the DTD, allowing a programmer to access declarations for elements, entities, notations, and attributes. Nodes may also exist for the XML declaration and document type declarations.

XML::Simple

The simplest tree model can be found in Grant McLean's module XML::Simple. It's designed to facilitate the job of reading and saving datafiles. The programmer doesn't have to know much about XML and parsers—only how to access arrays and hashes, the data structures used to store a document.

Example 6-1 shows a simple datafile that a program might use to store information.

Example 6-1. A program datafile

```
<preferences>
  <font role="default">
    <name>Times New Roman</name>
    <size>14</size>
  </font>
  <window>
    <height>352</height>
    <width>417</width>
    <locx>100</locx>
    <locy>120</locy>
  </window>
</preferences>
```

XML::Simple makes accessing information in the datafile remarkably easy. Example 6-2 extracts default font information from it.

Example 6-2. Program to extract font information

```
use XML::Simple;

my $simple = XML::Simple->new();          # initialize the object
my $tree = $simple->XMLin( './data.xml' );   # read, store document

# test access to the tree
print "The user prefers the font " . $tree->{ font }->{ name } . " at " .
    $tree->{ font }->{ size } . " points.\n";
```

First we initialize an XML::Simple object, then we trigger the parser with a call to its XMLin( ) method. This step returns a reference to the root of the tree, which is a hierarchical set of hashes. Element names provide keys to the hashes, whose values are either strings or references to other element hashes. Thus, we have a clear and concise way to access points deep in the document.

To illustrate this idea, let's look at the data structure, using Data::Dumper, a module that serializes data structures. Just add these lines at the end of the program:

```
use Data::Dumper;
print Dumper( $tree );
```

And here's the output:

```
$tree = {
        'font' => {
                    'size' => '14',
                    'name' => 'Times New Roman',
                    'role' => 'default'
                },
```

```
        'window' => {
                    'locx' => '100',
                    'locy' => '120',
                    'height' => '352',
                    'width' => '417'
                }
};
```

The $tree variable represents the root element of the tree, <preferences>. Each entry in
the hash it points to represents its child elements, <font> and <window>, accessible by
their types. The entries point to hashes representing the third tier of elements. Finally,
the values of these hash items are strings, the text found in the actual elements from
the file. The whole document is accessible with a simple string of hash references.

This example was not very complex. Much of the success of XML::Simple's interface
is that it relies on the XML to be simple. Looking back at our datafile, you'll note
that no sibling elements have the same name. Identical names would be impossible
to encode with hashes alone.

Fortunately, XML::Simple has an answer. If an element has two or more child elements with the same name, it uses a list to contain all the like-named children in a
group. Consider the revised datafile in Example 6-3.

Example 6-3. A trickier program datafile

```
<preferences>
  <font role="console">
    <size>9</size>
    <fname>Courier</fname>
  </font>
  <font role="default">
    <fname>Times New Roman</fname>
    <size>14</size>
  </font>
  <font role="titles">
    <size>10</size>
    <fname>Helvetica</fname>
  </font>
</preferences>
```

We've thrown XML::Simple a curve ball. There are now three <font> elements in a row.
How will XML::Simple encode that? Dumping the data structure gives us this output:

```
$tree = {
        'font' => [
                {
                  'fname' => 'Courier',
                  'size' => '9',
                  'role' => 'console'
                },
                {
                  'fname' => 'Times New Roman',
                  'size' => '14',
```

```
                    'role' => 'default'
                },
                {
                    'fname' => 'Helvetica',
                    'size' => '10',
                    'role' => 'titles'
                }
            ]
    };
```

Now the font entry's value is a reference to a list of hashes, each modeling one of the <font> elements. To select a font, you must iterate through the list until you find the one you want. This iteration clearly takes care of the like-named sibling problem.

This new datafile also adds attributes to some elements. These attributes have been incorporated into the structure as if they were child elements of their host elements. Name clashes between attributes and child elements are possible, but this potential problem is resolved the same way as like-named sibling elements. It's convenient this way, as long as you don't mind if elements and attributes are treated the same.

We know how to input XML documents to our program, but what about writing files? XML::Simple also has a method that outputs XML documents, XML_Out( ). You can either modify an existing structure or create a new document from scratch by building a data structure like the ones listed above and then passing it to the XML_Out( ) method.

Our conclusion? XML::Simple works well with simple XML documents, but runs into trouble with more complex markup. It can't handle elements with both text and elements as children (mixed content). It doesn't pay attention to node types other than elements, attributes, and text (like processing instructions or CDATA sections). Because hashes don't preserve the order of items, the sequence of elements may be scrambled. If none of these problems matters to you, then use XML::Simple. It will serve your needs well, minimizing the pain of XML markup and keeping your data accessible.

XML::Parser's Tree Mode

We used XML::Parser in Chapter 4 as an event generator to drive stream processing programs, but did you know that this same module can also generate tree data structures? We've modified our preference-reader program to use XML::Parser for parsing and building a tree, as shown in Example 6-4.

Example 6-4. Using XML::Parser to build a tree

```
# initialize parser and read the file
use XML::Parser;
$parser = new XML::Parser( Style => 'Tree' );
my $tree = $parser->parsefile( shift @ARGV );
```

Example 6-4. Using XML::Parser to build a tree (continued)

```
# dump the structure
use Data::Dumper;
print Dumper( $tree );
```

When run on the file in Example 6-4, it gives this output:

```
$tree = [
            'preferences', [
                {}, 0, '\n',
                'font', [
                    { 'role' => 'console' }, 0, '\n',
                    'size', [ {}, 0, '9' ], 0, '\n',
                    'fname', [ {}, 0, 'Courier' ], 0, '\n'
                ], 0, '\n',
                'font', [
                    { 'role' => 'default' }, 0, '\n',
                    'fname', [ {}, 0, 'Times New Roman' ], 0, '\n',
                    'size', [ {}, 0, '14' ], 0, '\n'
                ], 0, '\n',
                'font', [
                    { 'role' => 'titles' }, 0, '\n',
                    'size', [ {}, 0, '10' ], 0, '\n',
                    'fname', [ {}, 0, 'Helvetica' ], 0, '\n',
                ], 0, '\n',
            ]
        ];
```

This structure is more complicated than the one we got from XML::Simple; it tries to preserve everything, including node type, order of nodes, and mixed text. Each node is represented by one or two items in a list. Elements require two items: the element name followed by a list of its contents. Text nodes are encoded as the number 0 followed by their values in a string. All attributes for an element are stored in a hash as the first item in the element's content list. Even the whitespace between elements has been saved, represented as 0, \n. Because lists are used to contain element content, the order of nodes is preserved. This order is important for some XML documents, such as books or animations in which elements follow a sequence.

XML::Parser cannot output XML from this data structure like XML::Simple can. For a complete, bidirectional solution, you should try something object oriented.

XML::SimpleObject

Using built-in data types is fine, but as your code becomes more complex and hard to read, you may start to pine for the neater interfaces of objects. Doing things like testing a node's type, getting the last child of an element, or changing the representation of data without breaking the rest of the program is easier with objects. It's not surprising that there are more object-oriented modules for XML than you can shake a stick at.

Dan Brian's `XML::SimpleObject` starts the tour of object models for XML trees. It takes the structure returned by `XML::Parser` in tree mode and changes it from a hierarchy of lists into a hierarchy of objects. Each object represents an element and provides methods to access its children. As with `XML::Simple`, elements are accessed by their names, passed as arguments to the methods.

Let's see how useful this module is. Example 6-5 is a silly datafile representing a genealogical tree. We're going to write a program to parse this file into an object tree and then traverse the tree to print out a text description.

Example 6-5. A genealogical tree

```
<ancestry>
  <ancestor><name>Glook the Magnificent</name>
    <children>
      <ancestor><name>Glimshaw the Brave</name></ancestor>
      <ancestor><name>Gelbar the Strong</name></ancestor>
      <ancestor><name>Glurko the Healthy</name>
        <children>
          <ancestor><name>Glurff the Sturdy</name></ancestor>
          <ancestor><name>Glug the Strange</name>
            <children>
              <ancestor><name>Blug the Insane</name></ancestor>
              <ancestor><name>Flug the Disturbed</name></ancestor>
            </children>
          </ancestor>
        </children>
      </ancestor>
    </children>
  </ancestor>
</ancestry>
```

Example 6-6 is our program. It starts by parsing the file with `XML::Parser` in tree mode and passing the result to an `XML::SimpleObject` constructor. Next, we write a routine begat( ) to traverse the tree and output text recursively. At each ancestor, it prints the name. If there are progeny, which we find out by testing whether the child method returns a non-undef value, it descends the tree to process them too.

Example 6-6. An XML::SimpleObject program

```
use XML::Parser;
use XML::SimpleObject;

# parse the data file and build a tree object
my $file = shift @ARGV;
my $parser = XML::Parser->new( ErrorContext => 2, Style => "Tree" );
my $tree = XML::SimpleObject->new( $parser->parsefile( $file ));

# output a text description
print "My ancestry starts with ";
begat( $tree->child( 'ancestry' )->child( 'ancestor' ), '' );
```

Example 6-6. An XML::SimpleObject program (continued)

```
# describe a generation of ancestry
sub begat {
    my( $anc, $indent ) = @_;

    # output the ancestor's name
    print $indent . $anc->child( 'name' )->value;

    # if there are children, recurse over them
    if( $anc->child( 'children' ) and $anc->child( 'children' )->children ) {
        print " who begat...\n";
        my @children = $anc->child( 'children' )->children;
        foreach my $child ( @children ) {
            begat( $child, $indent . '   ' );
        }
    } else {
        print "\n";
    }
}
```

To prove it works, here's the output. In the program, we added indentation to show the descent through generations:

```
My ancestry starts with Glook the Magnificent who begat...
    Glimshaw the Brave
    Gelbar the Strong
    Glurko the Healthy who begat...
        Glurff the Sturdy
        Glug the Strange who begat...
            Blug the Insane
            Flug the Disturbed
```

We used several different methods to access data in objects. child( ) returns a reference to an XML::SimpleObject object that represents a child of the source node. children( ) returns a list of such references. value( ) looks for a character data node inside the source node and returns a scalar value. Passing arguments in these methods restricts the search to just a few matching nodes. For example, child('name') specifies the <name> element among a set of children. If the search fails, the value undef is given.

This is a good start, but as its name suggests, it may be a little too simple for some applications. There are limited ways to access nodes, mostly by getting a child or list of children. Accessing elements by name doesn't work when more than one element has the same name.

Unfortunately, this module's objects lack a way to get XML back out, so outputting a document from this structure is not easy. However, for simplicity, this module is an easy OO solution to learn and use.

XML::TreeBuilder

XML::TreeBuilder is a factory class that builds a tree of XML::Element objects. The XML::Element class inherits from the older HTML::Element class that comes with the HTML::Tree package. Thus, you can build the tree from a file with XML::TreeBuilder and use the XML::Element accessor methods to move around, grab data from the tree, and change the structure of the tree as needed. We're going to focus on that last thing: using accessor methods to assemble a tree of our own.

For example, we're going to write a program that manages a simple, prioritized "to-do" list that uses an XML datafile to store entries. Each item in the list has an "immediate" or "long-term" priority. The program will initialize the list if it's empty or the file is missing. The user can add items by using -i or -l (for "immediate" or "long-term," respectively), followed by a description. Finally, the program updates the datafile and prints it out on the screen.

The first part of the program, listed in Example 6-7, sets up the tree structure. If the datafile can be found, it is read and used to build the tree. Otherwise, the tree is built from scratch.

Example 6-7. To-do list manager, first part

```
use XML::TreeBuilder;
use XML::Element;
use Getopt::Std;

# command line options
# -i          immediate
# -l          long-term
#
my %opts;
getopts( 'il', \%opts );

# initialize tree
my $data = 'data.xml';
my $tree;

# if file exists, parse it and build the tree
if( -r $data ) {
    $tree = XML::TreeBuilder->new( );
    $tree->parse_file($data);

# otherwise, create a new tree from scratch
} else {
    print "Creating new data file.\n";
    my @now = localtime;
    my $date = $now[4] . '/' . $now[3];
    $tree = XML::Element->new( 'todo-list', 'date' => $date );
    $tree->push_content( XML::Element->new( 'immediate' ));
    $tree->push_content( XML::Element->new( 'long-term' ));
}
```

A few notes on initializing the structure are necessary. The minimal structure of the datafile is this:

```
<todo-list date="DATE">
  <immediate></immediate>
  <long-term></long-term>
</todo-list>
```

As long as the <immediate> and <long-term> elements are present, we have somewhere to put schedule items. Thus, we need to create three elements using the XML::Element constructor method new( ), which uses its argument to set the name of the element. The first call of this method also includes an argument 'date' => $date to create an attribute named "date." After creating element nodes, we have to connect them. The push_content( ) method adds a node to an element's content list.

The next part of the program updates the datafile, adding a new item if the user supplies one. Where to put the item depends on the option used (-i or -l). We use the as_XML method to output XML, as shown in Example 6-8.

Example 6-8. To-do list manager, second part

```
# add new entry and update file
if( %opts ) {
    my $item = XML::Element->new( 'item' );
    $item->push_content( shift @ARGV );
    my $place;
    if( $opts{ 'i' }) {
        $place = $tree->find_by_tag_name( 'immediate' );
    } elsif( $opts{ 'l' }) {
        $place = $tree->find_by_tag_name( 'long-term' );
    }
    $place->push_content( $item );
}
open( F, ">$data" ) or die( "Couldn't update schedule" );
print F $tree->as_XML;
close F;
```

Finally, the program outputs the current schedule to the terminal. We use the find_by_tag_name( ) method to descend from an element to a child with a given tag name. If more than one element match, they are supplied in a list. Two methods retrieve the contents of an element: attr_get_i( ) for attributes and as_text( ) for character data. Example 6-9 has the rest of the code.

Example 6-9. To-do list manager, third part

```
# output schedule
print "To-do list for " . $tree->attr_get_i( 'date' ) . ":\n";
print "\nDo right away:\n";
my $immediate = $tree->find_by_tag_name( 'immediate' );
my $count = 1;
foreach my $item ( $immediate->find_by_tag_name( 'item' )) {
    print $count++ . '. ' . $item->as_text . "\n";
}
```

Example 6-9. To-do list manager, third part (continued)

```perl
print "\nDo whenever:\n";
my $longterm = $tree->find_by_tag_name( 'long-term' );
$count = 1;
foreach my $item ( $longterm->find_by_tag_name( 'item' )) {
    print $count++ . '. ' . $item->as_text . "\n";
}
```

To test the code, we created this datafile with several calls to the program (whitespace was added to make it more readable):

```xml
<todo-list date="7/3">
  <immediate>
    <item>take goldfish to the vet</item>
    <item>get appendix removed</item>
  </immediate>
  <long-term>
    <item>climb K-2</item>
    <item>decipher alien messages</item>
  </long-term>
</todo-list>
```

The output to the screen was this:

```
To-do list for 7/3:

Do right away:
1. take goldfish to the vet
2. get appendix removed

Do whenever:
1. climb K-2
2. decipher alien messages
```

XML::Grove

The last object model we'll examine before jumping into standards-based solutions is Ken MacLeod's XML::Grove. Like XML::SimpleObject, it takes the XML::Parser output in tree mode and changes it into an object hierarchy. The difference is that each node type is represented by a different class. Therefore, an element would be mapped to XML::Grove::Element, a processing instruction to XML::Grove::PI, and so on. Text nodes are still scalar values.

Another feature of this module is that the declarations in the internal subset are captured in lists accessible through the XML::Grove object. Every entity or notation declaration is available for your perusal. For example, the following program counts the distribution of elements and other nodes, and then prints a list of node types and their frequency.

First, we initialize the parser with the style "grove" (to tell XML::Parser that it needs to use XML::Parser::Grove to process its output):

```
use XML::Parser;
use XML::Parser::Grove;
use XML::Grove;

my $parser = XML::Parser->new( Style => 'grove', NoExpand => '1' );
my $grove = $parser->parsefile( shift @ARGV );
```

Next, we access the contents of the grove by calling the contents( ) method. This method returns a list including the root element and any comments or PIs outside of it. A subroutine called tabulate( ) counts nodes and descends recursively through the tree. Finally, the results are printed:

```
# tabulate elements and other nodes
my %dist;
foreach( @{$grove->contents} ) {
  &tabulate( $_, \%dist );
}
print "\nNODES:\n\n";
foreach( sort keys %dist ) {
  print "$_: " . $dist{$_} . "\n";
}
```

Here is the subroutine that handles each node in the tree. Since each node is a different class, we can use ref( ) to get the type. Attributes are not treated as nodes in this model, but are available through the element class's method attributes( ) as a hash. The call to contents( ) allows the routine to continue processing the element's children:

```
# given a node and a table, find out what the node is, add to the count,
# and recurse if necessary
#
sub tabulate {
  my( $node, $table ) = @_;

  my $type = ref( $node );
  if( $type eq 'XML::Grove::Element' ) {
    $table->{ 'element' }++;
    $table->{ 'element (' . $node->name . ')' }++;
    foreach( keys %{$node->attributes} ) {
      $table->{ "attribute ($_)" }++;
    }
    foreach( @{$node->contents} ) {
      &tabulate( $_, $table );
    }

  } elsif( $type eq 'XML::Grove::Entity' ) {
    $table->{ 'entity-ref (' . $node->name . ')' }++;

  } elsif( $type eq 'XML::Grove::PI' ) {
    $table->{ 'PI (' . $node->target . ')' }++;
```

```
    } elsif( $type eq 'XML::Grove::Comment' ) {
        $table->{ 'comment' }++;

    } else {
        $table->{ 'text-node' }++
    }
}
```

Here's a typical result, when run on an XML datafile:

```
NODES:
PI (a): 1
attribute (date): 1
attribute (style): 12
attribute (type): 2
element: 30
element (category): 2
element (inventory): 1
element (item): 6
element (location): 6
element (name): 12
element (note): 3
text-node: 100
```

DOM

In this chapter, we return to standard APIs with the Document Object Model (DOM). In Chapter 5, we talked about the benefits of using standard APIs: increased compatibility with other software components and (if implemented correctly) a guaranteed complete solution. The same concept applies in this chapter: what SAX does for event streams, DOM does for tree processing.

DOM and Perl

DOM is a recommendation by the World Wide Web Consortium (W3C). Designed to be a language-neutral interface to an in-memory representation of an XML document, versions of DOM are available in Java, ECMAscript,* Perl, and other languages. Perl alone has several implementations of DOM, including XML::DOM and XML::LibXML.

While SAX defines an interface of handler methods, the DOM specification calls for a number of classes, each with an interface of methods that affect a particular type of XML markup. Thus, every object instance manages a portion of the document tree, providing accessor methods to add, remove, or modify nodes and data. These objects are typically created by a *factory object*, making it a little easier for programmers who only have to initialize the factory object themselves.

In DOM, every piece of XML (the element, text, comment, etc.) is a node represented by a Node object. The Node class is extended by more specific classes that represent the types of XML markup, including Element, Attr (attribute), ProcessingInstruction, Comment, EntityReference, Text, CDATASection, and Document. These classes are the building blocks of every XML tree in DOM.

The standard also calls for a couple of classes that serve as containers for nodes, convenient for shuttling XML fragments from place to place. These classes are NodeList, an ordered list of nodes, like all the children of an element; and NamedNodeMap, an

---

* A standards-friendly language patterned after JavaScript.

unordered set of nodes. These objects are frequently required as arguments or given as return values from methods. Note that these objects are all *live*, meaning that any changes done to them will immediately affect the nodes in the document itself, rather than a copy.

When naming these classes and their methods, DOM merely specifies the outward appearance of an implementation, but leaves the internal specifics up to the developer. Particulars like memory management, data structures, and algorithms are not addressed at all, as those issues may vary among programming languages and the needs of users. This is like describing a key so a locksmith can make a lock that it will fit into; you know the key will unlock the door, but you have no idea how it really works. Specifically, the outward appearance makes it easy to write extensions to legacy modules so they can comply with the standard, but it does not guarantee efficiency or speed.

DOM is a very large standard, and you will find that implementations vary in their level of compliance. To make things worse, the standard has not one, but two (soon to be three) levels. DOM1 has been around since 1998, DOM2 emerged more recently, and they're already working on a third. The main difference between Levels 1 and 2 is that the latter adds support for namespaces. If you aren't concerned about namespaces, then DOM1 should be suitable for your needs.

DOM Class Interface Reference

Since DOM is becoming the interface of choice in the Perl-XML world, it deserves more elaboration. The following sections describe class interfaces individually, listing their properties, methods, and intended purposes.

 The DOM specification calls for UTF-16 as the standard encoding. However, most Perl implementations assume a UTF-8 encoding. Due to limitations in Perl, working with characters of lengths other than 8 bits is difficult. This will change in a future version, and encodings like UTF-16 will be supported more readily.

Document

The Document class controls the overall document, creating new objects when requested and maintaining high-level information such as references to the document type declaration and the root element.

Properties

doctype
    Document Type Declaration (DTD).

documentElement
    The root element of the document.

Methods

createElement, createTextNode, createComment, createCDATASection, createProcessingInstruction, createAttribute, createEntityReference
> Generates a new node object.

createElementNS, createAttributeNS (DOM2 only)
> Generates a new element or attribute node object with a specified namespace qualifier.

createDocumentFragment
> Creates a container object for a document's subtree.

getElementsByTagName
> Returns a NodeList of all elements having a given tag name at any level of the document.

getElementsByTagNameNS (DOM2 only)
> Returns a NodeList of all elements having a given namespace qualifier and local name. The asterisk character (*) matches any element or any namespace, allowing you to find all elements in a given namespace.

getElementById (DOM2 only)
> Returns a reference to the node that has a specified ID attribute.

importNode (DOM2 only)
> Creates a new node that is the copy of a node from another document. Acts like a "copy to the clipboard" operation for importing markup.

DocumentFragment

The DocumentFragment class is used to contain a document fragment. Its children are (zero or more) nodes representing the tops of XML trees. This class contrasts with Document, which has at most one child element, the document root, plus metadata like the document type. In this respect, DocumentFragment's content is not well-formed, though it must obey the XML well-formed rules in all other respects (no illegal characters in text, etc.)

No specific methods or properties are defined; use the generic node methods to access data.

DocumentType

This class contains all the information contained in the document type declaration at the beginning of the document, except the specifics about an external DTD. Thus, it names the root element and any declared entities or notations in the internal subset.

No specific methods are defined for this class, but the properties are public (but read-only).

Properties

name

    The name of the root element.

entities

    A `NamedNodeMap` of entity declarations.

notation

    A `NamedNodeMap` of notation declarations.

internalSubset (DOM2 only)

    The internal subset of the DTD represented as a string.

publicId (DOM2 only)

    The external subset of the DTD's public identifier.

systemId (DOM2 only)

    The external subset of the DTD's system identifier.

Node

All node types inherit from the class `Node`. Any properties or methods common to all node types can be accessed through this class. A few properties, such as the value of the node, are undefined for some node types, like `Element`. The generic methods of this class are useful in some programming contexts, such as when writing code that processes nodes of different types. At other times, you'll know in advance what type you're working with, and you should use the specific class's methods instead.

All properties but `nodeValue` and `prefix` are read-only.

Properties

nodeName

    A property that is defined for elements, attributes, and entities. In the context of elements this property would be the tag's name.

nodeValue

    A property defined for attributes, text nodes, CDATA nodes, PIs, and comments.

nodeType

    One of the following types of nodes: `Element`, `Attr`, `Text`, `CDATASection`, `EntityReference`, `Entity`, `ProcessingInstruction`, `Comment`, `Document`, `DocumentType`, `DocumentFragment`, or `Notation`.

parentNode

    A reference to the parent of this node.

childNodes

    An ordered list of references to children of this node (if any).

firstChild, lastChild
> References to the first and last of the node's children (if any).

previousSibling, nextSibling
> The node immediately preceding or following this one, respectively.

attributes
> An unordered list (`NamedNodeMap`) of nodes that are attributes of this one (if any).

ownerDocument
> A reference to the object containing the whole document—useful when you need to generate a new node.

namespaceURI (DOM2 only)
> A namespace URI if this node has a namespace prefix; otherwise it is `null`.

prefix (DOM2 only)
> The namespace prefix associated with this node.

Methods

insertBefore
> Inserts a node before a reference child element.

replaceChild
> Swaps a child node with a new one you supply, giving you the old one in return.

appendChild
> Adds a new node to the end of this node's list of children.

hasChildNodes
> True if there are children of this node; otherwise, it is false.

cloneNode
> Returns a duplicate copy of this node. It provides an alternate way to generate nodes. All properties will be identical except for `parentNode`, which will be undefined, and `childNodes`, which will be empty. Cloned elements will all have the same attributes as the original. If the argument `deep` is set to true, then the node and all its descendants will be copied.

hasAttributes (DOM2 only)
> Returns true if this node has defined attributes.

isSupported (DOM2 only)
> Returns true if this implementation supports a specific feature.

NodeList

This class is a container for an ordered list of nodes. It is "live," meaning that any changes to the nodes it references will appear in the document immediately.

Properties

length
> Returns an integer indicating the number of nodes in the list.

Methods

item
> Given an integer value *n*, returns a reference to the *n*th node in the list, starting at zero.

NamedNodeMap

This unordered set of nodes is designed to allow access to nodes by name. An alternate access by index is also provided for enumerations, but no order is implied.

Properties

length
> Returns an integer indicating the number of nodes in the list.

Methods

getNamedItem, setNamedItem
> Retrieves or adds a node using the node's `nodeName` property as the key.

removeNamedItem
> Takes a node with the specified name out of the set and returns it.

item
> Given an integer value *n*, returns a reference to the *n*th node in the set. Note that this method does not imply any order and is provided only for unique enumeration.

getNamedItemNS (DOM2 only)
> Retrieves a node based on a namespace-qualified name (a namespace prefix and local name).

removeNamedItemNS (DOM2 only)
> Takes an item out of the list and returns it, based on its namespace-qualified name.

setNamedItemNS (DOM2 only)
> Adds a node to the list using its namespace-qualified name.

CharacterData

This class extends `Node` to facilitate access to certain types of nodes that contain character data, such as `Text`, `CDATASection`, `Comment`, and `ProcessingInstruction`. Specific classes like `Text` inherit from this class.

Properties

data
> The character data itself.

length
> The number of characters in the data.

Methods

appendData
> Appends a string of character data to the end of the data property.

substringData
> Extracts and returns a segment of the data property from *offset* to *offset + count*.

insertData
> Inserts a string inside the data property at the location given by *offset*.

deleteData
> Sets the data property to an empty string.

replaceData
> Changes the contents of data property with a new string that you provide.

Element

This is the most common type of node you will encounter. An element can contain other nodes and has attribute nodes.

Properties

tagname
> The name of the element.

Methods

getAttribute, getAttributeNode
> Returns the value of an attribute, or a reference to the attribute node, with a given name.

setAttribute, setAttributeNode
> Adds a new attribute to the element's list or replaces an existing attribute of the same name.

removeAttribute, removeAttributeNode
> Returns the value of an attribute and removes it from the element's list.

getElementsByTagName
> Returns a NodeList of descendant elements who match a name.

normalize

Collapses adjacent text nodes. You should use this method whenever you add new text nodes to ensure that the structure of the document remains the same, without erroneous extra children.

getAttributeNS (DOM2 only)

Retrieves an attribute value based on its qualified name (the namespace prefix plus the local name).

getAttributeNodeNS (DOM2 only)

Gets an attribute's node by using its qualified name.

getElementsByTagNamesNS (DOM2 only)

Returns a NodeList of elements among this element's descendants that match a qualified name.

hasAttribute (DOM2 only)

Returns true if this element has an attribute with a given name.

hasAttributeNS (DOM2 only)

Returns true if this element has an attribute with a given qualified name.

removeAttributeNS (DOM2 only)

Removes and returns an attribute node from this element's list, based on its namespace-qualified name.

setAttributeNS (DOM2 only)

Adds a new attribute to the element's list, given a namespace-qualified name and a value.

setAttributeNodeNS (DOM2 only)

Adds a new attribute node to the element's list with a namespace-qualified name.

Attr

Properties

name

The attribute's name.

specified

If the program or the document explicitly set the attribute, this property is true. If it was set in the DTD as a default and not reset anywhere else, then it will be false.

value

The attribute's value, represented as a text node.

ownerElement (DOM2 only)

The element to which this attribute belongs.

Text

Methods

splitText
> Breaks the text node into two adjacent text nodes, each with part of the original text content. Content in the first node is from the beginning of the original up to, but not including, a character whose position is given by *offset*. The second node has the rest of the original node's content. This method is useful for inserting a new element inside a span of text.

CDATASection

CDATA Section is like a text node, but protects its contents from being parsed. It may contain markup characters (<, &) that would be illegal in text nodes. Use generic Node methods to access data.

ProcessingInstruction

Properties

target
> The target value for the node.

data
> The data value for the node.

Comment

This is a class representing comment nodes. Use the generic Node methods to access the data.

EntityReference

This is a reference to an entity defined by an Entity node. Sometimes the parser will be configured to resolve all entity references into their values for you. If that option is disabled, the parser should create this node. No explicit methods force resolution, but some actions to the node may have that side effect.

Entity

This class provides access to an entity in the document, based on information in an entity declaration in the DTD.

Properties

publicId

A public identifier for the resource (if the entity is external to the document).

systemId

A system identifier for the resource (if the entity is external to the document).

notationName

If the entity is unparsed, its notation reference is listed here.

Notation

`Notation` represents a notation declaration appearing in the DTD.

Properties

publicId

A public identifier for the notation.

systemId

A system identifier for the notation.

XML::DOM

Enno Derkson's `XML::DOM` module is a good place to start exploring DOM in Perl. It's a complete implementation of Level 1 DOM with a few extra features thrown in for convenience. `XML::DOM::Parser` extends `XML::Parser` to build a document tree installed in an `XML::DOM::Document` object whose reference it returns. This reference gives you complete access to the tree. The rest, we happily report, works pretty much as you'd expect.

Here's a program that uses DOM to process an XHTML file. It looks inside `<p>` elements for the word "monkeys," replacing every instance with a link to `monkeystuff.com`. Sure, you could do it with a regular expression substitution, but this example is valuable because it shows how to search for and create new nodes, and read and change values, all in the unique DOM style.

The first part of the program creates a parser object and gives it a file to parse with the call to `parsefile( )`:

```
use XML::DOM;

&process_file( shift @ARGV );

sub process_file {
    my $infile = shift;
    my $dom_parser = new XML::DOM::Parser;          # create a parser object
    my $doc = $dom_parser->parsefile( $infile );    # make it parse a file
    &add_links( $doc );                             # perform our changes
```

```
    print $doc->toString;                        # output the tree again
    $doc->dispose;                               # clean up memory
}
```

This method returns a reference to an XML::DOM::Document object, which is our gateway to the nodes inside. We pass this reference along to a routine called add_links( ), which will do all the processing we require. Finally, we output the tree with a call to toString( ), and then dispose of the object. This last step performs necessary cleanup in case any circular references between nodes could result in a memory leak.

The next part burrows into the tree to start processing paragraphs:

```
sub add_links {
    my $doc = shift;

    # find all the <p> elements
    my $paras = $doc->getElementsByTagName( "p" );
    for( my $i = 0; $i < $paras->getLength; $i++ ) {
        my $para = $paras->item( $i );

        # for each child of a <p>, if it is a text node, process it
        my @children = $para->getChildNodes;
        foreach my $node ( @children ) {
            &fix_text( $node ) if( $node->getNodeType eq TEXT_NODE );
        }
    }
}
```

The add_links( ) routine starts with a call to the document object's getElementsByTagName( ) method. It returns an XML::DOM::NodeList object containing all matching <p>s in the document (multilevel searching is so convenient) from which we can select nodes by index using item( ).

The bit we're interested in will be hiding inside a text node inside the <p> element, so we have to iterate over the children to find text nodes and process them. The call to getChildNodes( ) gives us several child nodes, either in a generic Perl list (when called in an array context) or another XML::DOM::NodeList object; for variety's sake, we've selected the first option. For each node, we test its type with a call to getNodeType and compare the result to XML::DOM's constant for text nodes, provided by TEXT_NODE( ). Nodes that pass the test are sent off to a routine for some node massaging.

The last part of the program targets text nodes and splits them around the word "monkeys" to create a link:

```
sub fix_text {
    my $node = shift;
    my $text = $node->getNodeValue;
    if( $text =~ /(monkeys)/i ) {

        # split the text node into 2 text nodes around the monkey word
        my( $pre, $orig, $post ) = ( $`, $1, $' );
        my $tnode = $node->getOwnerDocument->createTextNode( $pre );
```

```
        $node->getParentNode->insertBefore( $tnode, $node );
        $node->setNodeValue( $post );

        # insert an <a> element between the two nodes
        my $link = $node->getOwnerDocument->createElement( 'a' );
        $link->setAttribute( 'href', 'http://www.monkeystuff.com/' );
        $tnode = $node->getOwnerDocument->createTextNode( $orig );
        $link->appendChild( $tnode );
        $node->getParentNode->insertBefore( $link, $node );

        # recurse on the rest of the text node
        # in case the word appears again
        fix_text( $node );
    }
}
```

First, the routine grabs the node's text value by calling its getNodeValue( ) method. DOM specifies redundant accessor methods used to get and set values or names, either through the generic Node class or through the more specific class's methods. Instead of getNodeValue( ), we could have used getData( ), which is specific to the text node class. For some nodes, such as elements, there is no defined value, so the generic getNodeValue( ) method would return an undefined value.

Next, we slice the node in two. We do this by creating a new text node and inserting it before the existing one. After we set the text values of each node, the first will contain everything before the word "monkeys", and the other will have everything after the word. Note the use of the XML::DOM::Document object as a factory to create the new text node. This DOM feature takes care of many administrative tasks behind the scenes, making the genesis of new nodes painless.

After that step, we create an <a> element and insert it between the text nodes. Like all good links, it needs a place to put the URL, so we set it up with an href attribute. To have something to click on, the link needs text, so we create a text node with the word "monkeys" and append it to the element's child list. Then the routine will recurse on the text node after the link in case there are more instances of "monkeys" to process.

Does it work? Running the program on this file:

```
<html>
<head><title>Why I like Monkeys</title></head>
<body><h1>Why I like Monkeys</h1>
<h2>Monkeys are Cute</h2>
<p>Monkeys are <b>cute</b>. They are like small, hyper versions of
ourselves. They can make funny facial expressions and stick out their
tongues.</p>
</body>
</html>
```

produces this output:

```
<html>
<head><title>Why I like Monkeys</title></head>
```

```
<body><h1>Why I like Monkeys</h1>
<h2>Monkeys are Cute</h2>
<p><a href="http://www.monkeystuff.com/">Monkeys</a>
are <b>cute</b>. They are like small, hyper versions of
ourselves. They can make funny facial expressions and stick out their
tongues.</p>
</body>
</html>
```

XML::LibXML

Matt Sergeant's `XML::LibXML` module is an interface to the GNOME project's
LibXML library. It's quickly becoming a popular implementation of DOM, demon-
strating speed and completeness over the older `XML::Parser` based modules. It also
implements Level 2 DOM, which means it has support for namespaces.

So far, we haven't worked much with namespaces. A lot of people opt to avoid them.
They add a new level of complexity to markup and code, since you have to handle
both local names and prefixes. However, namespaces are becoming more important
in XML, and sooner or later, we all will have to deal with them. The popular transformation language XSLT uses namespaces to distinguish between tags that are
instructions and tags that are data (i.e., which elements should be output and which
should be used to control the output).

You'll even see namespaces used in good old HTML. Namespaces provide a way to
import specialized markup into documents, such as equations into regular HTML
pages. The MathML language (*http://www.w3.org/Math/*) does just that. Example 7-1
incorporates MathML into it with namespaces.

Example 7-1. A document with namespaces

```
<html>
<body xmlns:eq="http://www.w3.org/1998/Math/MathML">
<h1>Billybob's Theory</h1>
<p>
It is well-known that cats cannot be herded easily. That is, they do
not tend to run in a straight line for any length of time unless they
really want to. A cat forced to run in a straight line against its
will has an increasing probability, with distance, of deviating from
the line just to spite you, given by this formula:</p>
<p>
  <!-- P = 1 - 1/(x^2) -->
  <eq:math>
    <eq:mi>P</eq:mi><eq:mo>=</eq:mo><eq:mn>1</eq:mn><eq:mo>-</eq:mo>
    <eq:mfrac>
      <eq:mn>1</eq:mn>
      <eq:msup>
        <eq:mi>x</eq:mi>
        <eq:mn>2</eq:mn>
      </eq:msup>
    </eq:mfrac>
```

Example 7-1. A document with namespaces (continued)

```
    </eq:mfrac>
  </eq:math>
</p>
</body>
</html>
```

The tags with eq: prefixes are part of a namespace identified by the URI *http://www. w3.org/1998/Math/MathML*, defined in an attribute in the <body> element. Using a namespace helps the browser discern between what is native to HTML and what is not. Browsers that understand MathML route the qualified elements to their equation formatter instead of the regular HTML formatter.

Some browsers are confused by the MathML tags and render unpredictable results. One particularly useful utility is a program that detects and removes namespace-qualified elements that would gum up an older HTML processor. The following example uses DOM2 to sift through a document and strip out all elements that have a namespace prefix.

The first step is to parse the file:

```
use XML::LibXML;

my $parser = XML::LibXML->new( );
my $doc = $parser->parse_file( shift @ARGV );
```

Next, we locate the document element and run a recursive subroutine on it to ferret out the namespace-qualified elements. Afterwards, we print out the document:

```
my $mathuri = 'http://www.w3.org/1998/Math/MathML';
my $root = $doc->getDocumentElement;
&amp;purge_nselems( $root );
print $doc->toString;
```

This routine takes an element node and, if it has a namespace prefix, removes it from its parent's content list. Otherwise, it goes on to process the descendants:

```
sub purge_nselems {
  my $elem = shift;
  return unless( ref( $elem ) =~ /Element/ );
  if( $elem->prefix ) {
    my $parent = $elem->parentNode;
    $parent->removeChild( $elem );
  } elsif( $elem->hasChildNodes ) {
    my @children = $elem->getChildnodes;
    foreach my $child ( @children ) {
      &purge_nselems( $child );
    }
  }
}
```

You might have noticed that this DOM implementation adds some Perlish conveniences over the recommended DOM interface. The call to getChildnodes, in an array context, returns a Perl list instead of a more cumbersome NodeList object. Called in a scalar context, it would return the number of child nodes for that node, so NodeLists aren't really used at all.

Simplifications like this are common in the Perl world, and no one really seems to mind. The emphasis is usually on ease of use over rigorous object-oriented protocol. Of course, one would hope that all DOM implementations in the Perl world adopt the same conventions, which is why many long discussions on the *perl-xml* mailing list try to decide the best way to adopt standards. A current debate discusses how to implement SAX2 (which supports namespaces) in the most logical, Perlish way.

Matt Sergeant has stocked the XML::LibXML package with other goodies. The Node class has a method called findnodes( ), which takes an XPath expression as an argument, allowing retrieval of nodes in more flexible ways than permitted by the ordinary DOM interface. The parser has options that control how pedantically the parser runs, entity resolution, and whitespace significance. One can also opt to use special handlers for unparsed entities. Overall, this module is excellent for DOM programming.

CHAPTER 8

Beyond Trees: XPath, XSLT, and More

In the last chapter, we introduced the concepts behind handling XML documents as memory trees. Our use of them was kind of primitive, limited to building, traversing, and modifying pieces of trees. This is okay for small, uncomplicated documents and tasks, but serious XML processing requires beefier tools. In this chapter, we examine ways to make tree processing easier, faster, and more efficient.

Tree Climbers

The first in our lineup of power tools is the tree climber. As the name suggests, it climbs a tree for you, finding the nodes in the order you want them, making your code simpler and more focused on per-node processing. Using a tree climber is like having a trained monkey climb up a tree to get you coconuts so you don't have to scrape your own skin on the bark to get them; all you have to do is drill a hole in the shell and pop in a straw.

The simplest kind of tree climber is an *iterator* (sometimes called a *walker*). It can move forward or backward in a tree, doling out node references as you tell it to move. The notion of moving forward in a tree involves matching the order of nodes as they would appear in the text representation of the document. The exact algorithm for iterating forward is this:

- If there's no current node, start at the root node.
- If the current node has children, move to the first child.
- Otherwise, if the current node has a following sibling, move to it.
- If none of these options work, go back up the list of the current node's ancestors and try to find one with an unprocessed sibling.

With this algorithm, the iterator will eventually reach every node in a tree, which is useful if you want to process all the nodes in a document part. You could also implement this algorithm recursively, but the advantage to doing it iteratively is that you can stop in between nodes to do other things. Example 8-1 shows how one might implement an iterator object for DOM trees. We've included methods for moving both forward and backward.

Example 8-1. A DOM iterator package

```perl
package XML::DOMIterator;

sub new {
  my $class = shift;
  my $self = {@_};
  $self->{ Node } = undef;
  return bless( $self, $class );
}

# move forward one node in the tree
#
sub forward {
  my $self = shift;

  # try to go down to the next level
  if( $self->is_element and
      $self->{ Node }->getFirstChild ) {
    $self->{ Node } = $self->{ Node }->getFirstChild;

  # try to go to the next sibling, or an acestor's sibling
  } else {
    while( $self->{ Node }) {
      if( $self->{ Node }->getNextSibling ) {
        $self->{ Node } = $self->{ Node }->getNextSibling;
        return $self->{ Node };
      }
      $self->{ Node } = $self->{ Node }->getParentNode;
    }
  }
}

# move backward one node in the tree
#
sub backward {
  my $self = shift;

  # go to the previous sibling and descend to the last node in its tree
  if( $self->{ Node }->getPreviousSibling ) {
    $self->{ Node } = $self->{ Node }->getPreviousSibling;
    while( $self->{ Node }->getLastChild ) {
      $self->{ Node } = $self->{ Node }->getLastChild;
    }

  # go up
  } else {
    $self->{ Node } = $self->{ Node }->getParentNode;
  }
  return $self->{ Node };
}
```

Example 8-1. A DOM iterator package (continued)

```
# return a reference to the current node
#
sub node {
  my $self = shift;
  return $self->{ Node };
}

# set the current node
#
sub reset {
  my( $self, $node ) = @_;
  $self->{ Node } = $node;
}

# test if current node is an element
#
sub is_element {
  my $self = shift;
  return( $self->{ Node }->getNodeType == 1 );
}
```

Example 8-2 is a test program for the iterator package. It prints out a short description of every node in an XML document tree—first in forward order, then in backward order.

Example 8-2. A test program for the iterator package

```
use XML::DOM;

# initialize parser and iterator
my $dom_parser = new XML::DOM::Parser;
my $doc = $dom_parser->parsefile( shift @ARGV );
my $iter = new XML::DOMIterator;
$iter->reset( $doc->getDocumentElement );

# print all the nodes from start to end of a document
print "\nFORWARDS:\n";
my $node = $iter->node;
my $last;
while( $node ) {
  describe( $node );
  $last = $node;
  $node = $iter->forward;
}

# print all the nodes from end to start of a document
print "\nBACKWARDS:\n";
$iter->reset( $last );
describe( $iter->node );
while( $iter->backward ) {
  describe( $iter->node );
}
```

Example 8-2. A test program for the iterator package (continued)

```
# output information about the node
#
sub describe {
  my $node = shift;
  if( ref($node) =~ /Element/ ) {
    print 'element: ', $node->getNodeName, "\n";
  } elsif( ref($node) =~ /Text/ ) {
    print "other node: \"", $node->getNodeValue, "\"\n";
  }
}
```

Many tree packages provide automated tree climbing capability. XML::LibXML::Node has a method iterator( ) that traverses a node's subtree, applying a subroutine to each node. Data::Grove::Visitor performs a similar function.

Example 8-3 shows a program that uses an automated tree climbing function to test processing instructions in a document.

Example 8-3. Processing instruction tester

```
use XML::LibXML;

my $dom = new XML::LibXML;
my $doc = $dom->parse_file( shift @ARGV );
my $docelem = $doc->getDocumentElement;
$docelem->iterator( \&find_PI );

sub find_PI {
  my $node = shift;
  return unless( $node->nodeType == &XML_PI_NODE );
  print "Found processing instruction: ", $node->nodeName, "\n";
}
```

Tree climbers are terrific for tasks that involve processing the whole document, since they automate the process of moving from node to node. However, you won't always have to visit every node. Often, you only want to pick out one from the bunch or get a set of nodes that satisfy a certain criterion, such as having a particular element name or attribute value. In these cases, you may want to try a more selective approach, as we will demonstrate in the next section.

XPath

Imagine that you have an army of monkeys at your disposal. You say to them, "I want you to get me a banana frappe from the ice cream parlor on Massachusetts Avenue just north of Porter Square." Not being very smart monkeys, they go out and bring back every beverage they can find, leaving you to taste them all to figure out which is the one you wanted. To retrain them, you send them out to night school to learn a rudimentary language, and in a few months you repeat the request. Now the monkeys follow your directions, identify the exact item you want, and return with it.

We've just described the kind of problem XPath was designed to solve. XPath is one of the most useful technologies supporting XML. It provides an interface to find nodes in a purely descriptive way, so you don't have to write code to hunt them down yourself. You merely specify the kind of nodes that interest you and an XPath parser will retrieve them for you. Suddenly, XML goes from becoming a vast, confusing pile of nodes to a well-indexed filing cabinet of data.

Consider the XML document in Example 8-4.

Example 8-4. A preferences file

```
<plist>
  <dict>
    <key>DefaultDirectory</key>
    <string>/usr/local/fooby</string>
    <key>RecentDocuments</key>
    <array>
      <string>/Users/bobo/docs/menu.pdf</string>
      <string>/Users/slappy/pagoda.pdf</string>
      <string>/Library/docs/Baby.pdf</string>
    </array>
    <key>BGColor</key>
    <string>sage</string>
  </dict>
</plist>
```

This document is a typical preferences file for a program with a series of data keys and values. Nothing in it is too complex. To obtain the value of the key BGColor, you'd have to locate the <key> element containing the word "BGColor" and step ahead to the next element, a <string>. Finally, you would read the value of the text node inside. In DOM, you might do it as shown in Example 8-5.

Example 8-5. Program to get a preferred color

```
sub get_bgcolor {
    my @keys = $doc->getElementsByTagName( 'key' );
    foreach my $key ( @keys ) {
        if( $key->getFirstChild->getData eq 'BGColor' ) {
            return $key->getNextSibling->getData;
        }
    }
    return;
}
```

Writing one routine like this isn't too bad, but imagine if you had to do hundreds of queries like it. And this program was for a relatively simple document—imagine how complex the code could be for one that was many levels deep. It would be nice to have a shorthand way of doing the same thing, say, on one line of code. Such a syntax would be much easier to read, write, and debug. This is where XPath comes in.

XPath is a language for expressing a path to a node or set of nodes anywhere in a document. It's simple, expressive, and standard (backed by the W3C, the folks who brought you XML).* You'll see it used in XSLT for matching rules to nodes, and in XPointer, a technology for linking XML documents to resources. You can also find it in many Perl modules, as we'll show you soon.

An XPath expression is called a *location path* and consists of some number of path *steps* that extend the path a little bit closer to the goal. Starting from an absolute, known position (for example, the root of the document), the steps "walk" across the document tree to arrive at a node or set of nodes. The syntax looks much like a file-system path, with steps separated by slash characters (/).

This location path shows how to find that color value in our last example:

```
/plist/dict/key[text()='BGColor']/following-sibling::*[1]/text( )
```

A location path is processed by starting at an absolute location in the document and moving to a new node (or nodes) with each step. At any point in the search, a *current node* serves as the context for the next step. If multiple nodes match the next step, the search branches and the processor maintains a set of current nodes. Here's how the location path shown above would be processed:

- Start at the root node (one level above the root element).
- Move to a <plist> element that is a child of the current node.
- Move to a <dict> element that is a child of the current node.
- Move to a <key> element that is a child of the current node and that has the value BGColor.
- Find the next element after the current node.
- Return any text nodes belonging to the current node.

Because node searches can branch if multiple nodes match, we sometimes have to add a test condition to a step to restrict the eligible candidates. Adding a test condition was necessary for the <key> sampling step where multiple nodes would have matched, so we added a test condition requiring the value of the element to be BGColor. Without the test, we would have received all text nodes from all siblings immediately following a <key> element.

This location path matches all <key> elements in the document:

```
/plist/dict/key
```

Of the many kinds of test conditions, all result in a boolean true/false answer. You can test the position (where a node is in the list), existence of children and attributes, numeric comparisons, and all kinds of boolean expressions using AND and OR operators. Sometimes a test consists of only a number, which is shorthand for specifying an index into a node list, so the test [1] says, "stop at the first node that matches."

* The recommendation is on the Web at *http://www.w3.org/TR/xpath/*.

You can link multiple tests inside the brackets with boolean operations. Alternatively, you can chain tests with multiple sets of brackets, functioning as an AND operator. Every path step has an implicit test that prunes the search tree of blind alleys. If at any point a step turns up zero matching nodes, the search along that branch terminates.

Along with boolean tests, you can shape a location path with directives called *axes*. An axis is like a compass needle that tells the processor which direction to travel. Instead of the default, which is to descend from the current node to its children, you can make it go up to the parent and ancestors or laterally among its siblings. The axis is written as a prefix to the step with a double colon (::). In our last example, we used the axis following-sibling to jump from the current node to its next-door neighbor.

A step is not limited to frolicking with elements. You can specify different kinds of nodes, including attributes, text, processing instructions, and comments, or leave it generic with a selector for any node type. You can specify the node type in many ways, some of which are listed here:

Symbol	Matches
node( )	Any node
text( )	A text node
element::foo	An element named foo
foo	An element named foo
attribute::foo	An attribute named foo
@foo	An attribute named foo
@*	Any attribute
*	Any element
.	This element
..	The parent element
/	The root node
/*	The root element
//foo	An element foo at any level

Since the thing you're most likely to select in a location path step is an element, the default node type is an element. But there are reasons why you should use another node type. In our example location path, we used text( ) to return just the text node for the <value> element.

Most steps are *relative locators* because they define where to go relative to the previous locator. Although locator paths are comprised mostly of relative locators, they always start with an *absolute locator*, which describes a definite point in the document. This locator comes in two flavors: id( ), which starts at an element with a given ID attribute, and root( ), which starts at the root node of the document (an abstract node that is the parent of the document element). You will frequently see the shorthand "/" starting a path indicating that root( ) is being used.

Now that we've trained our monkeys to understand XPath, let's give it a whirl with Perl. The XML::XPath module, written by Matt Sergeant of XML::LibXML fame, is a solid implementation of XPath. We've written a program in Example 8-6 that takes two command-line arguments: a file and an XPath locator path. It prints the text value of all nodes it finds that match the path.

Example 8-6. A program that uses XPath

```
use XML::XPath;
use XML::XPath::XMLParser;

# create an object to parse the file and field XPath queries
my $xpath = XML::XPath->new( filename => shift @ARGV );

# apply the path from the command line and get back a list matches
my $nodeset = $xpath->find( shift @ARGV );

# print each node in the list
foreach my $node ( $nodeset->get_nodelist ) {
  print XML::XPath::XMLParser::as_string( $node ) . "\n";
}
```

That example was simple. Now we need a datafile. Check out Example 8-7.

Example 8-7. An XML datafile

```
<?xml version="1.0"?>
<!DOCTYPE inventory [
  <!ENTITY poison "<note>danger: poisonous!</note>">
  <!ENTITY endang "<note>endangered species</note>">
]>
<!-- Rivenwood Arboretum inventory -->
<inventory date="2001.9.4">
  <category type="tree">
    <item id="284">
      <name style="latin">Carya glabra</name>
      <name style="common">Pignut Hickory</name>
      <location>east quadrangle</location>
      &endang;
    </item>
    <item id="222">
      <name style="latin">Toxicodendron vernix</name>
      <name style="common">Poison Sumac</name>
      <location>west promenade</location>
      &poison;
    </item>
  </category>
  <category type="shrub">
    <item id="210">
      <name style="latin">Cornus racemosa</name>
```

Example 8-7. An XML datafile (continued)

```
      <name style="common">Gray Dogwood</name>
      <location>south lawn</location>
    </item>
    <item id="104">
      <name style="latin">Alnus rugosa</name>
      <name style="common">Speckled Alder</name>
      <location>east quadrangle</location>
      &endang;
    </item>
  </category>
</inventory>
```

The first test uses the path /inventory/category/item/name:

```
> grabber.pl data.xml "/inventory/category/item/name"
<name style="latin">Carya glabra</name>
<name style="common">Pignut Hickory</name>
<name style="latin">Toxicodendron vernix</name>
<name style="common">Poison Sumac</name>
<name style="latin">Cornus racemosa</name>
<name style="common">Gray Dogwood</name>
<name style="latin">Alnus rugosa</name>
<name style="common">Speckled Alder</name>
```

Every <name> element was found and printed. Let's get more specific with the path /inventory/category/item/name[@style='latin']:

```
> grabber.pl data.xml "/inventory/category/item/name[@style='latin']"
<name style="latin">Carya glabra</name>
<name style="latin">Toxicodendron vernix</name>
<name style="latin">Cornus racemosa</name>
<name style="latin">Alnus rugosa</name>
```

Now let's use an ID attribute as a starting point with the path //item[@id='222']/note. (If we had defined the attribute id in a DTD, we'd be able to use the path id('222')/note. We didn't, but this alternate method works just as well.)

```
> grabber.pl data.xml "//item[@id='222']/note"
<note>danger: poisonous!</note>
```

How about ditching the element tags? To do so, use this:

```
> grabber.pl data.xml "//item[@id='222']/note/text( )"
danger: poisonous!
```

When was this inventory last updated?

```
> grabber.pl data.xml "/inventory/@date"
 date="2001.9.4"
```

With XPath, you can go hog wild! Here's the path a silly monkey might take through the tree:

```
> grabber.pl data.xml "//*[@id='104']/parent::*/preceding-sibling::*/child::*[2]/
name[not(@style='latin')]/node( )"
Poison Sumac
```

The monkey started on the element with the attribute id='104', climbed up a level, jumped to the previous element, climbed down to the second child element, found a <name> whose style attribute was not set to 'latin', and hopped on the child of that element, which happened to be the text node with the value Poison Sumac.

We have just seen how to use XPath expressions to locate and return a set of nodes. The implementation we are about to see is even more powerful. XML::Twig, an ingenious module by Michel Rodriguez, is quite Perlish in the way it uses XPath expressions. It uses a hash to map them to subroutines, so you can have functions called automatically for certain types of nodes.

The program in Example 8-8 shows how this works. When you initialize the XML::Twig object, you can set a bunch of handlers in a hash, where the keys are XPath expressions. During the parsing stage, as the tree is built, these handlers are called for appropriate nodes.

As you look at Example 8-8, you'll notice that at-sign (@) characters are escaped. This is because @ can cause a little confusion with XPath expressions living in a Perl context. In XPath, @foo refers to an attribute named foo, not an array named foo. Keep this distinction in mind when going over the XPath examples in this book and when writing your own XPath for Perl to use—you must escape the @ characters so Perl doesn't try to interpolate arrays in the middle of your expressions.

If your code does so much work with Perl arrays and XPath attribute references that it's unclear which @ characters are which, consider referring to attributes in longhand, using the "attribute" XPath axis: attribute::foo. This raises the issue of the double colon and its different meanings in Perl and XPath. Since XPath has only a few hardcoded axes, however, and they're always expressed in lowercase, they're easier to tell apart at a glance.

Example 8-8. How twig handlers work

```
use XML::Twig;

# buffers for holding text
my $catbuf = '';
my $itembuf = '';

# initialize parser with handlers for node processing
my $twig = new XML::Twig( TwigHandlers => {
                          "/inventory/category"    => \&category,
                          "name[\@style='latin']"  => \&latin_name,
                          "name[\@style='common']" => \&common_name,
                          "category/item"          => \&item,
                                    });

# parse, handling nodes on the way
$twig->parsefile( shift @ARGV );
```

Example 8-8. How twig handlers work (continued)

```
# handle a category element
sub category {
  my( $tree, $elem ) = @_;
  print "CATEGORY: ", $elem->att( 'type' ), "\n\n", $catbuf;
  $catbuf = '';
}

# handle an item element
sub item {
  my( $tree, $elem ) = @_;
  $catbuf .= "Item: " . $elem->att( 'id' ) . "\n" . $itembuf . "\n";
  $itembuf = '';
}

# handle a latin name
sub latin_name {
  my( $tree, $elem ) = @_;
  $itembuf .= "Latin name: " . $elem->text . "\n";
}

# handle a common name
sub common_name {
  my( $tree, $elem ) = @_;
  $itembuf .= "Common name: " . $elem->text . "\n";
}
```

Our program takes a datafile like the one shown in Example 8-7 and outputs a summary report. Note that since a handler is called only after an element is completely built, the overall order of handler calls may not be what you expect. The handlers for children are called before their parent. For that reason, we need to buffer their output and sort it out at the appropriate time.

The result comes out like this:

```
CATEGORY: tree

Item: 284
Latin name: Carya glabra
Common name: Pignut Hickory

Item: 222
Latin name: Toxicodendron vernix
Common name: Poison Sumac

CATEGORY: shrub

Item: 210
Latin name: Cornus racemosa
Common name: Gray Dogwood

Item: 104
Latin name: Alnus rugosa
Common name: Speckled Alder
```

XPath makes the task of locating nodes in a document and describing types of nodes for processing ridiculously simple. It cuts down on the amount of code you have to write because climbing around the tree to sample different parts is all taken care of. It's easier to read than code too. We're happy with it, and because it is a standard, we'll be seeing more uses for it in many modules to come.

XSLT

If you think of XPath as a regular expression syntax, then XSLT is its pattern substitution mechanism. XSLT is an XML-based programming language for describing how to transform one document type into another. You can do some amazing things with XSLT, such as describe how to turn any XML document into HTML or tabulate the sum of figures in an XML-formatted table. In fact, you might not need to write a line of code in Perl or any language. All you really need is an XSLT script and one of the dozens of transformation engines available for processing XSLT.

The Origin of XSLT

XSLT stands for XML Style Language: Transformations. The name means that it's a component of the XML Style Language (XSL), assigned to handle the task of converting input XML into a special format called XSL-FO (the FO stands for "Formatting Objects"). XSL-FO contains both content and instructions for how to make it pretty when displayed.

Although it's stuck with the XSL name, XSLT is more than just a step in formatting; it's an important XML processing tool that makes it easy to convert from one kind of XML to another, or from XML to text. For this reason, the W3C (yup, they created XSLT too) released the recommendation for it years before the rest of XSL was ready.

To read the specification and find links to XSLT tutorials, look at its home page at *http://www.w3.org/TR/xslt*.

An XSLT transformation script is itself an XML document. It consists mostly of rules called *templates*, each of which tells how to treat a specific type of node. A template usually does two things: it describes what to output and defines how processing should continue.

Consider the script in Example 8-9.

Example 8-9. An XSLT stylesheet

```
<xsl:stylesheet
  xmlns:xsl="http://www.w3.org/1999/XSL/Transform"
  version="1.0">
```

Example 8-9. An XSLT stylesheet (continued)

```
    <xsl:template match="html">
      <xsl:text>Title: </xsl:text>
      <xsl:value-of select="head/title"/>
      <xsl:apply-templates select="body"/>
    </xsl:template>

    <xsl:template match="body">
      <xsl:apply-templates/>
    </xsl:template>

    <xsl:template match="h1 | h2 | h3 | h4">
      <xsl:text>Head: </xsl:text>
      <xsl:value-of select="."/>
    </xsl:template>

    <xsl:template match="p | blockquote | li">
      <xsl:text>Content: </xsl:text>
      <xsl:value-of select="."/>
    </xsl:template>
</xsl:stylesheet>
```

This transformation script converts an HTML document into ASCII with some extra text labels. Each `<xsl:template>` element is a rule that matches a part of an XML document. Its content consists of instructions to the XSLT processor describing what to output. Directives like `<xsl:apply-templates>` direct processing to other elements (usually descendants). We won't go into detail about XSLT syntax, as whole books on the subject are available. Our intent here is to show how you can combine XSLT with Perl to do powerful XML munching.

You might wonder, "Why do I need to use another language to transform XML when I can do that with the Perl I already know?" True, XSLT doesn't do anything you couldn't do in Perlish coding. Its value comes in the ease of learning the language. You can learn XSLT in few hours, but to do the same things in Perl would take much longer. In our experience writing software for XML, we found it convenient to use XSLT as a configuration file that nonprogrammers could maintain themselves. Thus, instead of viewing XSLT as competition for Perl, think of it more as a complementary technology that you can access through Perl when you need to.

How do Perl hackers employ the power of XSLT in their programs? Example 8-10 shows how to perform an XSLT transformation on a document using `XML::LibXSLT`, Matt Sergeant's interface to the super-fast GNOME library called LibXSLT, one of several XSLT solutions available from your CPAN toolbox.[*]

---

[*] Others that are currently available include the pure-Perl `XML::XSLT` module, and `XML::Sablotron`, based on the Expat and Sablotron C libraries (the latter of which is an XSLT library by the Ginger Alliance: *http://www.gingerall.com*).

Example 8-10. A program to run an XSLT transformation

```
use XML::LibXSLT;
use XML::LibXML;

# the arguments for this command are stylesheet and source files
my( $style_file, @source_files ) = @ARGV;

# initialize the parser and XSLT processor
my $parser = XML::LibXML->new( );
my $xslt = XML::LibXSLT->new( );
my $stylesheet = $xslt->parse_stylesheet_file( $style_file );

# for each source file: parse, transform, print out result
foreach my $file ( @source_files ) {
  my $source_doc = $parser->parse_file( $source_file );
  my $result = $stylesheet->transform( $source_doc );
  print $stylesheet->output_string( $result );
}
```

The nice thing about this program is that it parses the stylesheet only once, keeping it in memory for reuse with other source documents. Afterwards, you have the document tree to do further work, if necessary:

- Postprocess or preprocess the text of the document with search-replace routines.
- Pluck a piece of the document out to transform just that bit.
- Run an iterator over the tree to handle some nodes that would be too difficult to process in XSLT.

The possibilities are endless and, as always in Perl, whatever you want to do, there's more than one way to do it.

Optimized Tree Processing

The big drawback to using trees for XML crunching is that they tend to consume scandalous amounts of memory and processor time. This might not be apparent with small documents, but it becomes noticeable as documents grow to many thousands of nodes. A typical book of a few hundred pages' length could easily have tens of thousands of nodes. Each one requires the allocation of an object, a process that takes considerable time and memory.

Perhaps you don't need to build the entire tree to get your work done, though. You might only want a small branch of the tree and can safely do all the processing inside of it. If that's the case, then you can take advantage of the optimized parsing modes in XML::Twig (recall that we dealt with this module earlier in the section "XPath"). These modes allow you to specify ahead of time what parts (or "twigs") of the tree you'll be working with so that only those parts are assembled. The result is a hybrid of tree and event processing with highly optimized performance in speed and memory.

XML::Twig has three modes of operation: the regular old tree mode, similar to what we've seen so far; "chunk" mode, which builds a whole tree, but has only a fraction of it in memory at a time (sort of like paged memory); and multiple roots mode, which builds only a few selected twigs from the tree.

Example 8-11 demonstrates the power of XML::Twig in chunk mode. The data to this program is a DocBook book with some <chapter> elements. These documents can be enormous, sometimes a hundred megabytes or more. The program breaks up the processing per chapter so that only a fraction of the space is needed.

Example 8-11. A chunking program

```
use XML::Twig;

# initalize the twig, parse, and output the revised twig
my $twig = new XML::Twig( TwigHandlers => { chapter => \&process_chapter });
$twig->parsefile( shift @ARGV );
$twig->print;

# handler for chapter elements: process and then flush up the chapter
sub process_chapter {
  my( $tree, $elem ) = @_;
  &process_element( $elem );
  $tree->flush_up_to( $elem );  # comment out this line to waste memory
}

# append 'foo' to the name of an element
sub process_element {
  my $elem = shift;
  $elem->set_gi( $elem->gi . 'foo' );
  my @children = $elem->children;
  foreach my $child ( @children ) {
    next if( $child->gi eq '#PCDATA' );
    &process_element( $child );
  }
}
```

The program changes element names to append the string "foo" to them. Changing names is just busy work to keep the program running long enough to check the memory usage. Note the line in the function process_chapter( ):

```
$tree->flush_up_to( $elem );
```

We get our memory savings from this command. Without it, the entire tree will be built and kept in memory until the document is finally printed out. But when it is called, the tree that has been built up to a given element is dismantled and its text is output (called *flushing*). The memory usage never rises higher than what is needed for the largest chapter in the book.

To test this theory, we ran the program on a 3 MB document, first without and then with the line shown above. Without flushing, the program's heap space grew to over

30 MB. It's staggering to see how much memory an object-oriented tree processor needs—in this case ten times the size of the file. But with flushing enabled, the program hovered around only a few MB of memory usage, a savings of about 90 percent. In both cases, the entire tree is eventually built, so the total processing time is about the same. To save CPU cycles as well as memory, we need to use multiple roots mode.

Multiple roots mode works by specifying before parsing the roots of the twigs that you want built. You will save significant time and memory if the twigs are much smaller than the document as a whole. In our chunk mode example, we probably can't do much to speed up the process, since the sum of <chapter> elements is about the same as the size of the document. So let's focus on an example that fits the profile.

The program in Example 8-12 reads in DocBook documents and outputs the titles of chapters—a table of contents of sorts. To get this information, we don't need to build a tree for the whole chapter; only the <title> element is necessary. So for roots, we specify titles of chapters, expressed in the XPath notation chapter/title.

Example 8-12. A many-twigged program

```
use XML::Twig;

my $twig = new XML::Twig( TwigRoots => { 'chapter/title' => \&output_title });
$twig->parsefile( shift @ARGV );

sub output_title {
  my( $tree, $elem ) = @_;
  print $elem->text, "\n";
}
```

The key line here is the one with the keyword TwigRoots. It's set to a hash of handlers and works very similarly to TwigHandlers that we saw earlier. The difference is that instead of building the whole document tree, the program builds only trees whose roots are <title> elements. This is a small fraction of the whole document, so we can expect time and memory savings to be high.

How high? Running the program on the same test data, we saw memory usage barely reach 2 MB, and the total processing time was 13 seconds. Compare that to 30 MB memory usage (the size required to build the whole tree) and a full minute to grind out the titles. This conservation of resources is significant for both memory and CPU time.

XML::Twig can give you a big performance boost for your tree processing programs, but you have to know when chunking and multiple roots will help. You won't save much time if the sum of twigs is almost as big as the document itself. Chunking is not useful unless the chunks are significantly smaller than the document.

## CHAPTER 9

RSS, SOAP, and Other XML Applications

In the next couple of chapters, we'll cover, at long last, what happens when we pull together all the abstract tools and strategies we've discussed and start having XML dance for us. This is the land of the XML application, where parsers all have a bone to pick, picking up documents with a goal in mind. No longer satisfied with picking out the elements and attributes and calling it a day, these higher-level tools look for meaning in all that structure, according to directives that have been programmed into it.

When we say XML application, we are specifically referring to XML-based document formats, not the computer programs (applications of another sort) that do stuff with them. You may run across statements such as "GreenMonkeyML is an XML application that provides semantic markup for green monkeys." Visiting the project's home page at *http://www.greenmonkey-markup.com*, we might encounter documentation describing how this specific format works, example documents, suggested uses for it, a DTD or schema used to validate GreenMonkeyML documents, and maybe an online validation tool. This content would all fit into the definition of an XML application.

This chapter looks at XML applications that already have a strong presence in the Perl world, by way of publicly available Perl modules that know how to handle them.

XML Modules

The term *XML modules* narrows us down from the Perl modules on CPAN that send mail, process images, and play games, but it still leaves us with a very broad cross section. So far in this book, we have exhaustively covered Perl extensions that can perform general XML processing, but none that perform more targeted functions based on general processing. In the end, they hand you a plate of XML chunklets, free of any inherent meaning, and leave it to you to decide what happens next. In many of the examples we've provided so far in this book, we have written programs that do exactly this: invoke an XML parser to chew up a document and then cook up something interesting out of the elements and attributes we get back.

However, the modules we're thinking about here give you more than the generic parse-and-process module family by building on one of the parsers and abstracting the processing in a specific direction. They then provide an API that, while it might still contain hooks into the raw XML, concentrates on methods and routines particular to the XML application that they implement.

We can divide these XML application-mangling Perl modules into three types. We'll examine an example of each in this chapter, and in the next chapter, we'll try to make some for ourselves.

XML application helpers

Helper modules are the humblest of the lot. In practice, they are often little more than wrappers around raw XML processors, but sometimes that's all you need. If you find yourself writing several programs that need to read from and write to a specific XML-based document format, a helper module can provide common methods, freeing the programmer from worrying about the application's exact document format or its well-formedness in generated output. The module will take care of all that.

Programming helpers that use XML

This small but growing category describes Perl extensions that use XML to do cool stuff in your program, even if your program's input or output has little to do with XML. Currently, the most prominent examples involve the terrifying, DBI-like powers of XML::SAX, the whole PerlSAX2 family, and individual tools like the XML::Generator::DBI module, which crossbreeds existing Perl modules for database manipulation and SAX processing.

Full-on applications that use XML

Finally, we have software that uses XML, but has so many layers of abstraction between its intended purpose and the underlying XML that calling it an XML application is like calling Microsoft Word a C application. For example, working with SOAP::Lite involves documents that are barely human-readable and exist only in memory until they're shot over the Internet via HTTP; the role of XML in SOAP is completely transparent.

XML::RSS

By *helper modules*, we mean more focused versions of the XML processors we've already pawed through in our Perl and XML toolbox. In a way, XML::Parser and its ilk are helper applications since they save you from approaching each XML-chomping job with Perl's built-in file-reading functions and regular expressions by turning documents into immediately useful objects or event streams. Also, XML::Writer and friends replace plain old print statements with a more abstract and safer way to create XML documents.

However, the XML modules we cover now offer their services in a very specific direction. By using one of these modules in your program, you establish that you plan to use XML, but only a small, clearly defined subsection of it. By submitting to this restriction, you get to use (and create) software modules that handle all the toil of working with raw XML, presenting the main part of your code with methods and routines specific only to the application at hand.

For our example, we'll look at XML::RSS—a little number by Jonathan Eisenzopf.

Introduction to RSS

RSS (short for Rich Site Summary or Really Simple Syndication, depending upon whom you ask) is one of the first XML applications whose use became rapidly popular on a global scale, thanks to the Web. While RSS itself is little more than an agreed-upon way to summarize web page content, it gives the administrators of news sites, web logs, and any other frequently updated web site a standard and sweat-free way of telling the world what's new. Programs that can parse RSS can do whatever they'd like with this document, perhaps telling its masters by mail or by web page what interesting things it has learned in its travels. A special type of RSS program is an aggregator, a program that collects RSS from various sources and then knits it together into new RSS documents combining the information, so that lazier RSS-parsing programs won't have to travel so far.

Current popular aggregators include Netscape, by way of its customizable *my. netscape.com* site (which was, in fact, the birthplace of the earliest RSS versions) and Dave Winer's *http://www.scripting.com* (whose aggregator has a public frontend at *http://aggregator.userland.com/register*). These aggregators, in turn, share what they pick up as RSS, turning them into one-stop RSS shops for other interested entities. Web sites that collect and present links to new stuff around the Web, such as the O'Reilly Network's Meerkat (*http://meerkat.oreillynet.com*), hit these aggregators often to get information on RSS-enabled web sites, and then present it to the site's user.

Using XML::RSS

The XML::RSS module is useful whether you're coming or going. It can parse RSS documents that you hand it, or it can help you write your own RSS documents. Naturally, you can combine these abilities to parse a document, modify it, and then write it out again; the module uses a simple and well-documented object model to represent documents in memory, just like the tree-based modules we've seen so far. You can think of this sort of XML helper module as a tricked-out version of a familiar general XML tool.

In the following examples, we'll work with a notional web log, a frequently updated and Web-readable personal column or journal. RSS lends itself to web logs, letting them quickly summarize their most recent entries within a single RSS document.

Here are a couple of web log entries (admittedly sampling from the shallow end of the concept's notional pool, but it works for short examples). First, here is how one might look in a web browser:

```
Oct 18, 2002 19:07:06

Today I asked lab monkey 45-X how he felt about his recent chess
victory against Dr. Baker. He responded by biting my kneecap. (The
monkey did, I mean.) I
think this could lead to a communications breakthrough. As well as
painful swelling, which is unfortunate.

Oct 27, 2002 22:56:11

On a tangential note, Dr. Xing's research of purple versus green monkey
trans-sociopolitical impact seems to be stalled, having gained no
ground for several weeks. Today she learned that her lab assistant
never mentioned on his job application that he was colorblind. Oh well.
```

Here it is again, as an RSS v1.0 document:

```
<?xml version="1.0" encoding="UTF-8"?>

<rdf:RDF
 xmlns:rdf="http://www.w3.org/1999/02/22-rdf-syntax-ns#"
 xmlns="http://purl.org/rss/1.0/"
 xmlns:dc="http://purl.org/dc/elements/1.1/"
 xmlns:taxo="http://purl.org/rss/1.0/modules/taxonomy/"
 xmlns:syn="http://purl.org/rss/1.0/modules/syndication/"
>

<channel rdf:about="http://www.jmac.org/linklog/">
<title>Link's Log</title>
<link>http://www.jmac.org/linklog/</link>
<description>Dr. Lance Link's online research journal</description>
<dc:language>en-us</dc:language>
<dc:rights>Copright 2002 by Dr. Lance Link</dc:rights>
<dc:date>2002-10-27T23:59:15+05:00</dc:date>
<dc:publisher>llink@jmac.org</dc:publisher>
<dc:creator>llink@jmac.org</dc:creator>
<dc:subject>llink</dc:subject>
<syn:updatePeriod>daily</syn:updatePeriod>
<syn:updateFrequency>1</syn:updateFrequency>
<syn:updateBase>2002-03-03T00:00:00+05:00</syn:updateBase>
<items>
 <rdf:Seq>
  <rdf:li rdf:resource="http://www.jmac.org/linklog?2002-10-27#22:56:11" />
  <rdf:li rdf:resource="http://www.jmac.org/linklog?2002-10-18#19:07:06" />
 </rdf:Seq>
</items>
</channel>

<item rdf:about="http://www.jmac.org/linklog?2002-10-27#22:56:11">
<title>2002-10-27 22:56:11</title>
```

```
<link>http://www.jmac.org/linklog?2002-10-27#22:56:11</link>
<description>
Today I asked lab monkey 45-X how he felt about his recent chess
victory against Dr. Baker. He responded by biting my kneecap. (The
monkey did, I mean.) I
think this could lead to a communications breakthrough. As well as
painful swelling, which is unfortunate.
</description>
</item>

<item rdf:about="http://www.jmac.org/linklog?2002-10-18#19:07:06">
<title>2002-10-18 19:07:06</title>
<link>http://www.jmac.org/linklog?2002-10-18#19:07:06</link>
<description>
On a tangential note, Dr. Xing's research of purple versus green monkey
trans-sociopolitical impact seems to be stalled, having gained no
ground for several weeks. Today she learned that her lab assistant
never mentioned on his job application that he was colorblind. Oh well.
</description>
</item>

</rdf:RDF>
```

Note RSS 1.0's use of various metadata-enabling namespaces before it gets into the meat of laying out the actual content.[*] The curious may wish to point their web browsers at the URIs with which they identify themselves, since they are good little namespaces who put their documentation where their mouth is. ("dc" is the Dublin Core, a standard set of elements for describing a document's source. "syn" points to a syndication namespace—itself a sub-project by the RSS people—holding a handful of elements that state how often a source refreshes itself with new content.) Then the whole document is wrapped up in an RDF element.

Parsing

Using XML::RSS to read an existing document ought to look familiar if you've read the preceding chapters, and is quite simple:

```
use XML::RSS;

# Accept file from user arguments
my @rss_docs = @ARGV;

# For now, we'll assume they're all files on disk...
foreach my $rss_doc (@rss_docs) {
```

---

[*] I am careful to specify the RSS version here because RSS Version .9 and 0.91 documents are much simpler in structure, eschewing namespaces and RDF-encapsulated metadata in favor of a simple list of <item> elements wrapped in an <rss> element. For this reason, many people prefer to use pre-1.0 RSS, and socially astute RSS software can read from and write to all these versions. XML::RSS can do this, and as a side effect, allows easy conversion between these different versions (given a single original document).

```
# First, create a new RSS object that will represent the parsed doc
my $rss = XML::RSS->new;

# Now parse that puppy
$rss->parsefile($rss_doc);

# And that's all. Do whatever else we may want here.
}
```

Inheriting from XML::Parser

If that parsefile method looked familiar, it had good reason: it's the same one used by grandpappy XML::Parser, both in word and deed.

XML::RSS takes direct advantage of XML::Parser's inheritability right off the bat, placing this module into its @ISA array before getting down to business with all that map definition.

It shouldn't surprise those familiar with object-oriented Perl programming that, while it chooses to define its own new method, it does little more than invoke SUPER:: new. In doing so, it lets XML::Parser initialize itself as it sees fit. Let's look at some code from that module itself—specifically its constructor, new, which we invoked in our example:

```
sub new {
    my $class = shift;
    my $self = $class->SUPER::new(Namespaces   => 1,
                                  NoExpand      => 1,
                                  ParseParamEnt => 0,
                                  Handlers      => { Char    => \&handle_char,
                                                     XMLDecl => \&handle_dec,
                                                     Start   => \&handle_start})
    ;
    bless ($self,$class);
    $self->_initialize(@_);
    return $self;
}
```

Note how the module calls its parent's new with very specific arguments. All are standard and well-documented setup instructions in XML::Parser's public interface, but by taking these parameters out of the user's hands and into its own, the XML::RSS module knows exactly what it's getting—in this case, a parser object with namespace processing enabled, but not expansion or parsing of parameter entities—and defines for itself what its handlers are.

The result of calling SUPER:: new is an XML::Parser object, which this module doesn't want to hand back to its users—doing so would diminish the point of all this abstraction! Therefore, it reblesses the object (at this point, deemed to be a new $self for this class) using the Perl-itically correct two-argument method, so that the returned object claims fealty to XML::RSS, not XML::Parser.

The Object Model

Since we can see that XML::RSS is not very unique in terms of parser object construction and document parsing, let's look at where it starts to cut an edge of its own: through the shape of the internal data structure it builds and to which it applies its method-based API.

XML::RSS's code is made up mostly of accessors—methods that read and write to predefined places in the structure it's building. Using nothing more complex than a few Perl hashes, XML::RSS builds maps of what it expects to see in the document, made of nested hash references with keys named after the elements and attributes it might encounter, nested to match the way one might find them in a real RSS XML document. The module defines one of these maps for each version of RSS that it handles. Here's the simplest one, which covers RSS Version 0.9:

```perl
my %v0_9_ok_fields = (
    channel => {
        title       => '',
        description => '',
        link        => '',
        },
    image  => {
        title => '',
        url   => '',
        link  => ''
        },
    textinput => {
        title       => '',
        description => '',
        name        => '',
        link        => ''
        },
    items => [],
    num_items => 0,
    version         => '',
    encoding        => ''
);
```

This model is not entirely made up of hash references, of course; the top-level "items" key holds an empty array reference, and otherwise, all the end values for all the keys are scalars—all empty strings. The exception is num_items, which isn't among RSS's elements. Instead, it serves the role of convenience, making a small trade-off of structural elegance for the sake of convenience (presumably so the code doesn't have to keep explicitly dereferencing the items array reference and then getting its value in scalar context).

On the other hand, this example risks going out of sync with reality if what it describes changes and the programmer doesn't remember to update the number when that happens. However, this sort of thing often comes down to programming style, which is far beyond the bounds of this book.

There's good reason for this arrangement, besides the fact that hash values have to be set to something (or undef, which is a special sort of something). Each hash doubles as a map for the module's subroutines to follow and a template for the structures themselves. With that in mind, let's see what happens when an XML::Parser item is constructed via this module's new class method.

Input: User or File

After construction, an XML::RSS is ready to chew through an RSS document, thanks to the parsing powers afforded to it by its proud parent, XML::Parser. A user only needs to call the object's parse or parsefile methods, and off it goes—filling itself up with data.

Despite this, many of these objects will live long* and productive lives without sinking their teeth into an existing XML document. Often RSS users would rather have the module help build a document from scratch—or rather, from the bits of text that programs we write will feed to it. This is when all those accessors come in handy.

Thus, let's say we have a SQL database somewhere that contains some web log entries we'd like to RSS-ify. We could write up this little script:

```perl
#!/usr/bin/perl

# Turn the last 15 entries of Dr. Link's Weblog into an RSS 1.0 document,
# which gets pronted to STDOUT.

use warnings;
use strict;

use XML::RSS;
use DBIx::Abstract;

my $MAX_ENTRIES = 15;

my ($output_version) = @ARGV;
$output_version ||= '1.0';
unless ($output_version eq '1.0' or $output_version eq '0.9'
                         or $output_version eq '0.91') {
  die "Usage: $0 [version]\nWhere [version] is an RSS version to output:
0.9, 0 .91, or 1.0\nDefault is 1.0\n";
}

my $dbh = DBIx::Abstract->connect({dbname=>'weblog',
                                   user=>'link',
                                   password=>'dirtyape'})
  or die "Couln't connect to database.\n";
```

---

* Well, a few hundredths of a second on a typical whizbang PC, but we mean long in the poetic sense.

```perl
my ($date) = $dbh->select('max(date_added)',
                          'entry')->fetchrow_array;
my ($time) = $dbh->select('max(time_added)',
                          'entry')->fetchrow_array;

my $time_zone = "+05:00"; # This happens to be where I live. :)
my $rss_time = "${date}T$time$time_zone";
# base time is when I started the blog, for the syndication info
my $base_time = "2001-03-03T00:00:00$time_zone";

# I'll choose to use RSS version 1.0 here, which stuffs some meta-information into
# 'modules' that go into their own namespaces, such as 'dc' (for Dublin Core) or
# 'syn' (for RSS Syndication), but fortunately it doesn't make defining the document
# any more complex, as you can see below...

my $rss = XML::RSS->new(version=>'1.0', output=>$output_version);

$rss->channel(
            title=>'Dr. Links Weblog',
            link=>'http://www.jmac.org/linklog/',
            description=>"Dr. Link's weblog and online journal",
            dc=> {
                  date=>$rss_time,
                  creator=>'llink@jmac.org',
                  rights=>'Copyright 2002 by Dr. Lance Link',
                  language=>'en-us',
                  },
            syn=> {
                  updatePeriod=>'daily',
                  updateFrequency=>1,
                  updateBase=>$base_time,
                  },
            );


$dbh->query("select * from entry order by id desc limit $MAX_ENTRIES");
while (my $entry = $dbh->fetchrow_hashref) {
  # Replace XML-naughty characters with entities
  $$entry{entry} =~ s/&/&amp;/g;
  $$entry{entry} =~ s/</&lt;/g;
  $$entry{entry} =~ s/'/&apos;/g;
  $$entry{entry} =~ s/"/&quot;/g;
  $rss->add_item(
        title=>"$$entry{date_added} $$entry{time_added}",
        link=>"http://www.jmac.org/weblog?$$entry{date_added}#$$entry{time_added}",
        description=>$$entry{entry},
              );
}

# Just throw the results into standard output. :)
print $rss->as_string;
```

Did you see any XML there? We didn't. Well, OK, we did have to give the truth of the
matter a little nod by tossing in those entity-escape regexes, but other than that, we

were reading from a database and then stuffing what we found into an object by way of a few method calls (or rather, a single, looped call to its `add_item` method). These calls accepted, as their sole argument, a hash made of some straightforward strings. While we (presumably) wrote this program to let our web log take advantage of everything RSS has to offer, no actual XML was munged in the production of this file.

Off-the-Cuff Output

By the way, `XML::RSS` doesn't use XML-generation-helper modules such as `XML::Writer` to product its output; it just builds one long scalar based on what the map-hash looks like, running through ordinary `if`, `else`, and `elsif` blocks, each of which tend to use the `.=` self-concatenation operator. If you think you can get away with it in your own XML-generating modules, you might try this approach, building up the literal document-to-be in memory and `printing` it to a filehandle; that way, you'll save a lot of overhead and gain control, but give up some safety in the process. Just be sure to test your output thoroughly for well-formedness. (If you're making a dual-purpose parser/generator like `XML::RSS`, you might try to have the module parse some of its own output and make sure everything looks as you'd expect.)

XML Programming Tools

Now we'll cover software that performs a somewhat inverse role compared to the ground we just covered. Instead of giving you Perl-lazy ways to work with XML documents, it uses XML standards to make things easier for a task that doesn't explicitly involve XML. Recently, some key folk in the community from the *perl-xml* mailing list have been seeking a mini-platform of universal data handling in Perl with SAX at its core. Some very interesting (and useful) examples have been born from this research, including Ilya Sterin's `XML::SAXDriver::Excel` and `XML::SAXDriver::CSV`, and Matt Sergeant's `XML::Generator::DBI`. All three modules share the ability to take a data format—Microsoft Excel files, Comma-Separated Value files, and SQL databases, respectively—and wrap a SAX API around it (the same sort covered in Chapter 5, so that any programmer can merrily pretend that the format is as well behaved and manageable as all the other XML documents they've seen (even if the underlying module is quietly performing acrobatics akin to medicating cats).

We'll look more closely at one of these tools, as its subject matter has some interesting implications involving recent developments, before we move on to this chapter's final section.

XML::Generator::DBI

`XML::Generator::DBI` is a fine example of a *glue module*, a simple piece of software whose only job is to take two existing (but not entirely unrelated) pieces of software and let them talk to one another. In this case, when you construct an object of this class, you hand it your additional objects: a DBI-flavored database handle and a SAX-speaking handler object.

XML::Generator::DBI does not know or care how or where the objects came from, but only trusts that they respond to the standard method calls of their respective families (either DBI, SAX, or SAX2). Then you can call an execute method on the XML::Generator::DBI object with an ordinary SQL statement, much as you would with a DBI-created database handle.

The following example shows this module in action. The SAX handler in question is an instance of Michael Koehne's XML::Handler::YAWriter module, a pleasantly configurable module that turns SAX events into textual output. Using this program, we can turn, say, a SQL table of CDs into well-formed XML and then have it printed to standard output:

```perl
#!/usr/bin/perl

use warnings;
use strict;

use XML::Generator::DBI;
use XML::Handler::YAWriter;

use DBI;

my $ya = XML::Handler::YAWriter->new(AsFile => "-");
my $dbh = DBI->connect("dbi:mysql:dbname=test", "jmac", "");
my $generator = XML::Generator::DBI->new(
                                  Handler => $ya,
                                  dbh => $dbh
                                  );
my $sql = "select * from cds";

$generator->execute($sql);
```

The result is this:

```xml
<?xml version="1.0" encoding="UTF-8"?><database>
 <select query="select * from cds">
  <row>
   <id>1</id>
   <artist>Donald and the Knuths</artist>
   <title>Greatest Hits Vol. 3.14159</title>
   <genre>Rock</genre>
  </row>
  <row>
   <id>2</id>
   <artist>The Hypnocrats</artist>
   <title>Cybernetic Grandmother Attack</title>
   <genre>Electronic</genre>
  </row>
  <row>
```

```
    <id>3</id>
    <artist>The Sam Handwich Quartet</artist>
    <title>Handwich a la Yogurt</title>
    <genre>Jazz</genre>
   </row>
  </select>
 </database>
```

This example isn't very interesting, but it looks good in print. The point is that we didn't have to use YAWriter. We could have used any SAX handler Perl package on our system, including ones we wrote ourselves, and tossed them into the mix when baking a new XML::Generator::DBI object. Given the same database table as the example above used, when the $genenerator object's execute method is called, it would act as if it had just parsed the previous XML document (modulo the whitespace that YAWriter inserted to make things more human-readable). It would act this way even though the actual source isn't an XML document at all, but a database table.

Further Ruminations on DBI and SAX

While we're on the subject, let's digress down the path of DBI and SAX, which may have more in common than mutual utility in data management.

The main reason why the Perl DBI earned its position as the preeminent Perl database interface involves its architecture. When installing DBI, one must obtain two separate pieces: DBI.pm contains all the code behind the DBI API and its documentation, but it alone won't let you drive a database with Perl; you also need at least one DBD module that is suitable to the type of database you plan to use. CPAN has many of these modules to choose from, DBD::MySQL, DBD::Oracle, and DBD::Pg for Postgres. While the programmer interacts only with the DBI module, feeding it SQL queries and receiving results from it, the appropriate DBD module communicates directly with the actual database. The DBD module turns the abstract DBI methods into highly specific and platform-dependent database commands. It does this far underneath the level at which the DBI user works, so that any Perl program using DBI will work on any database for which somebody has made available a DBD driver.[*]

A similar movement is on the ascent in the Perl and XML world, which started in 2001 with the SAX drivers mentioned at the start of this section and ended up with the XML::SAX module, a SAX2 implementation that works like DBI. Tell it you want a SAX parser, optionally specifying the SAX features your program's gotta have, and it roots around on your system to find the best tool for the job, which it instantiates

---

[*] Assuming, of course, that the programmer took care not to have the program rely on any queries unique to a given database. $sth->query('select last_insert_id() from foo') might work well when hacking on a MySQL database, but cause your friends using Postgres great pain. Consult O'Reilly's *Programming the Perl DBI* by Alligator Descartes and Tim Bunce for more information.

and hands back to you. Then you plug in the SAX handler package of your choice (much as with XML::Generator::DBI) and go to town.

Instead of a variety of DBD drivers that let you use a standard interface to pull data from a variety of databases, PerlSAX handlers let you use a standard interface to pull data from any imaginable data source. As with DBI, it requires only one intrepid hacker to wade through the data format in question, and suddenly other Perl programmers with a clue about SAX hacking can find themselves using a standard API to handle this once-alien format.

SOAP::Lite

Finally, we come to the category of Perl and XML software that is so ridiculously abstracted from the book's topic that it's almost not worth covering, but it's definitely much more worth showing off. This category describes modules and extensions that are similar to the XML::RSS class helper modules; they help you work with a specific variety of XML documents, but set themselves apart by the level of aggression they employ to keep programmers separated from the raw, element-encrusted data flowing underneath it. They involve enough layers of abstraction to make you forget that you're even dealing with XML in the first place.

Of course, they're perfectly valid in doing so; for example, if we want to write a program that uses the SOAP or XML-RPC protocols to use remote code, nothing could be further from our thoughts than XML. It's all a magic carpet, as far as we're concerned—we just want our program to work! (And when we do care, a good module lets us peek at the raw XML, if we insist.)

The Simple Object Access Protocol (SOAP) gives you the power of object-oriented web services[*] by letting you construct and use objects whose class definitions exist at the other end of a URI. You don't even need to know what programming language they use because the protocol magically turns the object's methods into a common, XML-based API. As long as the class is documented somewhere, with more details of the available class and object methods, you can hack away as if the class was simply another file on your hard drive, despite the fact that it actually exists on a remote machine.

At this point it's entirely too easy to forget that we're working with XML. At least with RSS, the method names of the object API more or less match those of the resulting output document; in this case, We don't even want to see the horrible

---

[*] Despite the name, web services don't have to involve the World Wide Web per se; a web service is simply a piece of software that listens patiently on a port to which a URI points, and, upon receiving a request, concocts a reply that makes sense to the requesting entity. A plain old HTTP-trafficking web server is the most common sort of web service, but the concept's more recent hype centers around its newfound ability to provide persistent access to objects and procedures (so that a programmer can use bits of code that exist on remote servers, tying them seamlessly into locally stored software).

machine-readable-only document any more than we'd want to see the numeric codes representing keystrokes that are sent to our machine's CPU.

SOAP::Lite's name refers to the amount of work you have to apply when you wish to use it, and does not reflect its own weight. When you install it on your system, it makes a long list of Perl packages available to you, many of which provide a plethora of transportation styles,* a mod_perl module to assist with SOAPy web serving, and a whole lot of documentation and examples. Then it does most of this all over again with a set of modules providing similar APIs for XML-RPC, SOAP's non-object-oriented cousin.† SOAP::Lite is one of those seminal all-singing, all-dancing tools for Perl programmers, doing for web service programming what CGI.pm does for dynamic web site programming.

Let's get our hands dirty with SOAP.

First Example: A Temperature Converter

Every book about programming needs some temperature-conversion code in it somewhere, right? Well, we don't quite have that here. In this example, lovingly ripped off from the SYNOPSIS section of the documentation for SOAP::Lite, we write a program whose main function, f2c, lives on whatever machine answers to the URI *http://services.soaplite.com/Temperatures*.

```
use SOAP::Lite;
print SOAP::Lite
    -> uri('http://www.soaplite.com/Temperatures')
    -> proxy('http://services.soaplite.com/temper.cgi')
    -> f2c(32)
    -> result;
```

Executing this program as a Perl script (on a machine with SOAP::Lite properly installed) gives the correct response: 0.

Second Example: An ISBN Lookup Engine

This example, which uses a little module residing on one of the author's personal web servers, is somewhat more object oriented. It takes an ISBN number and returns Dublin Core XML for almost any book that might match it:

```
my ($isbn_number) = @ARGV;
use SOAP::Lite +autodispatch=>
    uri=>'http://www.jmac.org/ISBN',
    proxy=>'http://www.jmac.org/projects/bookdb/isbn/lookup.pl';
```

---

* HTTP is the usual way to SOAP objects around, but if you want to use raw TCP, SMTP, or even Jabber, SOAP::Lite is ready for you

† And whose relationship with Perl is covered in depth in O'Reilly's *Programming Web Services with XML-RPC* by Simon St.Laurent, Joe Johnston, and Edd Dumbill.

```
my $isbn_obj = ISBN->new;

# The 'get_dc' method fetches Dublin Core information
my $result = $isbn_obj->get_dc($isbn_number);
```

The magic here is that the module on the host machine, *ISBN.pm*, isn't unusual in any way; it's a pretty straightforward Perl module that you could use in the usual fashion, if you happened to have a local copy. In other words, we can get the same results by logging into the machine and hammering out a little program like this:

```
my ($isbn_number) = @ARGV;
use ISBN; # This line replaces the long 'use SOAP::Lite' line
my $isbn_obj = ISBN->new;

# The 'get_dc' method fetches Dublin Core information
my $result = $isbn_obj->get_dc($isbn_number);
```

But, by invoking SOAP::Lite and mumbling a few extra incantations to aim our sights at a remote machine that's listening for SOAP-ish requests, you don't need a copy of that Perl module on your end to enjoy the benefits of its API. And, if we eventually went insane and reimplemented the module in Java, you'd probably never know it, since we'd keep the interface the same. In the language-independent world of web services, that's all that matters.

Where is the XML? We can switch on a valve and peek at the raw stuff roaring beneath this pleasant veneer. Let's see what actually happens with that ISBN class constructor call after we activate SOAP::Lite's outputxml option:

```
my ($isbn_number) = @ARGV;
use SOAP::Lite +autodispatch=>
    uri=>'http://www.jmac.org/ISBN', outputxml=>1,
    proxy=>'http://www.jmac.org/projects/bookdb/isbn/lookup.pl';
my $isbn_xml = ISBN->new;
print "$isbn_xml\n";
```

What we get back is something like this:

```
<?xml version="1.0" encoding="UTF-8"?><SOAP-ENV:Envelope xmlns:SOAP-ENC="http://
schemas.xmlsoap.org/soap/encoding/" SOAP-ENV:encodingStyle="http://schemas.xmlsoap.
org/soap/encoding/" xmlns:SOAP-ENV="http://schemas.xmlsoap.org/soap/envelope/" xmlns:
xsi="http://www.w3.org/1999/XMLSchema-instance" xmlns:xsd="http://www.w3.org/1999/
XMLSchema" xmlns:namesp1="http://www.jmac.org/ISBN"><SOAP-ENV:Body><namesp2:
newResponse xmlns:namesp2="http://www.jmac.org/ISBN"><ISBN xsi:type="namesp1:ISBN"/>
</namesp2:newResponse></SOAP-ENV:Body></SOAP-ENV:Envelope>
```

The second bit of example code had to stop short, of course, since it returned a scalar containing a pile of XML (which we then printed) instead of an object belonging to the SOAP::Lite class family. We can't well continue calling methods on it. We can fix this problem by passing the blob to the magic SOAP::Deserializer class, which turns SOAPy XML back into objects:

```
# Continuing from the previous snippet...
my $deserial = SOAP::Deserializer->new;
```

```
my $isbn_obj = $deserial->deserialize($isbn_xml);
# Now we can continue as with the first example.
```

A little extra work, then, nets us the raw XML as well as the black boxes of the SOAP::Lite objects. As you may expect, this feature has uses far beyond interesting book examples, as getting the raw XML in hand opens up the door to all kinds of interesting mischief on our end.

While SOAP::Lite the Perl module is magic in diverse ways, SOAP the protocol is just, well, a protocol, and all the strange namespaces, elements, and attributes seen in the XML generated by this module are compliant to the world-readable SOAP specification.[*] This compliance allows you to apply a cunning plan to your SOAP-using application, with which you let the SOAP::Lite module do its usual magic—but then your program leaps in, captures the raw XML, does something strange and wonderful with it (it can be parsed with any method we've covered so far), and then perhaps return control back to SOAP::Lite.

Admittedly, most of SOAP::Lite doesn't require a fingernail's width of knowledge about XML processing in Perl, as most applications will probably be content with its prepackaged functionality. If you want to get really tricky with it, though, it welcomes your meddling. Knowledge is power, my friend.

That's all for our sampling of Perl and XML applications. Next, we'll talk about some strategies for building our own applications.

---

[*] For Version 1.2, see *http://www.w3.org/TR/soap12-part1/*.

CHAPTER 10
Coding Strategies

This chapter sends you off by bringing this book's topics full circle. We return to many of the themes about XML processing in Perl that we introduced in Chapter 3, but in the context of all the detailed material that we've covered in the interceding chapters. Our intent is to take you on one concluding tour through the world of Perl and XML, with its strategies and its gotchas, before sending you on your way.

Perl and XML Namespaces

You've seen XML namespaces used since we first mentioned this concept back in Chapter 2. Many XML applications, such as XSLT, insist that all their elements claim fealty to a certain namespace. The deciding factor here usually involves how symbiotic the application is in its usual use: does it usually work on its own, with a one-document-per-application style, or does it tend to mix with other sorts of XML?

DocBook XML, for example, is not very symbiotic. An instance of DocBook is almost always a whole XML document, defining a book or an article, and all the elements within such a document that aren't explicitly tied to some other namespace are found in the official DocBook documentation.[*] However, within a DocBook document, you might encounter a clump of MathML elements making their home in a rather parasitic fashion, nestled in among the folds of the DocBook elements, from which it derives nourishing context.

This sort of thing is useful for two reasons: first, DocBook, while its element spread tries to cover all kinds of things you might find in a piece of technical documentation,[†] doesn't have the capacity to richly describe everything that might go into a mathematical equation. (It does have <equation> elements, but they are often used to

---

[*] See *http://www.docbook.org* or O'Reilly's *DocBook: The Definitive Guide.*

[†] Some would say, in fact, that it tries a little too hard; hence the existence of trimmed-down variants such as Simplified DocBook.

describe the nature of the graphic contained within them.) By adding MathML into the mix, you can use all the tags defined by that markup language's specification inside of a DocBook document, tucked away safely in their own namespace. (Since MathML and DocBook work so well together, the DocBook DTD allows a user to plug in a "MathML module," which adds a `<mml:math>` element to the mix. Within this mix, everything is handled by MathML's own DTD, which the module imports (along with DocBook's main DTD) into the whole DTD-space when validating.)

Second, and perhaps more interesting from the parser's point of view, tags existing in a given namespace work like embassies; while you stand on its soil (or in its scope), all that country's rules and regulations apply to you, despite the embassy's location in a foreign land. XML namespaces are also similar to Perl namespaces, which let you invoke variables, subroutines, and other symbols that live inside `Some::Other::Package`, though you may not have defined them within the default `main` package (or whatever package you are working in).

In other words, the presence of a namespace often indicates that another, separate XML application is invoked within the current one. Thus, if you are writing a processor to handle a type of XML application and you know that a certain namespace will probably pop up within it, you can save yourself a lot of work by passing off the work to another Perl module that knows how to handle things in that other application.

For example, let's say that on your machine you have an XML file whose document keeps a list of the monkeys living in your house. Much of this file contains elements of your own design, but because you are both crafty and lazy, your document also uses the Monkey Markup Language, a standard way to describe monkeys with XML. Because it's designed for use in larger documents, it defines its own namespace:

```
<?xml version="1.0">
<monkey-list>
 <monkey>
  <description xmlns:mm="http://www.jmac.org/projects/monkeys/mm/">
   <mm:monkey> <!-- start of monkey section -->
    <mm:name>Virtram</mm:name>
    <mm:color>teal</mm:color>
    <mm:favorite-foods>
     <mm:food>Banana</mm:food> <mm:food>Walnut</mm:food>
    </mm:favorite-foods>
    <mm:personality-matrix>
     F6 30 00 0A 1B E7 9C 20
    </mm:personality-matrix>
   </mm:monkey>
  </description>
  <location>Living Room</location>
  <job>Scarecrow</job>
 </monkey>
 <!-- Put more monkeys here later -->
</monkey-list>
```

URI Identifiers

Many XML technologies, such as XML namespaces, SAX2, and SOAP, rely on URIs as unique identifiers—strings that differentiate features or properties to prevent ideological conflicts. Any processor that reads it can be absolutely sure that it's referring to the technology intended by the author. URIs used in this way often look like URLs, usually of the *http://* variety, which implies that typing them into a web browser will cause something to happen. However, sometimes the only result is a disappointing HTTP 404 response. URIs, unlike URLs, don't have to point to an actual resource; they only have to be globally unique.

Developers who need to assign a new URI to something often base them on URLs leading to web sites they have some control over. For example, if you have exclusive control over *http://www.greenmonkey-markup.com/~jmac*, then you can assign URIs based on it, such as *http://www.greenmonkey-markup/~jmac/monkeyml/*. Even without a response, you are still guaranteed that nobody else will ever use that URI. However, polite developers tend to put something at these URIs—preferably documentation about the technology that uses them.

Another popular solution involves using a service such as *http://purl.org* (no relation to Perl), which can put a layer of indirection between a URI you use as a namespace and the location that houses its documentation, letting you change the latter at will while keeping the former constant.

Sometimes a URI does convey information besides mere uniqueness. For example, many XML application processors are sticklers about URIs used to declare XML namespaces, with good reason. XSLT processors, for example, usually don't care that all stylesheet XSLT elements have the usual `xsl:` prefix, as much as they care what URI that prefix is bound to, in the appropriate `xmlns:`-prefixed attribute. Knowing what URI the prefix is bound to assures the processor that you're using, for example, the W3C's most recent version of XSLT, and not a pre-1.0 version that some bleeding-edge processor adopted (that has its own namespace).

Robin Berjon's `XML::NamespaceSupport` module, available on CPAN, can help you process XML documents that use namespaces and manage their prefix-to-URI mappings.

Luckily, we have a Perl module on our system, `XML::MonkeyML`, that can parse a MonkeyML document into an object. This module is useful because the `XML::MonkeyML` class contains code for handling MonkeyML's `personality-matrix` element, which condenses a monkey's entire personality down to a short hexadecimal code. Let's write a program that predicts how all our monkeys will react in a given situation:

```
#!/usr/bin/perl

# This program takes an action specified on the command line, and
# applies it to every monkey listed in a monkey-list XML document
# (whose filename is also supplied on the command line)
```

```
use warnings;
use strict;

use XML::LibXML;
use XML::MonkeyML;

my ($filename, $action) = @ARGV;

unless (defined ($filename) and defined ($action)) {
  die "Usage: $0 monkey-list-file action\n";
}

my $parser = XML::LibXML->new;
my $doc = $parser->parse_file($filename);

# Get all of the monkey elements
my @monkey_nodes = $parser->documentElement->findNodes("//monkey/description/mm:
monkey");

foreach (@monkey_nodes) {
  my $monkeyml = XML::MonkeyML->parse_string($_->toString);
  my $name = $monkeyml->name . " the " . $monkeyml->color . " monkey";
  print "$name would react in the following fashion:\n";
  # The magic MonkeyML 'action' object method takes an English
  # description of an action performed on this monkey, and returns a
  # phrase describing the monkey's reaction.
  print $monkeyml->action($action); print "\n";
}
```

Here is the output:

```
$ ./money_action.pl monkeys.xml "Give it a banana"

Virtram the teal monkey would react in the following fashion:
Take the banana. Eat it. Say "Ook".
```

Speaking of laziness, let's look at how a programmer might create a helper module
like XML::MonkeyML.

Subclassing

When writing XML-hacking Perl modules, another path to laziness involves stand-
ing on (and reading over) the shoulders of giants by subclassing general XML parsers as a quick way to build application-specific modules.

You don't have to use object inheritance; the least complicated way to accomplish
this sort of thing involves constructing a parser object in the usual way, sticking it
somewhere convenient, and turning around whenever you want to do something
XMLy. Here is some bogus code for you:

```
package XML::MyThingy;

use strict; use warnings;
```

```
use XML::SomeSortOfParser;

sub new {
  # Ye Olde Constructor
  my $invocant = shift;
  my $self = {};
  if (ref($invocant)) {
    bless ($self, ref($invocant));
  } else {
    bless ($self, $invocant);
  }

  # Now we make an XML parser...
  my $parser = XML::SomeSortOfParser->new
      or die "Oh no, I couldn't make an XML parser. How very sad.";

  # ...and stick it on this object, for later reference.
  $self->{xml} = $parser;
  return $self;
}

sub parse_file {

  # We'll just pass on the user's request to our parser object (which
  # just happens to have a method named parse_file)...
  my $self = shift;
  my $result = $self->{xml}->parse_file;

  # What happens now depends on whatever a XML::SomeSortOfParser
  # object does when it parses a file. Let's say it modifies itself and
  # returns a success code, so we'll just keep hold of the now-modified
  # object under this object's 'xml' key, and return the code.
  return $result;
}
```

Choosing to subclass a parser has some bonuses, though. First, it gives your module
the same basic user API as the module in question, including all the methods for
parsing, which can be quite lazily useful—especially if the module you're writing is
an XML application helper module. Second, if you're using a tree-based parser, you
can steal—er, I mean embrace and extend—that parser's data structure representation of the parsed document and then twist it to better serve your own nefarious goal
while doing as little extra work as possible. This step is possible through the magic of
Perl's class blessing and inheritance functionality.

Subclassing Example: XML::ComicsML

For this example, we're going to set our notional MonkeyML aside in favor of the
grim reality of ComicsML, a markup language for describing online comics.* It shares

---

* See *http://comicsml.jmac.org/*.

a lot of features and philosophies with RSS, providing, among other things, a standard way for comics to share web-syndication information, so a ComicsML helper module might be a boon for any Perl hacker who wishes to write programs that work with syndicated web comics.

We will go down a DOMmish path for this example and pull XML::LibXML down as our internal mechanism of choice, since it's (mostly) DOM compliant and is a fast parser. Our goal is to create a fully object-oriented API for manipulating ComicsML documents and all the major child elements within them:

```
use XML::ComicsML;

# parse an existing ComicsML file
my $parser = XML::ComicsML::Parser->new;
my $comic = $parser->parsefile('my_comic.xml');

my $title = $comic->title;
print "The title of this comic is $title\n";

my @strips = $comic->strips;
print "It has ".scalar(@strips)." strips associated with it.\n";
```

Without further ado, let's start coding.

```
package XML::ComicsML;

# A helper module for parsing and generating ComicsML documents.

use XML::LibXML;
use base qw(XML::LibXML);

# PARSING

# We catch the output of all XML::LibXML parsing methods in our hot
# little hands, then proceed to rebless selected nodes into our own
# little clasees

sub parse_file {
  # Parse as usual, but then rebless the root element and return it.
  my $self = shift;
  my $doc = $self->SUPER::parse_file(@_);
  my $root = $doc->documentElement;
  return $self->rebless($root);
}

sub parse_string {
  # Parse as usual, but then rebless the root element and return it.
  my $self = shift;
  my $doc = $self->SUPER::parse_string(@_);
  my $root = $doc->documentElement;
  return $self->rebless($root);
}
```

What exactly are we doing, here? So far, we declared the package to be a child of XML::LibXML (by way of the use base pragma), but then we write our own versions of its three parsing methods. All do the same thing, though: they call XML::LibXML's own method of the same name, capture the root element of the returned document tree object, and then pass it to these internal methods:

```
sub rebless {

    # Accept  some kind of XML::LibXML::Node (or a subclass
    # thereof) and, based on its name, rebless it into one of
    # our ComicsML classes.
    my $self = shift;
    my ($node) = @_;

    # Define a has of interesting element types. (hash for easier searching.)
    my %interesting_elements = (comic=>1,
                                person=>1,
                                panel=>1,
                                panel-desc=>1,
                                line=>1,
                                strip=>1,
                                );

    # Toss back this node unless it's an Element, and Interesting. Else,
    # carry on.
    my $name = $node->getName;
    return $node unless ( (ref($node) eq 'XML::LibXML::Element')
        and (exists($interesting_elements{$name})) );

        # It is an interesting element! Figure out what class it gets, and rebless it.
        my $class_name = $self->element2class($name);
        bless ($node, $class_name);
    return $node;
}

sub element2class {

    # Munge an XML element name into something resembling a class name.
    my $self = shift;
    my ($class_name) = @_;
    $class_name = ucfirst($class_name);
    $class_name =~ s/-(.?)/uc($1)/e;
    $class_name = "XML::ComicsML::$class_name";
}
```

The rebless method takes an element node, peeks at its name, and sees if it appears on a hardcoded list it has of "interesting" element names. If it appears on the list, it chooses a class name for it (with the help of that silly element2class method) and reblesses it into that class.

This behavior may seem irrational until you consider the fact that XML::LibXML objects are not very persistent, due to the way they are bound with the low-level, C-based structures underneath the Perly exterior. If I get a list of objects representing some node's children, and then ask for the list again later, I might not get the same Perl objects, though they'll both work (being APIs to the same structures on the C library-produced tree). This lack of persistence prevents us from, say, crawling the whole tree as soon as the document is parsed, blessing the "interesting" elements into our own ComicsML-specific classes, and calling it done.

To get around this behavior, we do a little dirty work, quietly turning the Element objects that XML::LibXML hands us into our own kinds of objects, where applicable. The main advantage of this, beyond the egomaniacal glee of putting our own (class) name on someone else's work, is the fact that these reblessed objects are now subject to having some methods of our own design called on them. Now we can finally define these classes.

First, we will taunt you by way of the AUTOLOAD method that exists in XML::ComicsML:: Element, a virtual base class from which our "real" element classes all inherit. This glop of code lords it over all our element classes' basic child-element and attribute accessors; when called due to the invocation of an undefined method (as all AUTOLOAD methods answer to), it first checks to see if the method exists in that class's hard-coded list of legal child elements and attributes (available through the element() and attribute() methods, respectively); failing that, if the method had a name like add_ foo or remove_foo, it enters either constructor or destructor mode:

```
package XML::ComicsML::Element;

# This is an abstract class for all ComicsML Node types.
use base qw(XML::LibXML::Element);
use vars qw($AUTOLOAD @elements @attributes);

sub AUTOLOAD {
  my $self = shift;
  my $name = $AUTOLOAD;
  $name =~ s/^.*::(.*)$/$1/;
  my @elements = $self->elements;
  my @attributes = $self->attributes;
  if (grep (/^$name$/, @elements)) {

    # This is an element accessor.
    if (my $new_value = $_[0]) {
      # Set a value, overwriting that of any current element of this type.
      my $new_node = XML::LibXML::Element->new($name);
      my $new_text = XML::LibXML::Text->new($new_value);
      $new_node->appendChild($new_text);
      my @kids = $new_node->childNodes;
      if (my ($existing_node) = $self->findnodes("./$name")) {
        $self->replaceChild($new_node, $existing_node);
      } else {
        $self->appendChild($new_node);
      }
    }
  }
```

```perl
    # Return the named child's value.
    if (my ($existing_node) = $self->findnodes("./$name")) {
      return $existing_node->firstChild->getData;
    } else {
      return '';
    }

  } elsif (grep (/^$name$/, @attributes)) {
    # This is an attribute accessor.
    if (my $new_value = $_[0]) {
      # Set a value for this attribute.
      $self->setAttribute($name, $new_value);
    }

    # Return the names attribute's value.
    return $self->getAttribute($name) || '';

    # These next two could use some error-checking.
  } elsif ($name =~ /^add_(.*)/) {
    my $class_to_add = XML::ComicsML->element2class($1);
    my $object = $class_to_add->new;
    $self->appendChild($object);
    return $object;

  } elsif ($name =~ /^remove_(.*)/) {
    my ($kid) = @_;
    $self->removeChild($kid);
    return $kid;
  }

}

# Stubs

sub elements {
  return ();
}

sub attributes {
  return ();
}

package XML::ComicsML::Comic;
use base qw(XML::ComicsML::Element);

sub elements {
  return qw(version title icon description url);
}

sub new {
  my $class = shift;
  return $class->SUPER::new('comic');
}
```

```
sub strips {
  # Return a list of all strip objects that are children of this comic.
  my $self = shift;
  return map {XML::ComicsML->rebless($_)}  $self->findnodes("./strip");
}

sub get_strip {
  # Given an ID, fetch a strip with that 'id' attribute.
  my $self = shift;
  my ($id) = @_;
  unless ($id) {
    warn "get_strip needs a strip id as an argument!";
    return;
  }
  my (@strips) = $self->findnodes("./strip[attribute::id='$id']");
  if (@strips > 1) {
    warn "Uh oh, there is more than one strip with an id of $id.\n";
  }
  return XML::ComicsML->rebless($strips[0]);
}
```

Many more element classes exist in the real-life version of ComicsML—ones that deal with people, strips within a comic, panels within a strip, and so on. Later in this chapter, we'll take what we've written here and apply it to an actual problem.

Converting XML to HTML with XSLT

If you've done any web hacking with Perl before, then you've kinda-sorta used XML, since HTML isn't too far off from the well-formedness goals of XML, at least in theory. In practice, HTML is used more frequently as a combination of markup, punctuation, embedded scripts, and a dozen other things that make web pages act nutty (with most popular web browsers being rather forgiving about syntax).

Currently, and probably for a long time to come, the language of the Web remains HTML. While you can use bona fide XML in your web pages by clinging to the W3C's XHTML,[*] it's far more likely that you'll need to turn it into HTML when you want to apply your XML to the Web.

You can go about this in many ways. The most sledgehammery of these involves parsing your document and tossing out the results in a CGI script. This example reads a local MonkeyML file of my pet monkeys' names, and prints a web page to standard output (using Lincoln Stein's ubiquitous CGI module to add a bit of syntactic sugar):

```
#!/usr/bin/perl

use warnings;
```

---

[*] XHTML comes in two flavors. We prefer the less pendantic "transitional" flavor, which chooses to look the other way when one commits egregious sins (such as using the <font> tag instead of the preferred method of applying cascading stylesheets).

```
    use strict;
    use CGI qw(:standard);
    use XML::LibXML;

    my $parser = XML::XPath;
    my $doc = $parser->parse_file('monkeys.xml');

    print header;
    print start_html("My Pet Monkeys");
    print h1("My Pet Monkeys");
    print p("I have the following monkeys in my house:");
    print "<ul>\n";
    foreach my $name_node ($doc->documentElement->findnodes("//mm:name")) {
        print "<li>" . $name_node->firstChild->getData ."</li>\n";
    }

    print end_html;
```
Another approach involves XSLT.

XSLT is used to translate one type of XML into another. XSLT factors in strongly here because using XML and the Web often requires that you extract all the presentable pieces of information from an XML document and wrap them up in HTML. One very high-level XML-using application, Matt Sergeant's AxKit (*http:// www.axkit.org*), bases an entire application server framework around this notion, letting you set up a web site that uses XML as its source files, but whose final output to web browsers is HTML (and whose final output to other devices is whatever format best applies to them).

Example: Apache::DocBook

Let's make a little module that converts DocBook files into HTML on the fly. Though our goals are not as ambitious as AxKit's, we'll still take a cue from that program by basing our code around the Apache mod_perl module. mod_perl drops a Perl interpreter inside the Apache web server, and thus allows one to write Perl code that makes all sorts of interesting things happen with requests to the server.

We'll use a couple of mod_perl's basic features here by writing a Perl module with a handler subroutine, the standard name for mod_perl callbacks; it will be passed an object representing the Apache request, and from this object, we'll determine what (if anything) the user sees.

A frequent source of frustration for people running Perl and XML programs in an Apache environment comes from Apache itself, or at least the way it behaves if it's not given a few extra configuration directives when compiled. The standard Apache distribution comes with a version of the Expat C libraries, which it will bake into its binary if not explicitly told otherwise. Unfortunately, these libraries often conflict with XML::Parser's calls to Expat libraries elsewhere on the system, resulting in nasty errors (such as segmentation faults on Unix) when they collide.

The Apache development community has reportedly considered quietly removing this feature in future releases, but currently, it may be necessary for Perl hackers wishing to invoke Expat (usually by way of XML::Parser) to recompile Apache without it (by setting the EXPAT configuration option to no).

The cheaper workaround involves using a low-level parsing module that doesn't use Expat, such as XML::LibXML or members of the newer XML::SAX family.

We begin by doing the "starting to type in the module" dance, and then digging into that callback sub:

```
package Apache::DocBook;

use warnings;
use strict;

use Apache::Constants qw(:common);

use XML::LibXML;
use XML::LibXSLT;

our $xml_path;                        # Document source directory
our $base_path;                       # HTML output directory
our $xslt_file;                       # path to DocBook-to-HTML XSLT stylesheet
our $icon_dir;                        # path to icons used in index pages

sub handler {
  my $r = shift;                # Apache request object
  # Get config info from Apache config
  $xml_path = $r->dir_config('doc_dir') or die "doc_dir variable not set.\n";
  $base_path = $r->dir_config('html_dir') or die "html_dir variable not set.\n";
  $icon_dir = $r->dir_config('icon_dir') or die "icon_dir variable not set.\n";
  unless (-d $xml_path) {
    $r->log_reason("Can't use an xml_path of $xml_path: $!", $r->filename);
    die;
  }
  my $filename = $r->filename;

  $filename =~ s/$base_path\/?//;
  # Add in path info (the file might not actually exist... YET)
  $filename .= $r->path_info;
```

```
$xslt_file = $r->dir_config('xslt_file') or die "xslt_file Apache variable not set.
\n";

    # The subroutines we'll call after this will take care of printing
    # stuff at the client.

    # Is this an index request?
      if ( (-d "$xml_path/$filename") or ($filename =~ /index.html?$/) ) {
      # Why yes! We whip up an index page from the floating aethers.
      my ($dir) = $filename =~ /^(.*)(\/index.html?)?$/;
      # Semi-hack: stick trailing slash on URI, maybe.
      if (not($2) and $r->uri !~ /\/$/) {
        $r->uri($r->uri . '/');
      }
      make_index_page($r, $dir);
      return $r->status;
    } else {
      # No, it's a request for some other page.
      make_doc_page($r, $filename);
      return $r->status;
    }
    return $r->status;

}
```

This subroutine performs the actual XSLT transformation, given a filename of the original XML source and another filename to which it should write the transformed HTML output:

```
sub transform {
  my ($filename, $html_filename) = @_;

  # make sure there's a home for this file.
  maybe_mkdir($filename);

  my $parser = XML::LibXML->new;
  my $xslt = XML::LibXSLT->new;

  # Because libxslt seems a little broken, we have to chdir to the
  # XSLT file's directory, else its file includes won't work. ;b
  use Cwd;                       # so we can get the current working dir
  my $original_dir = cwd;
  my $xslt_dir = $xslt_file;
  $xslt_dir =~ s/^(.*)\/.*$/$1/;
  chdir($xslt_dir) or die "Can't chdir to $xslt_dir: $!";

  my $source = $parser->parse_file("$xml_path/$filename");
  my $style_doc = $parser->parse_file($xslt_file);

  my $stylesheet = $xslt->parse_stylesheet($style_doc);

  my $results = $stylesheet->transform($source);
```

```
  open (HTML_OUT, ">$base_path/$html_filename");
  print HTML_OUT $stylesheet->output_string($results);
  close (HTML_OUT);

  # Go back to original dir
  chdir($original_dir) or die "Can't chdir to $original_dir: $!";

}
```

Now we have a pair of subroutines to generate index pages. Unlike the document pages, which are the product of an XSLT transformation, we make the index pages from scratch, the bulk of its content being a table filled with information we grab from the document via XPath (looking first in the appropriate metadata element if present, and falling back to other bits of information if not).

```
sub make_index_page {
  my ($r, $dir) = @_;

  # If there's no corresponding dir in the XML source, the request
  # goes splat

  my $xml_dir = "$xml_path/$dir";
  unless (-r $xml_dir) {
    unless (-d $xml_dir) {
      # Whoops, this ain't a directory.
      $r->status( NOT_FOUND );
      return;
    }
    # It's a directory, but we can't read it. Whatever.
    $r->status( FORBIDDEN );
    return;
  }

  # Fetch mtimes of this dir and the index.html in the corresponding
  # html dir
  my $index_file = "$base_path/$dir/index.html";

  my $xml_mtime = (stat($xml_dir))[9];
  my $html_mtime = (stat($index_file))[9];

  # If the index page is older than the XML dir, or if it simply
  # doesn't exist, we generate a new one.
    if ((not($html_mtime)) or ($html_mtime <= $xml_mtime)) {
    generate_index($xml_dir, "$base_path/$dir", $r->uri);
    $r->filename($index_file);
    send_page($r, $index_file);
    return;
  } else {
    # The cached index page is fine. Let Apache serve it.
    $r->filename($index_file);
    $r->path_info('');
    send_page($r, $index_file);
    return;
  }
```

```
}

sub generate_index {
  my ($xml_dir, $html_dir, $base_dir) = @_;

  # Snip possible trailing / from base_dir
  $base_dir =~ s|/$||;

  my $index_file = "$html_dir/index.html";

  my $local_dir;
  if ($html_dir =~ /^$base_path\/*(.*)/) {
    $local_dir = $1;
  }


  # make directories, if necessary
  maybe_mkdir($local_dir);
  open (INDEX, ">$index_file") or die "Can't write to $index_file: $!";

  opendir(DIR, $xml_dir) or die "Couldn't open directory $xml_dir: $!";
  chdir($xml_dir) or die "Couldn't chdir to $xml_dir: $!";

  # Set icon files
  my $doc_icon = "$icon_dir/generic.gif";
  my $dir_icon = "$icon_dir/folder.gif";

  # Make the displayable name of $local_dir (probably the same)
  my $local_dir_label = $local_dir || 'document root';

  # Print start of page
  print INDEX <<END;
<html>
<head><title>Index of $local_dir_label</title></head>
<body>
<h1>Index of $local_dir_label</h1>
<table width="100%">
END

  # Now print one row per file in this dir

  while (my $file = readdir(DIR)) {
    # ignore dotfiles & directories & stuff
    if (-f $file && $file !~ /^\./) {
      # Create parser objects
      my $parser = XML::LibXML->new;

      # Check for well-formedness, skip if yukky:
      eval {$parser->parse_file($file);};
      if ($@) {
        warn "Blecch, not a well-formed XML file.";
        warn "Error was: $@";
        next;
      }
```

```
        my $doc = $parser->parse_file($file);

        my %info;                   # Will hold presentable info

        # Determine root type
        my $root = $doc->documentElement;
        my $root_type = $root->getName;

        # Now try to get an appropriate info node, which is named $FOOinfo
        my ($info) = $root->findnodes("${root_type}info");
        if ($info) {

          # Yay, an info element for us. Fill it %info with it.
          if (my ($abstract) = $info->findnodes('abstract')) {
            $info{abstract} = $abstract->string_value;
          } elsif ($root_type eq 'reference') {

              # We can usee first refpurpose as our abstract instead.
              if ( ($abstract) = $root->findnodes('/reference/refentry/refnamediv/
    refpurpose')) {
                $info{abstract} = $abstract->string_value;
              }
          }
          if (my ($date) = $info->findnodes('date')) {
            $info{date} = $date->string_value;
          }
        }
        if (my ($title) = $root->findnodes('title')) {
          $info{title} = $title->string_value;
        }

        # Fill in %info stuff we don't need the XML for...
        unless ($info{date}) {
          my $mtime = (stat($file))[9];
          $info{date} = localtime($mtime);
        }
        $info{title} ||= $file;

        # That's enough info. Let's build an HTML table row with it.
        print INDEX "<tr>\n";

        # Figure out a filename to link to -- foo.html
        my $html_file = $file;
        $html_file =~ s/^(.*)\..*$/$1.html/;
        print INDEX "<td>";
        print INDEX "<img src=\"$doc_icon\">" if $doc_icon;
        print INDEX "<a href=\"$base_dir/$html_file\">$info{title}</a></td> ";
        foreach (qw(abstract date)) {
          print INDEX "<td>$info{$_}</td> " if $info{$_};
        }
        print INDEX "\n</tr>\n";
      } elsif (-d $file) {

        # Just make a directory link.
        # ...unless it's an ignorable directory.
```

```
      next if grep (/^$file$/, qw(RCS CVS .)) or ($file eq '..' and not $local_dir);
      print INDEX "<tr>\n<td>";
      print INDEX "<a href=\"$base_dir/$file\"><img src=\"$dir_icon\">" if $dir_icon;
      print INDEX "$file</a></td>\n</tr>\n";
    }
  }


  # Close the table and end the page
  print INDEX <<END;
</table>
</body>
</html>
END

  close(INDEX) or die "Can't close $index_file: $!";
  closedir(DIR) or die "Can't close $xml_dir: $!";
}
```

These subroutines build on the transformation subroutine by generating the pages.
Note the use of caching by comparing the timestamps of the source DocBook file and
the destination HTML file and rewriting the latter only if it's older than the former.
(Of course, if there's no HTML at all, then it always creates a new web page.)

```
sub make_doc_page {
  my ($r, $html_filename) = @_;

  # Generate a source filename by replacing existing extension with .xml
  my $xml_filename = $html_filename;
  $xml_filename =~ s/^(.*)(?:\..*)$/$1.xml/;

  # If there's a problem reading the source XML file, so it goes with
  # the result HTML.
  unless (-r "$xml_path/$xml_filename") {
    unless (-e "$xml_path/$xml_filename") {
      $r->status( NOT_FOUND );
      return;
    } else {
      # Exists, but no read permissions, shrug.
      $r->status( FORBIDDEN );
      return;
    }
  }

  # Fetch mtimes of this file and corresponding html file
  my $xml_mtime = (stat("$xml_path/$xml_filename"))[9];
  my $html_mtime = (stat("$base_path/$html_filename"))[9];
  # If the html file is older than the xml XML file, or if it simply
  # doesn't exist, generate a new one

  if ((not($html_mtime)) or ($html_mtime <= $xml_mtime)) {
    transform($xml_filename, $html_filename);
    $r->filename("$base_path/$html_filename");
    $r->status( DECLINED );
```

```
      return;
    } else {
      # It's cached. Let Apache serve up the existing file.
      $r->status( DECLINED );
    }
  }

  sub send_page {
    my ($r, $html_filename) = @_;
    # Problem here: if we're creating the file, we can't just write it
    # and say 'DECLINED', cuz the default server handle hits us with a
    # file-not-found. Until I find a better solution, I'll just spew
    # the file, and DECLINE only known cache-hits.
    $r->status( OK );
    $r->send_http_header('text/html');

    open(HTML, "$html_filename") or die "Couldn't read $base_path/$html_filename: $!";
    while (<HTML>) {
      $r->print($_);
    }
    close(HTML) or die "Couldn't close $html_filename: $!";
    return;
  }
```

Finally, we have a utility subroutine to help us with a tedious task: copying the structure of subdirectories in the cache directory that mirrors that of the source XML
directory:

```
  sub maybe_mkdir {
    # Given a path, make sure directories leading to it exist, mkdir-ing
    # any that dont.
    my ($filename) = @_;
    my @path_parts = split(/\//, $filename);
    # if the last one is a filename, toss it out.
    pop(@path_parts) if -f $filename;
    my $traversed_path = $base_path;
    foreach (@path_parts) {
      $traversed_path .= "/$_";
      unless (-d $traversed_path) {
        mkdir ($traversed_path) or die "Can't mkdir $traversed_path: $!";
      }
    }
    return 1;
  }
```

A Comics Index

XSLT is one thing, but the potential for Perl, XML, and the Web working together is
as unlimited as, well, anything else you might choose to do with Perl and the Web.
Sometimes you can't just toss refactored XML at your clients, but must write Perl that
wrings interesting information out of XML documents and builds something Web-
bish out of the results. We did a little of that in the previous example, mixing the raw
XSLT usage when transforming the DocBook documents with index page generation.

Since we've gone through all the trouble of covering syndication-enabling XML technologies such as RSS and ComicsML in this chapter and Chapter 9, let's write a little program that uses web syndication. To prove (or perhaps belabor) a point, we'll construct a simple CGI program that builds an index of the user's favorite online comics (which, in our fantasy world, all have ComicsML documents associated with them):

```perl
#!/usr/bin/perl

# A very simple ComicsML muncher; given a list of URLs pointing to
# ComicsML documents, fetch them, flatten their strips into one list,
# and then build a web page listing, linking to, and possibly
# displaying these strips, sorted with newest first.

use warnings;
use strict;

use XML::ComicsML;              # ...so that we can build ComicsML objects
use CGI qw(:standard);
use LWP;
use Date::Manip;                # Cuz we're too bloody lazy to do our own date math

# Let's assume that the URLs of my favorite Internet funnies' ComicsML
# documents live in a plaintext file on disk, with one URL per line
# (What, no XML? For shame...)

my $url_file = $ARGV[0] or die "Usage: $0 url-file\n";

my @urls;                       # List of ComicsML URLs
open (URLS, $url_file) or die "Can't read $url_file: $!\n";
while (<URLS>) { chomp; push @urls, $_; }
close (URLS) or die "Can't close $url_file: $!\n";

# Make an LWP user agent
my $ua = LWP::UserAgent->new;
my $parser = XML::ComicsML->new;

my @strips; # This will hold objects representing comic strips

foreach my $url (@urls) {
  my $request = HTTP::Request->new(GET=>$url);
  my $result = $ua->request($request);
  my $comic;                    # Will hold the comic we'll get back
  if ($result->is_success) {
    # Let's see if the ComicsML parser likes it.
    unless ($comic = $parser->parse_string($result->content)) {
      # Doh, this is not a good XML document.
      warn "The document at $url is not good XML!\n";
      next;
    }
  } else {
    warn "Error at $url: " . $result->status_line . "\n";
    next;
  }
```

```
# Now peel all the strips out of the comic, pop each into a little
# hashref along with some information about the comic itself.
foreach my $strip ($comic->strips) {
    push (@strips, {strip=>$strip, comic_title=>$comic->title, comic_url=>$comic->
url}});
}
}

# Sort the list of strips by date.  (We use Date::Manip's exported
# UnixDate function here, to turn their unweildy Gregorian calendar
# dates into nice clean Unixy ones)
my @sorted = sort {UnixDate($$a{strip}->date, "%s") <=> UnixDate($$b{strip}->date,
"%s")} @strips;

# Now we build a web page!

print header;
print start_html("Latest comix");
print h1("Links to new comics...");

# Go through the sorted list in reverse, to get the newest at the top.
foreach my $strip_info (reverse(@sorted)) {
    my ($title, $url, $svg);
    my $strip = $$strip_info{strip};
    $title = join (" - ", $strip->title, $strip->date);
    # Hyperlink the title to a URL, if there is one provided
    if ($url = $strip->url) {
        $title = "<a href='$url'>$title</a>";
    }

    # Give similar treatment to the comics' title and URL
    my $comic_title = $$strip_info{comic_title};
    if ($$strip_info{comic_url}) {
        $comic_title = "<a href='$$strip_info{comic_url}'>$comic_title</a>";
    }

    # Print the titles
    print p("<b>$comic_title</b>: $title");

    print "<hr />";
}

print end_html;
```

Given the trouble we went through with that Apache::DocBook trifle a little earlier, this program might seem a tad too simple; it performs no caching, it contains no governors for how many strips it will process, and its sense of web page layout isn't much to write home about. For a quick hack, though, it works great and demonstrates the benefit of using helper modules like XML::ComicsML.

Our whirlwind tour of the world of Perl and XML ends here. As we said at the start of this book, the relationship between these two technologies is still young, and it only just started to reach for its full potential while we were writing this book, as new parsers like XML::LibXML and philosophies like PerlSAX2 emerged onto the scene during that time. We hope that we have given you enough information and encouragement to become part of this scene, as it will continue to unfold in increasingly interesting directions in the coming years.

```
<aloha>Happy hacking!</aloha>
```

Index

Symbols

< > (angle brackets), 16, 25
  parsers and, 35
  well-formed documents, checking, 41
( ) (parenthesis) in PYX notation, 74
[ ] (square brackets), 20
& (ampersands), 21, 60
  parsers and, 35
  well-formed documents, checking, 41
@ (at-sign) characters, 151
<! (delimiters), 57
:: (double colon), using boolean tests in XPath, 148
- (hyphen) in PYX notation, 75
? (question mark) in PYX notation, 75
; (semicolons), 35
/ (slashes), 26
  well-formed documents and, 41
  XPath expressions, 147

A

A (attribute) in PYX notation, 75
absolute locator in XPath, 148
ActiveState, 7
add_links( ) method, 137
add_parser( ) function, 101
addresses (code points), 64
American National Standards Institute (ANSI), 13
ampersands (&), 21, 60
  parsers and, 35
  well-formed documents, checking, 41
ancestor nodes, 115

angle brackets (< >), 16, 25
  parsers and, 35
  well-formed documents, checking, 41
ANSI (American National Standards Institute), 13
appendChild method for Node class (DOM), 131
appendData method for CharacterData class (DOM), 133
application helpers (XML), 159
arrays in Perl, 40
ASCII character encodings, 9, 22
at-sign characters (@), 151
attlist_decl method for PerlSAX DTD handlers, 89
Attr class (DOM), 134
attribute list declarations, 26
attributes
  in PYX notation, 75
  in XML, 15, 26–27
attributes property for Node class (DOM), 131
awk program working with XML::PYX, 74

B

base alphabetical glyphs, 64
base classes (handlers), 96–111
  XML::Handler::YAWriter module, 98
Berjon, Robin, 99
best matching rules, 31
BOM (byte order mark), 68
boolean operations in XPath, 148
Brian, Dan, 120

We'd like to hear your suggestions for improving our indexes. Send email to *index@oreilly.com*.

C

C programming language, 1
  parsers, writing in, 43
  XML::LibXML module and, 52
call-back functions, using Subs parsing
    styles, 45
CDATA (Character DATA) section, 24, 115
CDATASection class (DOM), 135
Character data node type, 115
character encodings, 9, 22, 63–69
character entities, 21
CharacterData class (DOM), 132
characters( ) method, 60, 104
  SAX event handlers, 83
child( ) method, 121
childNodes property for Node class
    (DOM), 130
children( ) method, 121
Chinese characters, 22
Clark, James, 43
cloneNode method for Node class
    (DOM), 131
code points in Unicode, 64
comment( ) method, 59, 106
Comment class (DOM), 135
Comment node type, 115
comment SAX method, 83
comments for XML, 24
Comprehensive Perl Archive Network (see
    CPAN)
container nodes in XML trees, 115
content handlers for SAX, 101–105
content models, 26
context lists, 51
conversions (encoding), 66–69
converter program for stream processing, 73
CPAN (Comprehensive Perl Archive
    Network), ix, 1
  modules, finding, 42
  XML programming tool and, 169
createAttribute method, 129
createAttributeNS method, 129
createCDATASection method, 129
createComment method, 129
createDocumentFragment method, 129
createElement method, 129
createElementNS method, 129
createEntityReference method, 129
createProcessingInstruction method, 129
createTextNode method, 129
current nodes in XPath expressions, 147
custom parsing style, 46

D

data parameters, 23
data property
  CharacterData class (DOM), 133
  ProcessingInstruction class (DOM), 135
Database Interface (DBI), 169
dataElement( ) Writer method, 60
Data::Grove::Visitor module, 145
DBD::MySQL module, 169
DBD::Oracle module, 169
DBD::Pg module, 169
DBI (Database Interface), 169
debug parsing style, 45
declaration handlers for SAX, 101
declarations (XML), 9, 23
  elements, 26
deleteData method for CharacterData class
    (DOM), 133
delimiters (<!), 57
depth-first order in stacks, 40
Derkson, Enno, 136
descendant nodes, 115
destination formats, 12
diacritical marks, 64
<dict> element, 147
DocBook, 14, 156, 174
  converting XML to HTML, 30, 73
  tree-based processing and, 156
doctype( ) Writer method, 59
DOCTYPE keyword, 20
doctype property, 128
doctype_decl method for PerlSAX DTD
    handlers, 89
Document class in DOM, 128
document elements, 20, 25
document instance, 56
Document Object Model (see DOM)
document prologs in DTD handlers, 89
Document Type Descriptions (see DTDs)
document validation, 56
documentElement property, 128
DocumentFragment class (DOM), 129
documents (XML), 8
DocumentType class (DOM), properties
    of, 129
DOM (Document Object Model), 52,
    127–141
  class interface reference, 128–136
  XML::DOM module, 136–138
double colon (::), using boolean tests in
    XPath, 148
drivers for non-XML sources, 93–96

H

Hampton, Kip, 99
Han Chinese characters, 22
handlers, 49, 71
    base classes for, 96–111
    DTD, 89–92
    lexical event, 105
    for SAX, 83–89, 101–107
    stream parsing styles, using, 46
    XML::Parser module and, 80
hasAttribute method for Element node, 134
hasAttributeNS method for Element
    node, 134
hasAttributes method for Node class
    (DOM), 131
hasChildNodes method for Node class
    (DOM), 131
helper modules, 159
hexadecimal character entities, 21
HTML (Hypertext Markup Language), 14
    converting, 30, 154, 183–191
    well-formed documents and, 36
Hypertext Markup Language (see HTML)
hyphen (-) in PYX notation, 75

I

iconv library, 67
id( ) module, 148
ideographic glyphs, 64
ignorable_whitespace( ), 104
importNode method, 129
input, when using XML::RSS module, 165
insertBefore method for Node class
    (DOM), 131
insertData method for CharacterData class
    (DOM), 133
instances (document), 56
internal subsets, 20
internalSubset for DocumentType class
    (DOM), 130
Internet (see World Wide Web)
invalid XML documents, 37
ISO Latin-1 characters, 22
isSupported method for Node class
    (DOM), 131
item( ) method, 137
item class for Node class (DOM), 132
item method for NodeList class (DOM), 132
iterators (tree climbers), 142

J

Java programming language, 2, 83, 127
JavaScript programming language, 2

K

<key> element, 147

L

lastChild property for Node class
    (DOM), 131
last-in, first-out (LIFO), 40
Learning Perl, Third Edition, ix
length property
    CharacterData class (DOM), 133
    NameNodeMap class (DOM), 132
    NodeList class (DOM), 132
lexical handlers, 101, 105
LibXML library, 139
libxml2, 52, 100
LIFO (last-in, first-out), 40
location paths in XPath expressions, 147
locators in XPath, 148
LogDriver directory, installing parsers, 112
loops, checking XML markup objects, 38
Lorie, Raymond, 13

M

MacLeod, Ken, 124
Makefile.PL, installing parsers, 112
markup languages, 11–17
    elements and structure for, 15–17
MathML elements, 174
McLean, Grant, 2, 115
Megginson, David, 82
methods (DOM), 132
    Document class, 129
    Elements node, 133
    Node class, 131
    NodeList class, 132
<mml:math> element, 175
modules, 6–9
    CPAN and, 1
    XML, 158
Mosher, Edward, 13

N

name property
    Attr class (DOM), 134
    DocumentType class (DOM), 130

About the Authors

Erik T. Ray has worked for O'Reilly & Associates as a software developer and XML specialist since 1995. He helped to establish a complete publishing solution using DocBook XML and Perl to produce books in print, on CD-ROM, and for the new Safari web library of books. As the author of the O'Reilly bestseller *Learning XML* and numerous articles for technical journals, Erik is known for his clear and entertaining writing style. When not hammering out code, he enjoys playing card games, reading about hemorrhagic fevers, practicing Buddhist meditation, and collecting toys. He lives in Saugus, Massachusetts with his wife Jeannine and seven parrots.

Jason McIntosh worked alongside Erik at O'Reilly for about a year, doing about the same sort of thing; this book is the chemical byproduct of their time together at O'Reilly. Currently, Jason earns his living as a freelance writer/hacker, with an occasional article popping up on the O'Reilly Network. He has various shenanigans on display at his personal web site, *http://www.jmac.org*. Jason lives in Cambridge, Massachusetts.

Colophon

Our look is the result of reader comments, our own experimentation, and feedback from distribution channels. Distinctive covers complement our distinctive approach to technical topics, breathing personality and life into potentially dry subjects.

The animals on the cover of *Perl and XML* are West African green monkeys. The green monkey, more commonly known as a vervet, is named for its yellow to olive-green fur. Most vervets live in semi-arid regions of sub-Saharan Africa, but some colonies, thought to be descendants of escaped pets, exist in St. Kitts, Nevis, and Barbados. The vervet's diet mainly consists of fruit, seeds, flowers, leaves, and roots, but it sometimes eats small birds and reptiles, eggs, and insects. The largely vegetarian nature of the vervet's diet creates problems for farmers sharing its land, who often complain of missing fruits and vegetables in areas where vervets are common. To control the problem, some farmers resort to shooting the monkeys, who often leave small orphan vervets behind. Some of these orphans are, controversially, sold as pets around the world. Vervets are also bred for use in medical research; some vervet populations are known to carry immunodeficiency viruses that might be linked to similar human viruses.

The green monkey uses a sophisticated set of vocalizations and visual cues to communicate a wide range of emotions, including anger, alarm, pain, excitement, and sadness. The animal is considered highly intelligent and, like other primates, its ability to express intimacy and anxiety is similar to that of humans.

Ann Schirmer was the production editor and copyeditor for *Perl and XML*. Emily Quill was the proofreader. Claire Cloutier and Leanne Soylemez provided quality control. Phil Dangler, Julie Flanagan, and Sarah Sherman provided production assistance. Joe Wizda wrote the index.

Ellie Volckhausen designed the cover of this book, based on a series design by Edie Freedman. The cover image is a 19th-century engraving from the Royal Natural History. Emma Colby produced the cover layout with QuarkXPress 4.1 using Adobe's ITC Garamond font.

Melanie Wang designed the interior layout, based on a series design by David Futato. Neil Walls converted the files from Microsoft Word to FrameMaker 5.5.6 using tools written in Perl by Erik Ray, Jason McIntosh, and Neil Walls. The text font is Linotype Birka; the heading font is Adobe Myriad Condensed; and the code font is LucasFont's TheSans Mono Condensed. The illustrations that appear in the book were produced by Robert Romano and Jessamyn Read using Macromedia Free-Hand 9 and Adobe Photoshop 6. The tip and warning icons were drawn by Christopher Bing. This colophon was written by Ann Schirmer.

More Titles from O'Reilly

Perl

Learning Perl, 3rd Edition

By Randal Schwartz & Tom Phoenix
3rd Edition July 2001
330 pages, ISBN 0-596-00132-0

Learning Perl is the quintessential tutorial for the Perl programming language. The third edition has not only been updated to Perl Version 5.6, but has also been rewritten from the ground up to reflect the needs of programmers learning Perl today. Other books may teach you to program in Perl, but this book will turn you into a Perl programmer.

Mastering Regular Expressions

By Jeffrey E. F. Friedl
1st Edition January 1997
368 pages, ISBN 1-56592-257-3

Regular expressions, a powerful tool for manipulating text and data, are found in scripting languages, editors, programming environments, and specialized tools. In this book, author Jeffrey Friedl leads you through the steps of crafting a regular expression that gets the job done. He examines a variety of tools and uses them in an extensive array of examples, with a major focus on Perl.

Learning Perl on Win32 Systems

By Randal L. Schwartz, Erik Olson & Tom Christiansen
1st Edition August 1997
306 pages, ISBN 1-56592-324-3

In this carefully paced course, leading Perl trainers and a Windows NT practitioner teach you to program in the language that promises to emerge as the scripting language of choice on NT. Based on the "llama" book, this book features tips for PC users and new NT-specific examples, along with a foreword by Larry Wall, the creator of Perl, and Dick Hardt, the creator of Perl for Win32.

Perl/Tk Pocket Reference

By Stephen Lidie
1st Edition November 1998
103 pages, ISBN 1-56592-517-3

The *Perl/Tk Pocket Reference* is a companion volume to *Learning Perl/Tk*. This handy reference book describes every Perl/Tk graphical element, including general widget and variable information, callbacks, geometry management, bindings, events, and window management, as well as composite widget, font, and image creation and manipulation commands.

Mastering Perl/Tk

By Steve Lidie & Nancy Walsh
1st Edition January 2002
768 pages, ISBN 1-56592-716-8

Beginners and seasoned Perl/Tk programmers alike will find *Mastering Perl/Tk* to be the definitive book on creating graphical user interfaces with Perl/Tk. After a fast-moving tutorial, the book goes into detail on creating custom widgets, working with bindings and callbacks, IPC techniques, and examples using many of the nonstandard add-on widgets for Perl/Tk (including Tix widgets). Every Perl/Tk programmer will need this book.

Perl Cookbook

By Tom Christiansen & Nathan Torkington
1st Edition August 1998
794 pages, ISBN 1-56592-243-3

The *Perl Cookbook* is a comprehensive collection of problems, solutions, and practical examples for anyone programming in Perl. You'll find hundreds of rigorously reviewed Perl "recipes" for manipulating strings, numbers, dates, arrays, and hashes; pattern matching and text substitutions; references, data structures, objects, and classes; signals and exceptions; and much more.

Perl

Perl & LWP

By Sean M. Burke
1st Edition, July 2002 (est.)
400 pages (est.), 0-596-00178-9

This comprehensive guide to LWP and its
applications comes with many practical
examples. Topics include programmatically
fetching web pages, submitting forms, using
various techniques for HTML parsing, handling cookies, and authentication. With the
knowledge in Perl & LWP, you can automate any task on the Web,
from checking the prices of items at online stores to bidding at
auctions automatically.

Perl Graphics Programming

By Shawn Wallace
1st Edition, August 2002 (est.)
504 pages (est.), 0-596-00219-X

This insightful volume focuses on scripting
programs that enable programmers to
manipulate graphics for the Web. The book
also helps demystify the manipulation of
graphics formats for web newcomers with a
practical, resource-like approach. While
most of the examples use Perl as a scripting language, the concepts are applicable to any programming language. The book
documents ways to use several powerful Perl modules for generating graphics, including GD, PerlMagick, and GIMP.

Computer Science & Perl Programming: Best of The Perl Journal

Edited by Jon Orwant
1st Edition, May 2002 (est.)
600 pages, ISBN 0-596-00310-2

The first of three volumes from the archives
of The Perl Journal that O'Reilly has exclusive rights to distribute, this book is a compi-
lation of the best from TPJ: 71 articles
providing a comprehensive tour of how
experts implement computer science concepts
in the real world, with code walkthroughs, case studies, and
explanations of difficult techniques that can't be found in any
other book.

Web, Graphics & Perl/Tk: Best of The Perl Journal

Edited by Jon Orwant
1st Edition July 2002 (est.)
504 pages (est.), ISBN 0-596-00311-0

Web, Graphics & Perl/Tk Programming, the
second volume of The Perl Journal series,
covers topics not included in O'Reilly's other
Perl books. Half of the articles in this volume
deal with essential issues faced by web developers using Perl, such as CGI scripting,
mod_perl programming, and content management with the
Apache web server. Remaining articles offer top-to-bottom coverage of how Perl programmers can create graphical applications
with Perl/Tk and Gnome. TPJ's archives go back as far as 1996
and the material is still vital today.

Games, Diversions & Perl Culture: Best of the Perl Journal

Edited by Jon Orwant
1st Edition August 2002 (est.)
504 pages (est.), ISBN 0-596-00312-9

Games, Diversions & Perl Culture, focuses
on entertaining topics that make Perl users
such fanatics about the language. Inside, you
will find all of the playful features TPJ offered
over the years, including the Obfuscated Perl
Contests, Perl Quiz Shows, humor articles,
and renowned one-line recipes.

XML

XML in a Nutshell

By Elliotte Rusty Harold & W. Scott Means
1st Edition December 2000
400 pages, ISBN 0-596-00058-8

XML in a Nutshell is just what serious XML developers need in order to take full advantage of XML's incredible potential: a comprehensive, easy-to-access desktop reference to the fundamental rules that all XML documents and authors must adhere to. This book details the grammar that specifies where tags may be placed, what they must look like, which element names are legal, how attributes attach to elements, and much more.

Java and XSLT

By Eric M. Burke
1st Edition September 2001
528 pages, ISBN 0-596-00143-6

Learn how to use XSL transformations in Java programs ranging from stand-alone applications to servlets. *Java and XSLT* introduces XSLT and then shows you how to apply transformations in real-world situations, such as developing a discussion forum, transforming documents from one form to another, and generating content for wireless devices.

Learning XML

By Erik T. Ray with Christopher R.Maden
1st Edition January 2001
368 pages, ISBN 0-596-00046-4

XML (Extensible Markup Language) is a flexible way to create "self-describing data"—and to share both the format and the data on the World Wide Web, intranets, and elsewhere. In *Learning XML*, the authors explain XML and its capabilities succinctly and professionally, with references to real-life projects and other cogent examples. *Learning XML* shows the purpose of XML markup itself, the CSS and XSL styling languages, and the XLink and XPointer specifications for creating rich link structures.

XSLT

By Doug Tidwell
1st Edition August 2001
473 pages, ISBN 0-596-00053-7

XSLT (Extensible Stylesheet Language Transformations) is a critical bridge between XML processing and more familiar HTML, and dominates the market for conversions between XML vocabularies. Useful as XSLT is, its complexities can be daunting. Doug Tidwell, a developer with years of XSLT experience, eases the pain by building from the basics to the more complex and powerful possibilities of XSLT, so you can jump in at your own level of expertise.

Java & XML, 2nd Edition

By Brett McLaughlin
2nd Edition September 2001
528 pages, ISBN 0-596-00197-5

New chapters on Advanced SAX, Advanced DOM, SOAP, and data binding, as well as new examples throughout, bring the second edition of *Java & XML* thoroughly up to date. Except for a concise introduction to XML basics, the book focuses entirely on using XML from Java applications. It's a worthy companion for Java developers working with XML or involved in messaging, web services, or the new peer-to-peer movement.

XML Pocket Reference, 2nd Edition

By Robert Eckstein with Michel Casabianca
2nd Edition April 2001
102 pages, ISBN 0-596-00133-9

The *XML Pocket Reference* is both a handy introduction to XML terminology and syntax, and a quick reference to XML instructions, attributes, entities, and datatypes. Although XML itself is complex, its basic concepts are simple. This small book combines a perfect tutorial for learning the basics of XML with a reference to the XML and XSL specifications. The new edition introduces information on XSLT (Extensible Stylesheet Language Transformations) and Xpath.

XML

Perl & XML

By Erik T. Ray, Jason McIntosh
1st Edition April 2002 (est.)
325 pages (est.), ISBN 0-596-00205-X

Perl & XML is aimed at Perl programmers
who need to work with XML documents and
data. This book gives a complete, comprehensive tour of the landscape of Perl and
XML, making sense of the myriad of modules,
terminology, and techniques. The last two
chapters of Perl and XML give complete examples of XML applications, pulling together all the tools at your disposal.

Programming Jabber

By DJ Adams
1st Edition January 2002
480 pages, ISBN 0-596-00202-5

This book will offer programmers a chance
to learn and understand the Jabber technology
and protocol from an implementer's point of
view. Every detail of every part of the Jabber
client protocol is introduced, explained, discussed, and covered in the form of recipes,
mini-projects or simple and extended examples in Perl, Python,
and Java. *Programming Jabber* provides a walk-through of the
foundation elements that are common to any messaging solution,
including a detailed overview of the Jabber server architecture.

Python & XML

By Christopher A. Jones & Fred Drake
1st Edition December 2001
378 pages, ISBN 0-596-00128-2

This book has two objectives: to provide a
comprehensive reference on using XML with
Python and to illustrate the practical applications of these technologies (often coupled
with cross-platform tools) in an enterprise
environment. Loaded with practical exam-
ples, it also shows how to use Python to create scalable XML con-
nections between popular distributed applications such as
databases and web servers. Covers XML flow analysis and details
ways to transport XML through a network.

Programming Web Services with SOAP

By James Snell, Doug Tidwell & Pavel Kulchenko
1st Edition December 2001
264 pages, ISBN 0-596-00095-2

In typical O'Reilly fashion this book moves
beyond the theoretical and explains how to
build and implement SOAP web services.
The book begins with a solid introduction to
SOAP, detailing its history and structure, followed by an introduction to the three major
types of SOAP applications: SOAP-RPC, SOAP-Messaging, and
SOAP-Intermediaries. Each SOAP application is illustrated with an
in-depth implementation.

O'REILLY®

TO ORDER: **800-998-9938** • **order@oreilly.com** • **www.oreilly.com**
ONLINE EDITIONS OF MOST O'REILLY TITLES ARE AVAILABLE BY SUBSCRIPTION AT **safari.oreilly.com**
ALSO AVAILABLE AT MOST RETAIL AND ONLINE BOOKSTORES

XML

SAX2

By David Brownell
1st Edition January 2002
240 pages, ISBN 0-596-00237-8

This concise book gives you information you need to effectively use the Simple API for XML (SAX2), the dominant API for efficient XML processing with Java. With SAX2, developers have access to information in XML documents as they are read without imposing major memory constraints or a large code footprint. SAX2 gives you the detail and examples required to use SAX2 to its full potential.

SVG Essentials

By J. David Eisenberg
1st Edition, February 2002
368 pages, ISBN 0-596-00223-8

SVG Essentials shows developers how to take advantage of SVG's open text-based format. Although SVG is much more approachable than the binary or PostScript files that have dominated graphics formats so far, developers need a roadmap to get started creating and processing SVG files. This book provides an introduction and reference to the foundations developers need to use SVG, and demonstrates techniques for generating SVG from other XML formats.

Web Services Essentials

By Ethan Cerami
1st Edition February 2002
304 pages, ISBN 0-596-00224-6

This concise book gives programmers both a concrete introduction and handy reference to XML web services. It explains the foundations of this new breed of distributed services, demonstrates quick ways to create services with open-source Java tools, and explores four key emerging technologies: XML-RPC, SOAP, UDDI, and WSDL. If you want to break through the Web Services hype and find useful information on these evolving technologies, look no further.

Programming Web Services with XML-RPC

By Simon St.Laurent, Joe Johnston & Edd Dumbill
Foreword by Dave Winer
1st Edition June 2001
230 pages, ISBN 0-596-00119-3

XML-RPC, a simple yet powerful system built on XML and HTTP, lets developers connect programs running on different computers with a minimum of fuss. Java programs can talk to Perl scripts, which can talk to ASP applications, and so on. With XML-RPC, developers can provide access to functionality without having to worry about the system on the other end, so it's easy to create web services.

How to stay in touch with O'Reilly

1. Visit Our Award-Winning Web Site

http://www.oreilly.com/

★ "Top 100 Sites on the Web" —PC Magazine
★ CIO Magazine's Web Business 50 Awards

Our web site contains a library of comprehensive product information (including book excerpts and tables of contents), downloadable software, background articles, interviews with technology leaders, links to relevant sites, book cover art, and more. File us in your bookmarks or favorites!

2. Join Our Email Mailing Lists

Sign up to get email announcements of new books and conferences, special offers, and O'Reilly Network technology newsletters at:
elists.oreilly.com.
It's easy to customize your free elists subscription so you'll get exactly the O'Reilly news you want.

3. Get Examples from Our Books

To find example files for a book, go to:
http://www.oreilly.com/catalog
select the book, and follow the "Examples" link.

4. Contact Us via Email

order@oreilly.com
For answers to problems regarding your order or our products. To place a book order online visit:
http://www.oreilly.com/order_new/

catalog@oreilly.com
To request a copy of our latest catalog.

booktech@oreilly.com
For book content technical questions or corrections.

proposals@oreilly.com
To submit new book proposals to our editors and product managers.

international@oreilly.com
For information about our international distributors or translation queries. For a list of our distributors outside of North America check out:
http://international.oreilly.com/distributors.html

5. Work with Us

Check out our web site for current employment opportunites:
http://jobs.oreilly.com/

6. Register your book

Register your book at:
http://register.oreilly.com

O'Reilly & Associates, Inc.
1005 Gravenstein Hwy North
Sebastopol, CA 95472 USA
TEL 707-827-7000 or 800-998-9938
 (6am to 5pm PST)
FAX 707-829-0104

International Distributors

http://international.oreilly.com/distributors.html • international@oreilly.com

UK, EUROPE, MIDDLE EAST, AND AFRICA (EXCEPT FRANCE, GERMANY, AUSTRIA, SWITZERLAND, LUXEMBOURG, AND LIECHTENSTEIN)

INQUIRIES
O'Reilly UK Limited
4 Castle Street
Farnham
Surrey, GU9 7HS
United Kingdom
Telephone: 44-1252-711776
Fax: 44-1252-734211
Email: information@oreilly.co.uk

ORDERS
Wiley Distribution Services Ltd.
1 Oldlands Way
Bognor Regis
West Sussex PO22 9SA
United Kingdom
Telephone: 44-1243-843294
UK Freephone: 0800-243207
Fax: 44-1243-843302 (Europe/EU orders)
or 44-1243-843274 (Middle East/Africa)
Email: cs-books@wiley.co.uk

FRANCE

INQUIRIES & ORDERS
Éditions O'Reilly
18 rue Séguier
75006 Paris, France
Tel: 33-1-40-51-71-89
Fax: 33-1-40-51-72-26
Email: france@oreilly.fr

GERMANY, SWITZERLAND, AUSTRIA, LUXEMBOURG, AND LIECHTENSTEIN

INQUIRIES & ORDERS
O'Reilly Verlag
Balthasarstr. 81
D-50670 Köln, Germany
Telephone: 49-221-973160-91
Fax: 49-221-973160-8
Email: anfragen@oreilly.de (inquiries)
Email: order@oreilly.de (orders)

CANADA

(FRENCH LANGUAGE BOOKS)
Les Éditions Flammarion ltée
375, Avenue Laurier Ouest
Montréal, QC H2V 2K3 Canada
Tel: 1-514-277-8807
Fax: 1-514-278-2085
Email: info@flammarion.qc.ca

HONG KONG

City Discount Subscription Service, Ltd.
Unit A, 6th Floor, Yan's Tower
27 Wong Chuk Hang Road
Aberdeen, Hong Kong
Tel: 852-2580-3539
Fax: 852-2580-6463
Email: citydis@ppn.com.hk

KOREA

Hanbit Media, Inc.
Chungmu Bldg. 210
Yonnam-dong 568-33
Mapo-gu
Seoul, Korea
Tel: 822-325-0397
Fax: 822-325-9697
Email: hant93@chollian.dacom.co.kr

PHILIPPINES

Global Publishing
G/F Benavides Garden
1186 Benavides Street
Manila, Philippines
Tel: 632-254-8949/632-252-2582
Fax: 632-734-5060/632-252-2733
Email: globalp@pacific.net.ph

TAIWAN

O'Reilly Taiwan
1st Floor, No. 21, Lane 295
Section 1, Fu-Shing South Road
Taipei, 106 Taiwan
Tel: 886-2-27099669
Fax: 886-2-27038802
Email: mori@oreilly.com

INDIA

Shroff Publishers & Distributors PVT. LTD.
C-103, MIDC, TTC Pawane
Navi Mumbai 400 701
India
Tel: (91-22) 763 4290, 763 4293
Fax: (91-22) 768 3337
Email: spdorders@shroffpublishers.com

CHINA

O'Reilly Beijing
SIGMA Building, Suite B809
No. 49 Zhichun Road
Haidian District
Beijing, China PR 100080
Tel: 86-10-8809-7475
Fax: 86-10-8809-7463
Email: beijing@oreilly.com

JAPAN

O'Reilly Japan, Inc.
Yotsuya Y's Building
7 Banch 6, Honshio-cho
Shinjuku-ku
Tokyo 160-0003 Japan
Tel: 81-3-3356-5227
Fax: 81-3-3356-5261
Email: japan@oreilly.com

SINGAPORE, INDONESIA, MALAYSIA, AND THAILAND

TransQuest Publishers Pte Ltd
30 Old Toh Tuck Road #05-02
Sembawang Kimtrans Logistics Centre
Singapore 597654
Tel: 65-4623112
Fax: 65-4625761
Email: wendiw@transquest.com.sg

AUSTRALIA

Woodslane Pty., Ltd.
7/5 Vuko Place
Warriewood NSW 2102
Australia
Tel: 61-2-9970-5111
Fax: 61-2-9970-5002
Email: info@woodslane.com.au

NEW ZEALAND

Woodslane New Zealand, Ltd.
21 Cooks Street (P.O. Box 575)
Waganui, New Zealand
Tel: 64-6-347-6543
Fax: 64-6-345-4840
Email: info@woodslane.com.au

ARGENTINA

Distribuidora Cuspide
Suipacha 764
1008 Buenos Aires
Argentina
Phone: 54-11-4322-8868
Fax: 54-11-4322-3456
Email: libros@cuspide.com

ALL OTHER COUNTRIES

O'Reilly & Associates, Inc.
1005 Gravenstein Hwy North
Sebastopol, CA 95472 USA
Tel: 707-827-7000
Fax: 707-829-0104
Email: order@oreilly.com

O'REILLY®

TO ORDER: **800-998-9938** • **order@oreilly.com** • **www.oreilly.com**
ONLINE EDITIONS OF MOST O'REILLY TITLES ARE AVAILABLE BY SUBSCRIPTION AT **safari.oreilly.com**
ALSO AVAILABLE AT MOST RETAIL AND ONLINE BOOKSTORES